Spirit Life & Science

Understanding Your Gifts of Healing and Mediumship

Spirit Life & Science

Understanding Your Gifts of Healing and Mediumship

Mahãn Hannes Jacob

BOOKS

Winchester, UK
Washington, USA

JOHN HUNT PUBLISHING

First published by O-Books, 2022
O-Books is an imprint of John Hunt Publishing Ltd., 3 East St., Alresford,
Hampshire SO24 9EE, UK
office@jhpbooks.com
www.johnhuntpublishing.com
www.o-books.com

For distributor details and how to order please visit the 'Ordering' section on our website.

Text copyright: Mahān Hannes Jacob 2021

ISBN: 978 1 78904 315 0
978 1 78904 316 7 (ebook)
Library of Congress Control Number: 2020938260

A CIP catalogue record for this book is available from the British Library.

The information in this book is not intended or implied to be a substitute for professional medical advice, diagnosis or treatment.

Design: Stuart Davies

Printed and bound in Malta by Gutenberg Press Ltd.

We operate a distinctive and ethical publishing philosophy in all areas of our business, from our global network of authors to production and worldwide distribution.

Contents

Other titles by this author

Au-delà d'un défunt – Médiumnité et Guérison au quotidien
(EAN-13: 9 782882 562043)

Spiritualität & Wissenschaft – Heilung und Medialität im Alltag
(ISBN-13: 978-3-03922-032-8)

Barbara, la petite chenille – Est-ce qu'on vole comme un papillon quand on meurt?
(ISBN-10: 283992683-6, EAN-13: 9 782839 926836)

Barbara, die kleine Raupe – Fliege ich wie ein Schmetterling, wenn ich sterbe?
(ISBN-13: 978-3-03922-035-9)

Foreword

By Dr. Laura Martignon, professor at the University of Education in Ludwigsburg and research associate at the Max Planck Institute for Educational Research.

The book contains biographical accounts of the author's life. These accounts are important, as they provide the background to his motivation. They also introduce the most pertinent topics in the book, but above all, they provide highly concrete examples of how these notions can be applied in everyday life.

H. Jacob's book is both a spiritual study and a scientific treatise. Indeed, the intention is obviously a spiritual one, yet his work adroitly overcomes a double challenge: that of bringing together and captivating the reader with esoteric leanings, the therapist, and also the scientist, each one respectively seeking explanations for phenomena that are still looked upon as enigmatic; and that of providing a text and vocabulary which are accessible to the layperson who is interested in spiritual development as well as informed scientific elements of interest to the scholarly specialist. His accounts allow a great many notions to be demystified and take the reader on a parallel journey filled with magic – the magic of Life!

The author advocates humility as the highest virtue of the aspiring medium. The reader will see that the author is a great medium, one who is both humble and confident throughout the book. He writes with verve, tremendous precision and rigor. His claims are founded, and so should be taken very seriously.

Readers of all levels, whether they wish to begin, consolidate or develop their practice, will be delighted with the practical exercises. Thus this is also a workbook. As a specialist in the study of education, I know a valuable teaching tool when I see one.

This book is extremely clear and well-written. It is an excellent introduction to a field that is often amalgamated with esoteric activities or opinions. It shows us that modern humans need to take spiritual life more seriously than they do in their mad daily rush. It invites the reader to take a break, to meditate and even to pray.

I am delighted to share this book with anyone who wishes to learn about the essence of life and to practice mediumship, as well as with my scientific colleagues. I confess that I am surprised to have found no research on the Hannes Jacob Syndrome up to now, nor any on the physical and psychic disorders that some sensitives can suffer from. I am happy and reassured to see that these disorders are not inevitable and that there are solutions. I am convinced that the innovative ideas presented in this book deserve to receive funding and attention from interested researchers in order to successfully carry out further studies.

When I decided to read this book, it was first out of curiosity, but then it awakened two things in me: the desire to learn more and above all a real hope. Many people tend to separate the two lobes of the brain by attributing specific characteristics to each: intellect and thought to the left, intuition and creativity to the right. In a similar manner, we mistakenly tend to want to separate classical medicine from complementary medicine. I do not share that opinion. We must accept that the two lobes complete each other while retaining their own specificities. In the same way, we have to accept that whereas classical medicine and alternative medicine have their specific fields of application, they are nonetheless complementary.

My hope springs from the style of writing in this book and from the way in which each subject is approached. If there is so little collaboration these days between the two fields, it is because there is still a tremendous lack of dialogue and listening on both sides. The solution to this deadlock and to this real barrier between these universes must be found. Indeed, at the level of the brain, the dialogues and exchanges between the hemispheres are continual, multiple, rich and infinite. The solution that will bring the two together lies not only in communication, meetings, or discussions but also in patience. Interpersonal communication is always the most powerful. May the disciplines that oppose each other today allow themselves to come together in this meeting that will lead them both down the path of knowledge. Humphrey Bogart would say, *"This is the beginning of a beautiful friendship."*

Laura Martignon, PhD

Acknowledgments

My gratitude stretches back many years. I cannot count the number of times that I have tried to put my thoughts and experiences into writing...

This book would never have become a reality without the help of my assistant and best friend Mélanie Engetschwiler. I will never be able to say enough to thank her for the countless nights she spent correcting my "Greek French from the Swiss Appenzell", as well as for her suggestions with respect to the content and its organization.

Anne Renaud was the first to transcribe my recordings. Years later, Maribel Torrent provided constructive comments on my drafts. In addition, I want to thank the Park Hotel Elefante in Verona for treating me as one of their own when I went into retreat there to finish my writing.

Many professors have trained and forged me. Maharaj Swamiji Dharmananda Saraswati taught me meditation and Kriya Yoga. She also gave me my spiritual name, "Mahãn". The late Glyn Edwards (who left us in 2015) provided guidance while I was learning mediumship. Chris Denton trained me in healing and trance. I am deeply indebted to each of my spiritual masters and my teachers for everything they taught me.

I owe the greatest respect to Therese Furrer and to Dr. Donatus Rüetschi for their patience with the nonconformist student that I was when I attended their school of mediumship in the 1990s. In hindsight, I think I must have been the ultimate pest. Thanks to their example and support, I try to be as patient with my students as these instructors were with me.

Thank you to Dr. François Moll, psychiatrist in Bienne, who had the courage to stick his neck out for me with his colleagues so I would be granted access to various laboratories in order to carry out experiments. Thank you also to the head physician in the neurology department in Bienne, Dr. Ralph Hassink, who supervised and commented on my experiments in distance healing and who was brave enough to appear in front of a TV camera on my behalf. I am also grateful to Dr. A. Amsel, doctor in psychiatry and then head of outpatient psychiatry in Bern, who encouraged me many times not to give up and who also made observations about the positive behavior of a patient during my treatment, and to Dr. Helen Burach in Bienne. My thanks go as well to Dr. Laura Martignon of the Max Planck Institute and the late Dr. Ulla Mitzdorfer who submitted, on my behalf, my writing on the "Hannes Jacob Syndrome" which is described in this book in the chapter on sensitive disorder. In addition, I extend my gratitude to Dr. Nathalie Calame for overseeing the medical section of the book.

Thank you to my parents in Speicher, Appenzell, who always supported me, even though they had to put up with the fluctuating career objectives of a son who first studied at the Swiss Police Academy, then became a hotel owner (without wanting a hotel), after which he turned into an inventor of snow skates ("Sled Dog" snow skates, videos of which can be viewed on YouTube) and eventually continued on the wave of international marketing to become a promoter. All of this to finally be faced with the fact that their son was fed up with that and would henceforth be a healer and, moreover, would speak with the dead...

Finally, my gratitude goes to Dr. Catherine Bourquin who encouraged and accompanied me when I was launching my project "*fréquences – Swiss School of Mediumship*" in 2005. Thank you also to Roland Bühlmann, healer in Bienne, partner in the *fréquences* adventure and my calm and grounded talisman in every wavering moment, and to Marlis Seligmann, Viviane Kuhn, and Aurélie Cuttat for their contributions.

Thank you, thank you all... and to those I may have omitted and who have supported me, my heartfelt thanks as well.

Introduction

In my acknowledgments, I have mentioned the living. Quite obviously, I also owe tremendous thanks to the spiritual world, and first of all to my guides Jonathan and White Feather who have influenced my writing and guided my pen.

If you should come across any nonsense in this book, believe me it does not come from the spirit world; rather, it is due to my own ignorance. All my knowledge is based on what has happened to me and on what I have observed. Thus it is possible that there may be errors with regard to the absolute truth, if it exists, as well as omissions. If I have hurt anyone, I never meant to do so. Of course, since my only sources are my actions and experiences, I am therefore obliged to talk about myself as well, but that is not the intention of this book.

Rest assured that beyond this statement and the confidence that you will see as you get to know me, I fully realize that there are multiple aspects of which I am not yet aware – but one has to start somewhere…

I had first written a book on my pilgrimage to Venice. When I reread it today, I am yet again entranced by the magic of travel. When you want to save the world, people think you are crazy, and maybe you are… Yet it was that journey that triggered my faith. Afterwards, I kept a diary of my trips to Greece and the mysticism that accompanied them. Maybe one day they will be published as the account of an initiatory journey.

What finally led me to compile my personal research and experience into this book is the tremendous amount of prejudice that is shown towards mediumship and healing, and also my wish to remedy the lack of information and clear up all the misunderstanding there is about these beautiful careers. Above all, the goal is to break down the preconceived idea that mediumship and healing are only old wives' tales.

Indeed, I deeply regret the poor reputation that may often accompany the term "medium", even if in many cases I understand the reason for this prejudice. Some people immediately disappear as soon as you say you are a medium, while others have a very whimsical idea of the profession and believe it has capacities that are far from realistic. The title of this book, *Spirit Life & Science: Understanding Your Gifts of Healing and Mediumship*, was expressly chosen because mediumship goes beyond just entering into contact with the spirit world; it encompasses a domain that is so much broader, which I hope you will discover with pleasure.

In order to be as clear as possible in the different statements that I make in this book, it is impossible for me to speak about medical or mediumistic topics without having first clarified the terms as well as the different subjects relating to sensitivity in general. You will discover them as you read. By becoming familiar with the vocabulary used in the field and the basic facts about the various functions of the etheric body or mind, the subjects we will be discussing will be easier to assimilate.

These terms are presented so that my students and readers can relate their practices to the medical consequences and thus better evaluate the importance of sensitivity in their own health as well as that of their patients.

I have done my best to cover this vast subject and hope to dispel many misunderstandings, but above all I have put all my heart into this book in order to reveal the beauty of our mind and our very existence.

Death
Lift the veil of your despair
Have mercy on our fate
So that we can leave our ignorance behind
And praise
For all eternity
Life

Chapter 1

Let's call him John

John was a close friend for some 20 years. He was a brilliant research scientist who morphed into a great clown as soon as he had had one drink. We played, ate, drank and went on holiday together every year... until the day I told him what I was going through in terms of healing and mediumship.

He then warned all his friends and family to be wary around me, that I might be in a sect, or be a charlatan, or lead them down the path of delusion and disappointment.

We never saw each other again.

Of course it was an extremely painful experience, but it was also beneficial in that it forced me to look beyond it.

How can you be angry with a blind person if he or she does not participate in a discussion on color or image depth?

How can you judge a deaf person if he or she doesn't coordinate his or her dance steps with yours?

How can you be hurt by ignorance?

Every person is surrounded with Johns; every person's name is John; depending on the subject, I am John...

Long live John!

Chapter 2

My introduction to mediumship

My conscience and my entire mind was flying through different dimensions and eventually came down to Earth on a steppe. I then found myself above a black panther that was running through the grass and brush. Little by little, as he ran, our minds grew closer. Suddenly, they fused and I blended into him. I was now inside him; I sensed the universe surrounding me through his senses. Not only was I seeing through his eyes, but I felt the high grass and the thin twigs of the bushes whip across my muzzle and face.

Another time, when meditating with the Guides, my view expanded and I found myself in the middle of a tropical forest. On a small pond, a fairy or goddess appeared – I have no other way to describe it. She was young, about 20 – if, however, it were possible to determine her age. A pearl necklace had been braided into her hair and her beauty was almost inhuman.

"Who are you?" I asked.

"A friend," she said.

I was going to address her as "Princess" but before I could say the word, she smiled at me and said, "Shiva." Immediately afterwards her image disappeared, to be replaced by that of a large white swan: calm, majestic and peaceful.

These experiences happened to me and therefore I know they were real. I can believe it as firmly as "two and two are four". I am a Cartesian thinker.

In a way, the longest experience occurred while I was meditating at home and happened over several mornings during a six-week period. When I was seated, I saw, two meters in front of me, a man with long brown hair, dressed in a long robe, both hands resting on the hilt of a large saber with the point on the ground. I ignored him despite his repeated appearances, telling myself it was only a mental projection.

One day, however, I asked him somewhat humorously and with a touch of skepticism, "Who are you? Some sort of Jesus?" "No," he replied, to my surprise. "I am Michael; you are working in my energy." Taken aback, I asked him again, "Are you Michael the angel?" "Yes." For a split second, symbolic wings appeared before my eyes, and then Michael disappeared.

Our universe is made up of several dimensions of existence and consciousness. These different layers overlap and penetrate each other, existing together in the same place. Matter believes itself king; yet there is nothing more ephemeral. It is worked, shaped and destroyed at will by the elements of Nature. This process is true for the entire universe and man is subjected to the same rules. For me, accessing these other dimensions did not happen effortlessly from one day to the next.

The first signs

My path to mediumship began at the end of my adolescence, when I was about 17 or 18. I was first interested in chirology – the interpretation of the lines on the hand. By reading a lot and examining many hands, I was able, in a few years, to acquire a solid foundation in the subject: reading the lines on anyone's hand can tell me a lot about that person, and most of it is accurate. I never do fortune-telling or palmistry.

Shortly after, I was initiated by a gypsy woman into the art of water dowsing and the use of the pendulum. The results were also positive as soon as I began doing this. However, despite these auspicious beginnings, I quickly became aware that I was not mature enough yet to do any serious work. Indeed, I was not doing it for deep-seated reasons but to amuse myself. Moreover, I was asking questions about subjects that were none of my business, for example, the future of people I knew. I soon realized that it was not the right time for me to get further involved in such a serious subject. I therefore stopped using the pendulum, but I continued to read people's hands at parties, though again for my sole amusement.

The flow

It was only on a day in the early 1990s, as I was meditating in a very simple manner in which one fills one's body with energy, that I felt a new and very powerful sensation in my body. I felt as though a switch had been flipped and a flow had started. I immediately knew that it was there to heal people, or to help me to heal them. After this discovery, and without telling anyone, I trained myself in various exercises in conscious energy in an attempt to master the new energy within me. I would transfer energy from one hand to the other, or I would hold my hand over a flame for as long as I could without burning myself. This went on for some time, until the day I started treating my close relatives and the neighboring farmer's cows. It was then that the first results appeared. Since then, I have never once stopped working with this energy.

My vision expands – The perception of energy

One morning, although I had not been thinking of anything in particular, I woke up with a different vision. I could see a light, luminous rain falling through the places in which I found myself. At first this seemed strange to me and I was concerned I might be having problems with my eyes. Later, I understood it was just natural energy, which some call *Prana*, others *Chi*, and yet others "universal energy", depending on which of the many different cultures it appears in. This energy surrounds us and flows through us all; it feeds us and plays an essential role in our existence. This perception has stayed with me; I see this golden light in the air, fields, rooms or around plants and people. It looks a lot like the very light rain that appeared in the dream I will describe later. This light is the energy that is around us and in us. I do not know all the possibilities this energy has to offer, but one thing is sure, and that is that the flow from my hands helps me heal people. I know that this energy is good for me because I can see it and feel it through my senses and not through religious beliefs.

I then discovered that I was capable of distance healing, although I had not yet begun any training or courses. This new resource also often allowed me to obtain, intuitively and without being able to explain why, sufficient information about what the other person was suffering from. Yet alas, to this day I still make frequent mistakes when it comes to making personal decisions, simply because as soon as my mental acuity is implicated, the answer is provided by my intellect and not my spirit.

The machine project

For years, I devoted myself completely to marketing. I was in charge of the promotion and sales of consumer goods such as winter sports equipment for important international events like the world ski championships or the winter Olympic Games. This said, little by little my career orientation changed, leading me to become involved in benevolent endeavors with a different meaning. I therefore cannot refrain from mentioning a great dream of mine, a philanthropic project that was dear to my heart.

Thus, along with my main activities, I put my heart and soul into developing an exciting and highly ambitious advertising project. It involved producing a machine that was capable of tracing advertising content in the grass grown on sports fields, the kind on which soccer, American football, cricket or rugby is played. This machine was supposed to move the blades of grass in different directions to cause the messages to appear, without any addition of color. These gigantic grassy spaces have enormous advertising potential with extremely large financial means at stake (nine-figure amounts and higher).

However, I had little interest in the latter aspect except for how the financial income would be used for projects with an ethical, humanitarian or ecological scope. I was planning to create "the five-star foundation" with as its logo a star with five branches, each representing a philanthropic field: humanitarian, nutrition, education, wildlife conservation and the protection of natural resources.

That's what made me tick at the time: this machine's potential for communication... I tried everything to convince financial institutions, directors of sports associations, politicians – even to contact the Swiss federal representatives – to support me in this endeavor. I needed their help, not only to produce the machine but also for it to be politically accepted on the playing fields. I only planned to approach FIFA and the big sports federations after I had obtained the advertising agencies' support as well as the status of NGO (Non-Governmental Organization). I did not want to risk any leaks before I had the completed project well in hand. However, although I searched for several years, I found neither adequate support nor any investor who was ready to put up several hundred thousand Swiss francs and then watch the profits be donated to charitable activities, a sector which by definition does not make a profit. Given the corruption scandals of which FIFA is currently the object, such a project would allow them to redeem themselves in the public's eyes.

Knowledgeable people are aware that "billions are just lying around in this way" and that all you have to do is simply to bend down and pick them up.

Yet, one night I became convinced that I was actually going to be able to carry out this project that was so important to me. While I was sitting in my living room, I saw over my partner's shoulder an advert for "MEXX" that caught my eye. It showed a black man hugging a white woman. This image immediately made me think of Benetton, the director of the fashion house. One of the advertisements for this brand of clothing shows a white horse being bred to a black horse. The long collaboration between Luciano Benetton and the nonconformist publicity agent, Oliviero Toscani, is still remembered today. If the first images were pretty, colorful ones depicting children from many races, united and smiling, the later campaigns took a different tack to deliver strong messages about extremely delicate subjects like war or the death penalty, with images that were more and more provocative and even shocking in some people's opinions. I was therefore convinced that Luciano Benetton was the man I was looking for, the one who would be willing to place advertising at the service of humanitarian and ecological causes.

Logo of the "Champions League": the image is very clear despite a poorly-kept playing field. Imagine what Coca-Cola would pay to see its logo shown to an audience of millions. We really would have GREEN COKE then...

The dream

That same night, I had a very strange dream, a sort of waking dream that was to play an essential role in the rest of my career. I was sitting in a clearing and a voice was speaking to me, without my being able to see where it was coming from. This voice was saying, "Luciano Benetton." Luciano brings to mind "*Luce*", the light, and Benetton, the "*bon ton*" (literally "good tone" in French). Immediately after that, I saw golden light raining down, and in that clearing, bathed in this soft luminosity, I was happy and deeply touched. What was happening was right and meaningful. I then woke up in the middle of the night, remembering each detail of this strange and beautiful dream. The voice seemed to remain with me in the bedroom. At that moment, I knew that the only thing to do was to go and see Mr. Benetton to persuade him to participate in my project.

The next day, I decided to call Luciano Benetton. The lady who answered the phone made it clear that Mr. Benetton did not know me and asked why I was calling. I told her I wanted to tell the CEO directly, but she rudely replied that this was not possible and that I had to write to him. "You know, madam," I said to her, "some things cannot be written either as a fax or a letter."

Having said this, and after thinking about it, I nevertheless decided to send a fax which essentially said, "I'd like to speak with you about a very important matter, which will take only ten minutes…" These few sentences were accompanied by three letters of recommendation: one from the international charity Caritas, one from WWF International and one from the Banque Alternative, attesting to the pertinence of my project and assuring Mr. Benetton that he would be able to listen to what I had to say with all due confidence. Two days later, having heard nothing in return, I called again. The same person replied, "We have received your fax, but the way you presented it, it is of no use to us." And she hung up on me.

I was a little upset; I did not know what to do. Then a sign came to me from heaven, without my having to look for it. I knew there was a way... a way; and then everything clicked into place – I would walk to Venice, because an investment of one or two months' hiking in order to get Benetton to sit down and listen to my project for ten minutes seemed to me to be quite fair.

Now that I knew I would be walking to Venice, and to train myself in the patience I would need on the journey, I created a special painting on which I wrote, in tiny letters and an incalculable number of times, the statement that came to me and which read, *"If patience were not tested, it would not be patience."*

To finish the exercise in a meditative state, I washed each of the leaves of my houseplants with warm water. And there are a lot of leaves...

You want to test my faith?
You have to find it first!
Where does faith begin?
Where does stubbornness end?
Hope and despair,
Hand in hand
Believing
Is believing to the very end
If God does not exist
He at least exists in me.

Venice

Thus I left on 5 February 1997. It was raining cats and dogs that morning, but I had set a rule that forbade me to take any form of public transport.

For the entire 800km hike across Switzerland and over the snow-covered Alps, then across northern Italy all the way to Venice, I suffered right from the first day from sharp pains in my feet and joints. It wasn't because of the blisters, because after the nineteenth blister, I had stopped counting. At any time, conscious of and surrounded by that magnificent bright rain, my faith carried me despite all my aches and pains. At times it took everything I had to get back on my feet after a rest.

And yet, during that long 800km walk, those 40 days of solitude, and despite the physical agony, my perceptions grew sharper. I heard that voice which, for weeks, had seemed to come from my own thoughts. It became clearer and clearer, correcting me if I took the wrong road, providing philosophical and instructive food for thought. That voice even told me when the hotel I had chosen would be closed that day. That voice was never wrong.

At one point, after playing the Devil's advocate many times, I finally had to accept that the voice was not coming from my head, but from the spirit world. When I had got past Verona and came to a small village, I sat down under a tree in San Benedetto square and the voice said:

Life is like a card game:
Your past deals them,
The player does his best
But whatever happens in the end
All the cards will again be
In the hands of the Great Spirit.

After exactly 40 days' walk, I arrived at the Benetton offices, where I was very poorly received. I was not even allowed to sit down on the grass outside his company building:

"*Proprieta private*," they said as they kicked me out. I left hastily, shocked because I had been so sure of myself, of having been sent by the Light. Afterwards I stopped in front of a large statue of Jesus, and asked him what "all this foolishness" meant. No answer, just a beatific smile.

Strangely enough, that very same night, I was surprised to catch myself singing in the shower. I was in a good mood, as if everything were all right. But after I had returned by train to Neuchâtel, I was overcome with depression. I feared all these signs were the result of some sort of psychosis. The voice became weaker; the vision, on the other hand, became clearer and clearer.

One morning at about two o'clock I got out of bed to use the toilet. As I was going back to my room, I came upon a Native American in the middle of my hallway!!! Complete with his feather headdress and his regalia with the hair pipe breastplate! There he was, unmoving and peaceful. He was as he was when alive, he was alive! Even today I do not understand my reaction: rather than bowing down, or kneeling or breaking down with emotion, my only thought was: "Ah, so that's him? That's how my guide looks?" and I went back to bed. Imagine my shame the next day!

This Native American, whose name was "White Feather" (as I later learnt), apparently did not hold it against me, because he is still present today during my treatments and continues to teach me. On the other hand, after the night he appeared, he never again appeared to me in his full form, but more subjectively, that is to say, inside my bubble, in the same way that I feel the energy from Michael, from my other guides or the way that I can see the deceased.

Chapter 3

Mental mediumship in everyday life

My late friend Rina

On 26 October 1999, I woke up as usual at 5:00 or 5:30 in the morning to do my three or four hours of daily meditation. While I was in deep meditation, Rina, a friend of mine who had died of cancer about three years previously, came to me. She had left her husband, Steve, and her son, Robin, who was at the time about eleven years old. In those three years she had already paid me a few friendly visits from the other world; but this time, our exchange was of a different nature. Rina began the conversation by saying, "Robin, my son, is feeling abandoned." When I asked her what I could do, her reply was simple and direct: "Talk to Steve." I was quite astonished at this request and unsure whether I had clearly understood, so I asked her to give me a sign, as described in *Meditation with the Guides, The question*, and which is found in the corresponding chapter and which would signify that the message had been correctly understood: "Show me an unusual object that I will come across or see today." And in the very same second, Rina showed me a toy, a red fire truck. I then replied to her, "All right, Rina, if I see a red fire truck today I will go and talk to Steve, but not otherwise." She simply said, "Thank you." That was all; the energy then dissipated and I continued my meditation.

At noon already, my daughter brought me her little red wooden truck so that I could glue the wheel back on.

I jumped slightly, but quickly composed myself. It was not the sign I was waiting for; Rina had spoken to me of a red fire truck and not another truck. Though I paid attention, I saw nothing the whole day, neither in town nor in a window, nor anywhere else. That evening, I switched on the television. There was a film with

Michelle Pfeiffer, a Hollywood production with a happy ending. Suddenly I exclaimed, "The truck! The fire truck!" Michelle Pfeiffer's son, who was sitting on some stairs, was indeed holding a toy in his lap, which was none other than a red fire truck! At that moment, I knew I had correctly understood what Rina had told me; I was truly touched, even overwhelmed.

I thought it over for a few days, but the most difficult thing was to muster the courage to contact Steve. When I decided to do it, his new girlfriend told me where I could reach him. The following Sunday, I went to his workplace, where he was very busy. I briefly suggested we make an appointment to discuss an important matter. Though we only were acquaintances, he accepted without question to meet the day after next, on Tuesday. At that moment I sent a thought out to Rina: "You'll be there, you won't let me down." The second I thought that, I felt a sort of energy run through me, like a pleasantly warm shiver. I had just grasped that she was already there and would be on Tuesday as well.

That day, just before the appointment, I asked Rina what I should say to Steve. She replied, "Just tell him to pay more attention to Robin; that's enough."

When the time came for the meeting, I was more nervous than ever. When Steve got there, though I had already been to the men's room twice, I excused myself to go again. After that, I asked him how Robin was. "He's doing fine, really well." His answer did not allow me to beat around the bush and I plunged straight in: "Listen, Steve, I'm a medium. I don't know everything but something important has taken place with Rina. She came to visit me." I told him about the message about Robin and I also mentioned the test with the fire truck. Steve looked at me with big eyes and answered simply, "You know, you're right. For a while now, I've been worried about Robin's behavior: he comes home from school and shuts himself in his room, all alone in the dark. He doesn't talk to me anymore. When I ask him if he wants to do something with me, he refuses. Since his reaction makes me angry, I don't insist and I leave him alone. We haven't had a talk in a long time and I don't have the courage to bring it up with him any longer." At the end of this talk, I told him that he could take it as he wished, but that his late wife was asking him to pay attention to his son.

The time we spent together in the café was a very powerful one and when we left a strong bond had been created between us, an understanding that went beyond what had been said. When I saw Steve again sometime later, I understood that the commitment he had made to be more attentive to his son had been successful. "We've sorted things out," he told me. "Robin's taken an interest in life again. I've got my boy back and now we have a fantastic relationship."

With this experience, I started to understand the reason for all the years of work, why I had learnt to communicate with the other world. Now things were falling into place and I could be useful to the people around me.

The day after seeing Steve, while meditating, my inner voice spoke to me and brought me back to that wonderful dream about the clearing, the one that had led me to go to Venice. I had a sort of epiphany and I finally understood the real meaning of what I had heard in that clearing: the journey had been the path to my initiation. Luciano = light; Benetton = the *"bon ton"*, the "good tone". I work in the light and the tone, the sound is that of the other dimension which is more beneficial. There is no real link with this Luciano Benetton. It was just a metaphor. If I had not believed in my dream, endured agonizing pain, and been dead tired, I would not be where I am today. The interpretation I made at the time could not have been more mistaken, and after all these events I am writing this book today… The joy I felt at that moment! How great it was! Believing means believing to the very end. He who believes until the end shall cease to believe, for he will know!

Looking for my roots

My origins are Greek, and I was lucky to have been adopted by a wonderful family in Appenzell who took me out of the orphanage. One day, I grew interested in my roots and what they may have been. It was not at all to complete something I felt was lacking in my life in Appenzell, but simply the need to learn about where I came from. The story I am about to tell would be worthy of its own book; I will therefore try to be concise.

In 2000, I took my courage in both hands and began my research. Soon after I had made my first inquiries, the Greek officials informed me that my birth mother was living in Switzerland. But in Switzerland the residential police showed me documents that proved she had returned to Greece. Nevertheless, I had her name and her parents' names. The story could have stopped there... yet it did not! As I continued my quest, first in the Peloponnesus, then elsewhere in the Greek islands, I let myself be guided by my intuition. I spoke to many people to see whether my mother's name was familiar. My psychiatrist friend Aspasia, a lovely and distinguished silver-haired lady of 72 years, went with me. Greece is a vast country. And yet, during one of my solitary strolls, I was led to a man in a shop in Delphi. As I passed by this boutique, it was as if I had been pushed inside, though there was neither any wind nor anyone near me. Yorgos, the owner of the shop, took an interest in my fate. After one or two bottles of Metaxa – a Greek brandy – had been drunk while I explained my story and how far I had come in my research, he promised in an alcoholic fog to find my mother. Of course, I did not believe him. I went back to Switzerland empty-handed and continued my own search.

Two years later, I went back to Greece because a certain Mr. Rieder from the Valais had given me the names of two possible towns in which my mother might be living, which he had located using a pendulum. One of these was Arachova, near Delphi. Aspasia went with me again. My Greek friend and I had questioned countless numbers of people but we had not obtained any satisfactory answers. I went back to Delphi to visit my drinking friend Yorgos. The latter did not welcome me with open arms – quite the opposite: he was angry. I was totally shaken. "Don't you recognize me?" I asked him. "Oh yes, I recognize you! I did everything I could to find your family and I have succeeded. You, however, have not even called me once!" he replied. After several months' work and more than 80 telephone calls, Yorgos had indeed found my family. We quickly made peace and he promised Aspasia he would give her my family's phone number, which he did not have on hand. There were five days left before my flight back to Switzerland, so I looked at the map of Greece to see where I could have a holiday and I saw the words "Cape Sounio", a place below Keratea, a good hour's drive from Athens. The word "Sounio" made me think of "sunshine" and at the same time I saw a sun in front of my third eye. So I went there and stayed at the Aegeon Hotel. But Aspasia had advised me to go to Mykonos, Santorin, Naxos or even elsewhere. Though it had never happened before, we got into an argument over where I should go, because I stuck to my decision. She said there was nothing to see in Sounio except for Poseidon's temple and visiting it would only take one hour. It made no difference to me; I had to go to Cape Sounio. At the Aegeon Hotel, I was welcomed like a son by Simeon, the owner, though I did not even know him. I spent hours with the old man, telling my long story and drinking Metaxa, until he would fall asleep at the table! The next day, he took me to meet his brother Koukos, owner of the restaurant just up the road from the hotel, at Poseidon's temple. I had no idea why Simeon wanted me to meet his brother. His hotel had rooms for 200 guests and was full of tourists. So why me? Koukos asked me to sit down and served me a free drink while he talked business with his brother. Each time I tried to ask him about my family, to find out if he knew the name "Athanassopoulos", he had to get back to the business at hand and I could not decently interrupt while he was talking to his brother, so I was unable to ask him the question I was dying so much to ask.

The Aegeon Hotel, below Poseidon's temple

Poseidon's temple

I finally went back to Switzerland. In the meantime, Yorgos had given Aspasia my uncle's phone number. I say my uncle's number, because I learned my birth mother had passed away! My friend called him for me, spoke to him in Greek and then told me my uncles were expecting me with joy.

Two weeks later, I was back in Greece, in Keratea, the town in which they lived. They welcomed me home like a prodigal son. With my arrival, it was like part of their beloved sister, who had died tragically, had come back to them. Before I met them, I had sent photos and documents proving my Greek identity. When I told my uncles that a few weeks' earlier I had stayed at the Aegeon Hotel in Sounio, only 20 minutes away, they both shouted at the same time, "Simon and Koukos are our closest friends!" They immediately got out a lot of photos of their two friends. It was really crazy! Greece is such a big country! When I was staying in Sounio, if Simeon had not fallen asleep after having drunk too much and if Koukos had not been so busy, my uncles and I would have already been able to meet!

Through two different approaches and at two different times, I had found my family: once with Yorgos' help and once through the two brothers. Simply thanks to my intuition which had been led by my ancestors, with no help from the authorities, with no administrative paperwork...

Many months later, my deceased mother appeared to me for the first time. I asked her why she had not told me she had died much earlier, and she replied, "If I had told you, you wouldn't have gone looking for me, and I wouldn't have been able to guide you to your relatives!"

And now I have a brother, a sister, uncles and cousins who have become part of the family I already had. I see my Greek family every year, and every time it is a genuine pleasure to explore my roots while I fish for octopus.

The story of the search for my roots proves that mediumship can be integrated into everyday life. It shows that our dear ones can help us and how much they still love us from wherever they are, just one frequency away, in the blink of an eye!

Chapter 4

Philosophical approaches

Thought

"In the beginning was the word."

Thus begins the Book of John in the Bible.

Yet, every word, every gesture, every plant, every animal or every man, every creation no matter how refined and subtle it is, originates, shall we say, with a first thought. Consequently, at the beginning was a thought.

Thought is at the origin of everything. It is thought that creates, transforms, and destroys. Wanting to know whether it is thought or information which is emitted first is like asking whether the chicken or the egg came first. In quantum physics, according to current understanding, Dr. Robert Lanza of Wake Forest University in North Carolina in the United States explains that neither time nor space exists, which is why the debate on which came first is senseless. In reality, things are much simpler. Each thought is the beginning and the end of everything. A thought generates another thought, which in turn generates another, according to the process of auto-production. It is what people call God.

Who am I?

God does not influence the happiness or the misfortune of human beings. Indeed, the latter punish themselves for their acts. Each act, be it positive or negative, is registered in our being. In other words, humans choose the experiences they want to live through in function of the level of evolution of their souls/spirits in order to learn to have faith and compassion in certain circumstances. Therefore the greatest gift that God could give to humans is not that of the condition of our birth or our lives, but truly that of our free will. The latter's role is to direct us like a captain sails his ship. Depending on how we use it – to serve our own ego or to promote faith and compassion – our free will helps us to leave the cycle of dualities and reincarnations, thus allowing us to dissolve into the Great Spirit, the Pure Conscience, therefore the Essence.

The terms "soul" and "spirit" can be found in all religions. Some of them assimilate the spirit with a disincarnated state and the soul with an incarnated state. Others, like the Buddhists, consider the soul as an illusion, as the nucleus of the ego. Thus in Buddhism, the soul does not exist. I myself believe that in our culture, the soul is a metaphor which designates our divine essence. This viewpoint suggests that all our souls are identical but that spirit and body are obviously not.

Who am I, me? What is that? My body, my cells, change trillions of times per second; am I my body? At what precise time in this permanent change will I be my body? [Source: SN Goenka, Buddhist teacher.] My spirit travels through time, through lives, changes with each thought... Am I my spirit? At what precise time in this permanent change will I be my spirit? I cannot be my body; it is constantly changing. I cannot be my spirit; it is constantly changing.

"I" do not exist; "me" is an illusion as is "mine" or "my". An object, a person, cannot be "mine", even if I think I own it. Everything has an appearance for a fraction of a fraction of an instant... Who am I? What am I? Where does my conscience come from? Where does that Light come from? That Light which is so bright that it goes through my eyes, yet without blinding me. Where does this all-encompassing peace come from? This peace that is beyond my body, beyond my spirit. Why doesn't it change like my body and my spirit?

Where does this Love come from, the Love that fills my heart to exploding? This unconditional, pure love.

Because "I" am this light, this peace, this love. At all moments, through eternity! That is all I am!

I am a sponge in the ocean and the ocean is in the sponge. My body is in my spirit; my spirit is in my body. The sponge dissolves, but not the ocean. My spirit is in its essence; the essence is in my spirit. The spirit dissolves in the essence, like the sponge dissolves in the ocean. The essence, like the ocean, does not dissolve. I am the essence.

Why do we love our children more than those of other parents? Why do we love our children more if they behave as we expect them to do? Love does not imply desire or greed. So why do we think that to desire is to love? The relationships between parents and children, between lovers, between friends, should be exempt of greed in order to be truly Love.

Where does the illusion stop, if it is not in the essence?

Without the spirit, man could not think; his "thought" would be mere information, only a mechanism transported by neurons and limited to matter alone. Each thought is impregnated with particles of energy. Together these particles construct information. Outside of matter, there is no information without energy. In other words, any form of energy contains the information derived from thought.

This is the essential principle to understanding that the spirit exists. We have a spirit and the spirit is all around us. Not only is it capable of communicating with its environment and outside of it, but it is also connected with each thought. In return, each thought acts on the spirit. A simple remark such as, "You look nice today," or "You look tired," modifies our spirit, our energy field, and our body. Thoughts can be produced by the person himself or be felt by physical or energetic information.

Physical information is received and processed by the five senses. Energetic information is received via the spirit, often called the "sixth sense" or "extrasensory perception". Energetic information is processed by the brain. The result is sent to the intellect.

The spirit is in contact with all the thoughts. It is an intelligent memory, interactive, which exceeds by far the operations of the human body. This physical body is already itself an indescribable miracle of creation and divine essence, of origin and eternity. The lack of voluntary interaction between thoughts and the spirit is one of the major elements in human ignorance. It is the reflection of our evolutionary state. Thoughts are registered in our being by every thought. A simple and purely intellectual thought is registered in our being at any moment, in every situation. The "Great Thought" perceived by the spirit and translated by our higher conscience is only registered in silence.

Who am I again?

In my personal introspection, the question of the totality, or the aspect of a soul or spirit, is a recurring one. Does my incarnated spirit represent everything I am, or just a small part of it? If we consider our bodies as a glass and our spirit as the contents of that glass, all of the information collected throughout an entire life would be represented by the liquid in the glass, the water. All this water contains information. If we take a drop of that water, it would contain the same amount of information as the total amount of the water. Given this hypothesis, it may be that my incarnated spirit or the deceased person with whom I am in contact is only a fraction of the total of what we are.

This question on the aspect of the totality or the fraction that we might be also comes up when the subject of soul mates arises. What are soul mates? Are they just another aspect of me which is having that experience at that time, while I am having others and we find each other by chance or by destiny? Silver Birch, the entity that is channeled by Maurice Barbanell, spoke of a diamond cut according to different facets and said that each being was only a facet of the diamond. Ever since I heard that statement, it has been on my mind. One guide, other than my guide Jonathan, also mentioned these aspects of the personality. Jonathan has also shared his view of things related to aspect or totality [see the corresponding chapter]. I do not have the absolute proof to establish the aspect or the totality of our incarnated being. In my professional work I have not come face to face with this irrefutable proof. Aside from that, in my teaching, I do not know how to introduce the subject well, given that I do not base it on supposition or hypothesis. On the other hand, any philosophy surrounding this theme is always welcome. Quantum physics could provide some ideas and answers, supposing that an atom can be in several places at once.

There, where Nothing leans forward
There
Where he takes All in his arms
There
Where both unite in tender kisses
There
My love
Lives the moment

In his books on "Water Memory", Masaru Emoto does a fine job of representing thought, its registration and thus its memory. To show how thought influences water, he affixed a label with a word or sentence to a Petri dish filled with water. Then he placed the water in a freezer for three hours at -25°C. During that time, the water was impregnated with the word or sentence. After removing the dishes, Emoto examined the crystals that had formed. In general, water that had been exposed to words like "you disgust me" formed incomplete crystals or ones that were distorted like diarrhea. On the other hand, water that had been exposed to words like "love" or "peace" formed crystals that looked like splendid snowflakes. As usual, when the scientific world has to deal with pioneering assumptions or ones that upset established schemas, some scientists oppose the results. In fact, the experience was repeated several times, and the results obtained – the images – were only similar and not identical! When you look at the number of photos, the crystals cannot leave you unmoved. Since the scientific world did not validate his work, Emoto described it as an art and not as a science.

Thought alone modifies our scope and our conscience. Calming, meditative thoughts allow us to see through the fog caused by the emotions of greed and aversion. Our conscience leads us to personal success and, more essentially, to peace. If we are at peace, we perceive our true nature and the nature of all things more and more clearly, which is to say, in the end, that thought brings us to our essence; to the Great Spirit.

Chapter 5

Karma – Cause and effect

The past is written in the present
So much future depends on so little present
The present is everything
And the only moment we can influence.

According to the Buddhist and Hindu teachings on the continuity of life in the afterlife, and especially with respect to reincarnation, personal thought is registered.

The Sanskrit word "karma" simply means "cause and effect". In the Western world, "karma" is especially used to designate negative causes or effects. This very idea is false! Karma can be good or bad, and even neutral. Indeed, it is simply an event or a chain of events that lead to effects, a sort of logical series. We have the ability to grasp the causes and effects in our present life. Yet we can hardly believe that some aspects of a past life can have effects on our present one.

Karma can be described in several ways. Sogyal Rinpoche, author of *The Tibetan Book on Living and Dying*, describes karma as a pile of playing dice. Each of the dice represents a different entity. Though each is different they are connected and dependent on each other in a logical manner. A candle flame is a good example of karma's cause and effect relation. Where we think we see only one flame, it is in fact millions of flames in succession, each one depending on the one before it. The information that is us resonates with some of the other information but not all of it. When we die, the spirit that is us leaves its charnel envelope with all the information it contains. By reincarnating, the spirit still contains all the information that has not been dissolved. The dissolution of this information can take place from birth to death, in order to get out of the cycle of reincarnation and become only essence. The Tibetan Buddhists call this process "bardo". This is why karma is a series of logical events organized by our own thought and our stored memory. God does not place anything we encounter in our path. He is not responsible for our destinies either. Our information resonates with people and situations. Like a magnet attracted to a piece of iron or the negative pole of another magnet. My convictions are forged by my personal experiences; they have completely convinced me that reincarnation really takes place!

A spirit that leaves the body when it dies has to have first been incorporated into it at birth. When my daughter was born, I witnessed her spirit enter her body. While my wife was in labor and the black tuft of my daughter's hair was already visible, a ball of lavender-colored light came down at great speed onto my wife's head. Suddenly it slowed – that could not be more precise! Then it swerved and came onto my wife's shoulder, leaning against her head. This ball stayed there for a few minutes like it was watching what was happening. Suddenly it entered the body of the baby girl that was still coming into the world. Since that experience which I saw with my own eyes, I am certain that the soul and the spirit enter the body at birth. Not before, during pregnancy. I am sure that the pretty lavender color of that ball of light is an indication of the evolutionary stage of the soul, or at least of the average level of information it contained at that specific moment.

I would like to draw particular attention to the work of the late Ian Stevenson, a Canadian doctor in psychiatry and professor at the University of Virginia School of Medicine in the United States. What I liked very much about his work was his scientific rigor. He was neither a religious person nor an esoteric one; he was factual. The goal of his work was to establish scientific proof of reincarnation. To provide factual proof of reincarnation, he interviewed over 3,000 children who claimed to have memories and reminders of a past life. To obtain these accounts, he covered 90,000 kilometers a year, from Africa to Alaska. Then, in order to verify the information provided by these children and to dismiss any psychosis, he used his global network. This network of people provided him with birth certificates, police reports and medical files. Ian Stevenson focused essentially on children between the ages of three and eight. According to him, in this age bracket, children remember their past lives better and more authentically. Ian Stevenson thought that most of the pathologies from which these children suffer originated in a traumatic experience in a past life or were the result of a traumatic death. Birthmarks may correspond to injuries from a previous life. Fears, paranoia or even gifts – the ability to play an instrument or speak an unknown language – may be inherited from a former existence.

One of the cases studied by Professor Stevenson (*Twenty Cases Suggestive of Reincarnation*) was that of a small boy who may have committed suicide in a previous life. Through studies carried out according to the child's accounts, his previous identity was found. Even his sister in the former life was found. As she was still alive, she confirmed that her brother had committed suicide with a bullet in the neck. Professor Stevenson read the autopsy report on the suicide. The bullet's exit hole was at the top of the skull. On examining the skull of the little boy, Stevenson found the scar from the bullet wound in the form of a birthmark.

Another similar case presented by Professor Stevenson was of a boy who said he had been murdered by a friend. Research done to corroborate his claims led Professor Stevenson to the murdered person and his murderer. He was also able to consult photos of the autopsy. On the body, the bullet had entered the stomach and made a small hole with a larger hole in the back as it exited. On examining the boy, there were two birthmarks in the same places and with the same shapes as the bullet holes seen in the autopsy photos.

In this book, I do not want to expound upon the phenomenon of reincarnation. The cases and analogies that I have presented should be used to understand the different connections that exist in parapsychology. Interpreting the facts is a purely professional thing. If you take the example of a child who suddenly begins to speak a foreign language that he has never learnt, anyone who believes in reincarnation will claim that is proof of a former life. The Catholic priest will begin his exorcism procedures since in his eyes the child is possessed by a demon or by the devil himself. The medium will be happy to observe a spontaneous trance in a child so young.

Chapter 6

ESP – Extrasensory perception

Before we delve into the extrasensory perceptions, or ESPs, let's take a short journey to explore our body and our spirit. We are all familiar with the five senses: sight, hearing, touch, smell and taste. Given that their tasks and capacities are well-known, I won't discuss them further. Buddhism expands on our Western definition of the five senses. The Buddhist definition makes it easier to understand and describe human nature by means of an additional sense, the sixth sense. In English, this sixth sense is called the "*Mind*". "*Mind*" can also be expressed as the "mental part" depending on the context. The most common synonym is "spirit". In Pali, the ancient Sanskrit dialect, the word "*vedana*" can be translated as "feelings", "sensations", or "perceptions". This word not only encompasses all the perceptions of the five physical senses, but also the information gathered by this sixth sense. This highly peculiar sense is divided into different clear-senses: clairvoyance, clairaudience, clairsentience or "clear feeling", clairolfactance, clairgustance and claircognizance or "clear knowing". The clear-senses can be trained, in particular by using the techniques included in the "Exercises" chapter in this book.

The spirit, or "*mind*" – the sixth sense – is infinite. It perceives the most subtle information. This information is registered and memorized in the energy field of a living or dead person, in an object, in a place, and more. This energetic registration allows us to read a person whether they are right in front of us or 20,000 kilometers away. I would even bet I could read an astronaut in a space station. Reading the subtle information in an energy field does not require a physical vector. This exploit is possible because the Mind is infinite. Time and distance only exist in physical laws.

To receive an ESP, I expand my conscious energy field by sending a ray from my aura to my target. This target can be the aura of another person, a place, another time or the field of a deceased person, for example. My energy will be focused on my target. My spirit has expanded and receives subtle information: the energetic recordings of the object of my reading. My brain is now in charge of translating the information that the ray from my aura has perceived to my intellect in a rational manner.

The ESPs and their potential are not only used by sensitives to help and support the people that consult them. They have also been employed by one of the most famous American intelligence agencies. Despite the CIA's efforts to keep the "Stargate project" a secret, one of its main subjects, Joseph McMoneagle, broke the silence and revealed the CIA's project to the general public.

In the early 1970s, McMoneagle, who was in the US Army at the time, discovered his sensitive faculties after a near-death experience. Following this discovery, he worked for some 20 years for the Army, but also for the CIA and other secret services involved in this governmental project. The applied practice was called "remote viewing". From the military base at which he was stationed, he supplied information that could not be accessed by "normal" means about the places in which hostages were detained, the locations in which the enemy had military bases or weapons, or where lost planes could be found. McMoneagle received several medals, notably the Legion of Merit for civil service. Today, he no longer works for the Army. He is pursuing his work on his own account. The procedure used here is classical ESP that reads a field, an object or a person at a distance.

I've also had similar experiences using a video conferencing application with people in New Delhi, Tokyo or Heidelberg, by reading what is inscribed in their recent memory. I did these readings though these people were hundreds, even thousands of kilometers away.

Whether I speak to a deceased person, read the aura of a living person near me or at a distance, or visit an unknown place, it is always MY memory that produces analogies with feelings, sounds, images or any other sensation…

The brain can only look into the memory of what it has experienced. It cannot translate information it does not know to the intellect. It cannot imagine anything unknown and describe it exactly. It is as if the brain was playing a sort of "Pictionary". All forms of telepathy go through this "subjective" filter.

If a medium has developed their objective clear-senses, they will be able to express themselves in a language that is unknown to their memory. They will be able to create new remedies and new technologies without having any scientific knowledge stored in their memory.

It is rare to come across adults that have objective ESP. Olivia Boa [see the chapter, The aura] is a remarkable representative of this group and a good example of an "objective" sensitive. "Objective" perceptions are present above all in children or in some teenagers. Most sensitives perceive things subjectively.

The big difficulty with subjective ESP is to put the mind aside and to recognize the reality of our perception. This may seem contradictory: the mind has to be set aside to let in information that is translated by the mind. Moreover, this information is supplied by the memory which is seated… in the mind. Putting the mind aside while continuing to work with it may seem highly ironical, and yet… The key lies in decoding the process that allows the mind to provide its information as well as that by which we manage to see how the information appears to our intellect [see exercises].

Objective perception is special and rare, but that does not mean it does not exist. With clairvoyance – thus with objective vision – the medium sees outside himself with his eyes wide open and not focused on his subjective inner screen. He sees in holograms, in three dimensions. The appearance of the dead, of places, or even of the patients' organs, are seen just as they are and not in their symbolic forms. It is a matter of correctly distinguishing between the objective perception of physical mediumship and the materialization it produces. We separate mental mediumship – which is only perceived by the medium – from physical mediumship in which the manifestation is perceived by the five physical senses, not only by the medium. An objective perception is therefore seeing what is real: hearing a real voice (even in an unknown language), tasting something, smelling something or even feeling another person's physical condition in your own body. Yes, you can be catapulted into another dimension, another reality, another frequency, and be there in three dimensions. And this is not due to some psychosis, or to schizophrenia! Out-of-Body Experiences (OBEs), astral voyages, Near-Death Experiences (NDEs), shamanic voyages – all of these are examples of objective ESP.

Here is one example among hundreds of an objective NDE: a boy was in the surgery of a hospital, surrounded by doctors and by both his parents. Even though he had been pronounced clinically dead, he came back to life. He then said he had arrived at a tunnel of light where he met his grandmother and his sister, who were very well. They told him he could not go with them because it was too soon for him. When the boy told this story to his parents, they did not take him seriously. Their daughter was at school. It was only that evening, when they got home, that the parents learned with great sadness that their daughter had died earlier in the day. The joy of knowing their beloved daughter was alive and with her grandmother was as great as the sadness they felt at losing her.

Innumerable people have experienced out-of-body experiences without being in a near-death state. A documentary relates the experience of a man who, during a safari, was surprised by a lion that charged out of a bush. The lion caught him by the back of his neck and shook him like a teddy bear.

This man watched the entire scene, three meters above his body, without feeling the slightest pain. This experience proves one thing: we are spirit; we can enter and leave our bodies!

The majority of mediums see in a subjective manner. It would be interesting to study blind people who are sensitives and to compare the cerebral images of a group of blind people who had previously been able to see with another group of blind people who have never been able to see. Which parts of the brain would be active? Would some regions of the brain that are usually dedicated to sight be used in that case for other functions or other senses, thus allowing the person to obtain the same information they would have if they had been able to see? Is objective clairvoyance possible for the sightless? This type of research would provide greater understanding of the cerebral correlations and movements in the different states. Some studies, notably the one by psychologist Kenneth Ring, PhD, and Sharon Cooper, MA of the University of Connecticut ("Near-Death and Out-of-Body Experiences in the Blind: A Study of Apparent Eyeless Vison"), have focused on the experiences of blind people during NDEs. Accounts of NDEs in blind people are perfectly similar to those of the sighted and the majority of them say they have "seen" even if it is difficult for them to describe this phenomenon which they have never experienced. In their numerous studies, the authors provide the testimonial by Vicki Umipeg, who was born blind and who, during an NDE and OBE, saw a physical body from her ceiling before realizing it was hers. She then passed through the roof of the hospital and was able to enjoy the magnificent panorama which spread before her...

Therefore this might very well mean that the spirit perceives in spite of the physical means of classical perception and that this subtle perception is accessible in a modified consciousness state. I would be delighted to work with these people, even if it were only to help them develop an extra sense.

The diagram below helps us to distinguish between the two main categories of mediumship. The ESPs are not included here. They are part of the mental category of mediumship. The latter is not limited to psychic reading. Spiritual healing can involve both categories: some phenomena are perceived by the five senses, by anyone, not only by the healer who is performing a treatment.

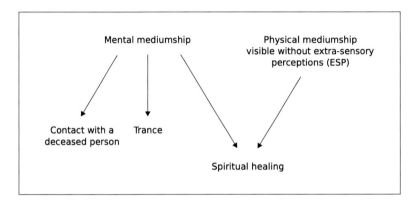

In the subjective perceptions, the greatest challenge is to respond to a question while disregarding the mind. There are so many opinions that can be given on the subject...

To prevent the mind from interfering and influencing the medium, it is easier to have no information that could feed it (not know which deceased person a client may have in his entourage, or what question(s) about his life a client may have). The most important thing for the medium is to remain outside of and detached from the client's expectations.

Chapter 7

The aura

When a spirit is incarnated, when a person is alive, an energy field emanates from them as a luminous halo made of layers of different colors. Some sensitive people are able to see this energy field which is called "aura". The four main layers are: the physical or etheric aura, the mental aura, the emotional aura and finally the spiritual aura. Each layer contains information about these different levels. For example, in the physical layer, you can see the first level of a person's current condition. The memory of former illnesses appears at a second level. Thus it is for each layer, within the informational domain it contains.

The eye sees auras in several steps. First of all, a white or light yellow halo appears around the physical body of the person.

As objective vision becomes more refined, we see colors that indicate the present state. This emanation is therefore a fluctuating one. Objective vision does not provide a precise reading of the aura at the level of the colors. Due to this lack of precision, an objective reading of the aura is senseless.

The belief that the different chakras have the colors of the rainbow is a joke. It's all very well to want to think they are colored. This belief may be useful in a subjective reading. But believe me, the chakras are a light golden-yellow color just like any pure energy. The yogis in India are the first to support my opinion on this matter, since long ago they received symbols that are very different from our colors. These symbols refer to evolutionary stages that are often represented as lotus petals. The base chakra "Mooladhara" has two petals. The number of petals doubles with each chakra as you move up. At the crown chakra "Sahasrara", the lotus flower has 28 petals.

The only person who has proven to me they have seen the energy emanating from a person beyond a simple perception of a colored field is Olivia Boa, therapist and artist in Fribourg (www.projetboa.com). She is a sensitive with the most objective clairvoyance I have ever seen. She has allowed me to consult her sketches of auras and fields. Using neurological devices, I have been able to test their precision. As you can read in some scientific studies, Olivia's diagnostics have turned out to be

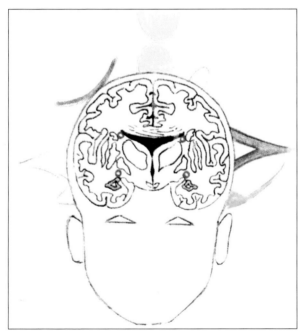

1. The intellect zone is shut down and shows little activity. The sensitivity zone is limited, as is the thalamus.

2. The connection between the two hemispheres is different. The planning, reasoning and personality zones are barely visible, even absent.

3. The cingulate cortex zone is paired with the auditory zone (hearing may switch to "automatic" mode) or the speech production zone (Broca's area).

4. The amygdala is joined to this pair of zones.

astonishingly precise! They support my experience that chakras do not have the colors certain esotericists attribute to them! Olivia Boa specifies that in her visions, she perceives energy like the heat rising from a candle, like a field under the summer sun, always moving. Pure energy in fact has no color!

Above is one of Olivia Boa's many drawings. It is illustrated in color so the reader can understand it, but this does not mean at all that the energy emanations are colored! This illustration is her drawing of me when I was in a trance.

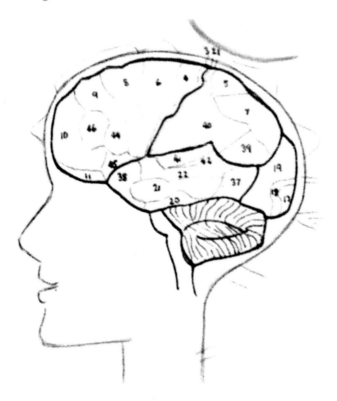

The SMA (supplementary motor area) is "shut down".

To summarize Olivia Boa's reading of my brain in these slow frequencies, thought is no longer possible in this head.

It is astonishing to see how precise a subjective vision can be. But that does not mean it happens in color.

However, this is not to say that an aura does not include colors; but that is another question. The colors in an aura – which show the physical condition or emotional state of the moment – are the result of a biochemical process. This has nothing at all to do with the color of a chakra. These colors are variable. They depend on the person's state. The rainbow colors of the chakras were invented by Western esotericists. This in itself is not a problem. If we look at the function of each of these chakras, we can easily accept their color as a description. For example, let's take the base chakra which has been described as red: its function is related to physical strength and to the forces of ancestral instincts such as anger or fear which are obviously driven by strong motor forces and energetic imbalances. At the same time, these instincts and these powers are the farthest from the energies of the higher consciousness.

For a precise and detailed reading of the aura, it is therefore essential to establish a personal and subjective range of each color and each layer of the aura. This may seem fastidious at first. It is a highly detailed task that is not done all at once. It takes practice as well to construct this range of colors. The task is also done with the colors you discover according to the different states of the person you are reading.

The mental layer provides elements relative to reasoning, intellect and its interests. This layer mainly reveals how a person functions. The emotional layer provides information on the person's affective experience, his joys and sorrows in the various periods of his life. Finally, the spiritual layer concerns what interests him in his particular domain, the importance of this with respect to his personal existence, sometimes religions, dogmas and the person's degree of evolution.

To establish your own range of colors organized by the layers of the aura, it is recommended to proceed in a pragmatic way.

So as not to influence the reader in the construction of his or her procedure, I will just give a brief example of my own range. Here is an extract of the physical layer:

A dirty yellow makes me think of pus; red makes me think of blood; green reminds me of nausea or stomach pains; gray, of the brain's gray matter, and so on.

When I evaluate a person, I proceed in an organized manner and decide what layer I will read. If I find the above-mentioned colors in that person, I see they are suffering from an infection, a blood disorder, a digestive problem, or a neurological or cerebral issue. The term "subjective" thus does not mean that the information perceived is false. It describes the way in which it is perceived. This term can be better understood through a study of mediumistic readings. To learn how to draw up a personal table of subjective colors, see the chapter on "exercises".

Chapter 8

Fortune-telling

Fortune-telling and predicting the future are often – mistakenly! – associated with mediumship. One of the illusions of the esoteric world is the interpretation of the word "medium" and its transposition to the practitioner of mediumship. There is still a misunderstanding between the medium and the fortune-teller who tells fortunes or predicts the future. Let me be clear about this: none of the forms of mediumship I am presenting in this book can be used to predict the future!

People who consult with fortune-tellers are looking for a message about their future whatever the cost. They are expecting a message that encourages them, a message that will confirm their wishes. This in itself is a positive approach. However, sometimes these people are hoping for a message that would allow them to deny or avoid personal responsibility. These clients are extremely gullible, even desperate. They can easily be manipulated.

A fortune-teller can receive false information, or even interpret it erroneously. The greatest damage is done by fortune-tellers who come close to the truth or who construct the past accurately. Indeed, if the past is established in a more or less accurate manner, how could a person who is in a fragile emotional or mental state not begin to believe the predictions about the future? I'm not talking about charlatans, because except for stories that are pure invention, they are not capable of providing accurate information. I have myself sometimes deviated, which means that the information I received was accurate, but the source was not what I expected. This story will be told later.

When the client is consulting with a fortune-teller, his discernment, his objectivity, or in a broader sense his logic, are completely dismissed. He may be wrongly influenced by the false information from the fortune-teller, or even by elements that are contrary to his best interests. All the discernment of the client is set aside, in particular if the first information provided by the fortune-teller was true.

To avoid this unpleasant situation, anyone who would like to learn more about his path in life in order to make thoughtful and relevant choices would be well advised to consult a trained "sensitive". The latter is quite capable of reading a person's energy field or aura and will be able to reveal the client's hidden potential. The sensitive will know how to encourage his client on the path to self-confidence and will be able to reveal their own potential in a positive manner, rather than by telling lies about the future.

Positive words sow positive seeds that sprout positive fruit!

Let's be fair and admit nevertheless that a good fortune-teller can see the future. Although the future is a relative notion, as, like distance, time does not exist. Predicting the precise moment that an event is going to happen is quite another story, another challenge... Time is a human or physical tool to describe movement, that's all. The Greek philosopher Plotinus said at the time: "All is in the one and the one is in all." So how to make space or time of it? Even if fortune-telling is possible, that does not prevent the problems and difficulties revealed in this chapter.

Fortune-telling or future prediction is one of the areas in which there are the most errors in reading information! Why are there so many inaccuracies and mistakes in predictions about the future, assuming that the future is written? Even if time or the future is predetermined, that does not mean we are puppets following a predetermined route. We can decide on our fate at any time.

Before continuing, I want to insist that it is practically impossible to discern the various sources from which information about the "future" emanates! It does not matter whether a fortune-teller has genuine perceptions, visions or feelings. The difficulty lies in knowing from which source it comes. That is great talent! And very rare!

But aside from that, many fortune-tellers I have met as students or through my research are absolutely incapable of carrying out a factual psychic reading. They simply lack solid basic training.

There are many sources of perception that can provide information and thus enable actual deduction or ESP, but that have nothing to do with the client's future:

- Gestures/mimics/appearance
- Psychology/rhetoric
- Personal fields:
  ○ Aura = memory: desires/aversions
  ○ The person's actual thoughts
- A deceased person whose level is not necessarily known
- A place
- An object or piece of jewelry
- The akashic records (see below)
- A past life
- Genealogy
- The future, perhaps
- And unfortunately the fortune-teller's mind.

The first source of perception to take into account is the medium's own mind. After that there are the client's mental projections – the thoughts he is having at the moment and which he is sending telepathically. There are also all the memories of past thoughts that are inscribed in the client's aura or divergence (see below) by the medium. The deceased people's opinions – whether or not they have transitioned to the spiritual world – may also be a source of perception. These opinions may be false or may vary according to the personality of the deceased. There is also the memory of places or things that have nothing to do with the client or his future and which are nevertheless inscribed in the field of his aura. For example, this might be a present offered by one person to another. Once all these sources of information have been identified, and only after that, the medium can perhaps access time, the future, a universal conscience, the memory of the above-mentioned "akashic record". The akashic record is mentioned in the Upanishads, texts which are in a sense the Hindu "bible". This is a sort of cosmic memory that records the world's events. Since time is an illusion, the future would be one as well.

Given these different sources of information, even the best-intentioned "fortune-teller" is incapable of perceiving the source that emits this information about his client's future...

The disillusionment is great when you find out that the images which were accessed were not those of the future. I myself experienced a great disillusionment about the future. In 2000, I was sitting one morning in deep meditation. I was doing my daily Kriya breathing exercises which I perform before my other practices. My thoughts were entirely focused on my meditation. Suddenly, I was catapulted into a bubble in which I saw the following scene in three dimensions. There were skyscrapers under water, beneath several meters of water. The sea was calm, so no tidal wave was taking place. Or maybe the scene took place after a tidal wave. On this image of underwater skyscrapers, "2014" was written in large numbers. Considering the layout of the city, I thought that New York or some other city with skyscrapers near the sea would be flooded. Whilst all over the world people were excited about 21 December 2012, the date announced by the Mayas as the end of the world, I was smiling sweetly. The end of the world expected by so many did not happen in 2012. Actually, it is now 2015 and no huge metropolis has been submerged beneath the waves. Did I confuse 2014 with 2004, the year that a huge tsunami did destroy parts of Asia?

This said, we can see that even in a deep and neutral state, we can still make a huge mistake! To date this has been my only experience with seeing into the future. Given the extent of the destruction that I saw, it's a good thing this vision was inaccurate. I am wondering why these visions were false, and I still can't explain why I feel that scene will occur someday. On the other hand, in terms of the study of how perception works, it's a pity I was wrong.

Earlier I spoke of divergence. Divergence is another example of how it is possible to make a mistake about the information received during a psychic reading. I had this experience once when I was in consultation with a client.

While I was doing a psychic reading, I was giving her information about her recent past. The information was acknowledged as correct; for example, the purchase of cleated soccer shoes for her son. During my reading, I clearly saw that she had played with or watched someone play with a kite. Whereas my entire reading was accurate, she denied the information about the kite. I was aware that my reading was accurate so I insisted and she kept on adamantly denying it. I even went so far as to smile and make a bet that she had to be suffering from memory loss because I knew the difference between a projection of my mind and a real ESP! She accepted the bet because she knew she was right. I kept thinking about it as the hours and days went by, until the moment when, a few days after the séance, I got a phone call from that client. I took the opportunity to ask about the kite, and she denied the information yet again. While we were talking, I suddenly thought of her son, who was my last source of accurate information, relating to the football shoes he had got. So I asked her if her son had played with a kite; she said he had not. Faced with her denial, I asked her to ask him. The next day I got a photo on my mobile phone of a show in which her son was playing with an enormous kite! This experience showed me that the kite was not in my client's field. In fact, the show was a surprise for the parents. Therefore my client could not have had the information about the kite. My spirit had, by itself, contacted the son's energy field when I spoke of the football shoes. My spirit had therefore left my client's energy field, her aura, and diverged!

Some time ago, I was approached by someone who offers remote fortune-telling on TV and who wished to recruit me. Despite the fact that I told him I did not believe in that and that I was not interested, this person – who calls himself a medium(!) – insisted. Very well, I met him, with my assistant, Mélanie. When we saw this man, we were forced to conclude that he had no idea what an ESP was and how it functions. His working method was purely intellectual! When I showed him how a real reading was done he was very surprised. When I contacted a deceased person for him, he became so afraid his forehead was beaded with perspiration. He begged me to stop immediately... Funny behavior for someone who calls himself a medium...

When I asked him if he had consulted his cards about me, to see if I was the right person for his project, he burst out laughing. He confided that he would never tell his own fortune because he DIDN'T BELIEVE IN IT!

Nevertheless, the big boss wanted to see me to test me. The meeting went more or less along the same lines as the one with the pseudo-medium. I showed him how a psychic reading was done after proper training. He was just as excited as his employee. At the end of the interview, the boss agreed that I was not operating on the same level as most of his employees. Our paths separated before they even merged because I never heard from him or his company again...

A psychic reading of the distant past cannot be done, unless there were major events with lasting effects. Every person has been happy, felt sad, lost a loved one, moved house, succeeded, and failed. The memory of the recent past is much more precise. Of course, a medium will have to refrain from bringing up information such as "you brushed your teeth and got dressed", or mentioning any other information that would correspond to everyone's logical daily routine anyway, or at least the routine that each person may often have. On the other hand, information like "you have just broken a cup, had a punctured tire, got ready for a journey, bought something specific" can be mathematically verified and calculated.

To summarize, this means information on a client's recent experience that is read in their energy must be accurate between 85 and 100% of the time. Guessing reaches 30% of the information that the client is interested in. If a fortune-teller is not able to give this type of information about the recent past, how then can it be supposed they can access the future?

Chapter 9

Mediumship: for whom and why?

My experience has taught me that it is possible to sort people who want to practice mediumship into four main groups.

The first group is made up of people who are or who feel like they are victims of their perceptions. I am not talking about hysterical or mentally ill people; I will return to that subject later. These people have begun – already in childhood or as adolescents – to see the dead, to feel others more intensely or to have premonitions. Very often, these perceptions that occur spontaneously are denied by the people around them – especially when the dead are perceived – and are associated with great fear. In many cases, when these perceptions begin in childhood, the parents do not understand what is happening to their children. These children will often end up being sent to psychiatrists [see "Hannes Jacob Syndrome – Sensitive Disorder"] and will be treated as though they were mentally ill. Whether they are adolescents or adults, these people will very often be locked into their fear, which is quite understandable, in fact. They have nonetheless found the courage to face these fears by deciding to manage their perceptions.

For this first group, the battle is already halfway won. When these people come to take classes in mediumship or in sensitivity, they understand and accept that they are not insane, in the medical sense of the word.

In the second group, we have the people who have lost one or more dearly loved ones. They are often incapable of overcoming their grief, of turning the page so to speak. So, rather than turning to a religion or to a medium, these people want to "perceive" for themselves. They want to meet the deceased ones and see if humans are truly immortal in nature, if there is really a life after death. Indeed, in the world of the living, there is much debate about the afterlife and its existence: "Nobody has come back to tell us whether there is life after death!" This saying is false: the dead have come back by the millions to tell us there is a life after death. There is even irrefutable proof, notably through physical mediumship and instrumental trance communication. [For more information, see the corresponding chapters.]

The third group is rather ignorant, even unhealthy. The people in this group choose to learn and practice mediumship with their intellect. They do so for money or to gain some delusional spiritual power. This group encounters the greatest frustrations because such people discover that learning to practice mediumship requires a genuine and consequential personal investment. Its study includes moments of great despair when the learner cannot manage to maintain the right frequency. The road to communication with the hereafter can be very rocky and filled with obstacles.

In my experience, I can generally say this: the people with the biggest egos cause the most damage in the expression of their "gift". When they understand that mediumship is a real learning process, or see that the training is not going the way they wanted it to, they run away.

Other students immediately start teaching as soon as they finish two years of study at the school *fréquences*. They do a lot of advertising for their activity and stop training themselves. There is a huge gap between knowing how to communicate with a deceased person and knowing what takes place in the energy field of a third person who is training. It takes a great deal of time to be able to get into contact with another person and know what is happening. It is insulting to teach innocent students without having the necessary skills. Who would want to train with a person that only has two years' experience?

I myself have been confronted with a deeply depressive client. She was placed in psychiatric care in an unstable condition. She had consulted a mediumship "professor" for a so-called "trance" or "channeling". This professor had given her the green light to commit suicide, affirming that her guides would accompany her and that there would be no problem. I was floored by her story! Her psychiatrist told it to me because I knew the "professor" who had come up with this "message". He advised me to denounce her to the cantonal doctor [chief medical officer of the region] or to the police. I did not do so as this is not my role. But after learning about this case, I am not surprised that mediumship has such a poor reputation.

The last group, doubtless the richest and most magnificent, is made up of people who want to serve and to help others. This genuine desire to serve, to make oneself available for the well-being of others, is a quality that is found much more often in the classes on healing. The egos of students of mediumship are generally more developed. These trends can be observed everywhere in Europe. And yet, there are students who decide to choose to develop this sense to serve even more than they now do.

Often these people want to better serve in the professional area in which they are already working. Not just in the areas of various treatments, education, therapy, or meditation but also in banking, farming, medicine, legal services or human resources. I have nevertheless been seeing a positive development in mediumship classes over the past few years. More and more students choose this education to train their senses in general. Not only to get into contact with the dead or open a clinic. They want to continue as teachers, nurses... to carry on practicing their jobs while mastering their subtle perceptions to better understand a student, a patient or a client. Thus the therapist trains to better hear the information from his guides and so on.

Still in terms of generalization, the individuals who are the shyest and most humble are often the most predisposed to mediumship. People who take the course in mediumship above all for personal development, those who attend classes with the genuine vocation to assist, those who have a high level of spiritual energy without realizing it – these are the people who become the most beautiful tools for Light. How glorious it is to observe them coming gently out of their shyness, opening like rosebuds in the sun, discovering themselves and further enriching their entourage. How beautiful it is to watch their incredulous yet happy faces as they describe, for the first time, a living person seated behind them, without seeing them and without making a mistake; or when they describe a deceased person by giving their exercise partner irrefutable proof of that presence in the afterlife. This fills me with joy. But the joy does not stop at the contact with a deceased person. It is the same when a novice gets unquestionable proof that his spiritual healing or Therapeutic Touch (TT) [see the chapter on healing] is producing results. When these people heal suddenly and inexplicably, the student's heart glows.

I am so happy to have participated in spreading this joy!

Communicating with the spiritual world is something that has to be learned. It's not just a question of frequencies. Indeed, if it were not possible to learn how to communicate in this way, my school would not be as successful. Mediumship is not a question of geographical location or placement within the spiritual world. It's not a gift for the select few. It's not a way to get to a certain spiritual level, either. A medium, alas, can have absolutely all the faults related to his humanity, all the negative traits that can be imagined: from the egotist to the pedophile, from the manipulator to the mythomaniac, from the cheater to the thief and all the addictions that may exist. When I was training, I met mediums – even some very well-known ones – who had these negative traits. I myself know my failings and acknowledge that I am not a saint, but I am capable of speaking with the dead.

Why isn't mediumship spiritual? As I have explained above, communicating with the spiritual world is done at a certain frequency that must be found and maintained. Looking for this frequency is not a spiritual act but a capacity that is to be developed and maintained. It's precisely like learning to walk a tightrope: you have to find your balance. The medium must find similar balance, but on a frequency. Once it is found, this balance must be maintained for a certain time. Here is the aerial acrobat – the medium. From the outset, let me make this clear: mediumship, or being able to speak with the deceased, is not the goal in itself, but simply a tool on the spiritual path. Talking to a deceased person is a magnificent thing, as much for the deceased as for the living and provides proof relating to the messages delivered. At the same time a medium's calling is to develop their sensitivity and perceptions in order to get closer to their essence, to themselves and thus to reach their potential. Mediumship can be learned quickly. Getting used to living with it takes more time, sometimes an entire life!

For a long time, I was one of those people who believed that a medium was a good, spiritual person... I don't dare recall the pain I felt when I discovered the truth! I will tell you about it so you will not experience the same disappointment. When beautiful people invest themselves in this magnificent path of mediumship or healing, I am deeply touched. It really warms my heart to meet people who want to serve, who are constantly working on their spiritual development, who suffer as they commit themselves to do good around them. Spiritual development is the key. Since training one's sensitivity has nothing to do with spiritual progression, it is even more important for the medium to work on his inner self. Working as a medium holds many responsibilities. The client or the patient will place all their hopes and expectations in the hands of their practitioner. The latter will be placed on a pedestal. It is the medium's responsibility to pursue their spiritual development, to cleanse themselves in order to not "take advantage" of the power they may hold. Through meditation and only through meditation, we can dissolve our deviant character traits. With a spirituality that rises gently, the use of mediumship will change. Service-related goals will become clearer, different, and the results will only be more beautiful!

The student or the patient who puts their professor on a pedestal can be a burden. Indeed, they worship the professor and credit him with all sorts of virtues. As soon as they discover that this professor is not the saint they had imagined, they destroy him. Of course a medium can be praised for the accuracy of his or her work, for his or her empathy, for the care he or she provides to clients but that's all! The only thing that can be judged is the result of the teacher's work. For the rest, we are all human, with the faults that are inherent to that condition. The student who is looking for teaching or treatment from a "Saint" will likely look for a long time and die before he finds it...

Mediumship is *the field* that best proves our survival, our life after death. It lets us see the loved ones we have lost, sometimes in horrible circumstances. This field shows that the religions are not all wrong in their approaches. Each of them tells the story of the spirit's or the soul's survival, with its own dogma which is so human in the end, since it was, precisely, written by humans. If I believe in eternal life, what more could I be afraid of? Physical suffering or starvation, if I lived in an underdeveloped country, but otherwise? With the irrefutable proof of my survival after the death of my physical body, knowing that my being is immortal, I would not know where to direct my fears. The medium can provide this proof of a life after death. He can describe the deceased; translate his joy at being in the spiritual world. He knows how to translate the peace that rules in the afterlife, just there, a wink away.

What beauty life offers us, eternal beauty...

What peace!

Life is a circle
But you see it as a line
That starts at birth
And ends in death

Reincarnations are a circle
They seem to start with one life
And end with another
One after the other like a necklace worn by the
Father
The path is a circle
Where we are born in ignorance
And finish in the truth
Faster or slower
Is up to you

Existence is a circle
That feeds itself
That is what you are
That is infinite like you
Whether you like it or not

Circle you always have been
Circle you are
Circle God
With no beginning or end

So if the beloved spirit comes to tell you
That he is alive
That he is in peace
What else than this circle that he is
Will you be?

Chapter 10

Communicating with the spirit

"Spirit, are you there?"
What a question, dear one
"Are you truly there?"
I walk beside you
always
whether you miss me or not
never more
than a wink away
a simple breath
a heartbeat
with you
before you can raise your eyes
faster than a thought
even before
you were able to ask me
I am spirit
your angel that guards you

Mediumship is not only a job that is done in a clinic by appointment. Many people train to have an extra tool for the job they already do every day. How does one train one's subtle perceptions? The tool has to remain pragmatic. The dad, the mom, and all the deceased acquaintances the client has known. In describing them accurately with the student client replying "yes" or "no" to information supplied by our perceptions, the latter helps us to understand if our working method is good. When I am able to trust my perceptions because it works when training, I will use them comfortably in my private and professional life in the service of others.

According to the French doctor Jean-Jacques Charbonier, it is stupid to claim that mediums must work for free under the pretext that they have received a divine gift. Go tell a professional football player he now has to play for free because God gifted him with a talent for kicking a ball! Or tell a doctor not to take payment for his services because he has a divine gift of being successful in his studies! Knowing how to sing, being able to write, or having acting skills and roles in films – all of these are gifts from God! Life is a gift from God. Each service rendered to society must be repaid in just measure, and easing grief by providing an accurate sign of acknowledgment from a loved one who has gone beyond the veil is a huge one. Moreover, for a maximum number of persons to be able to benefit from the gift of mediumship, you have to do it full time and thus make it your job. Yes, indeed: mediums are men and women like anyone else, and need to eat, drink, and have clothes and a roof over their heads. The money they make by working is not stolen. It is more than high time to give them the place they deserve in our society! Those I know set reasonable fees and apply them with tact. They even give free consultations to the poorest. There are also unfortunately many charlatans in the profession. They will be only eliminated from the circuit when mediumship is finally recognized by a spiritually underdeveloped Western society.

What type of training allows one to speak to the deceased? Let's take a tightrope walker. The tightrope walker has to find the rope on which to walk. Then he has to get onto it for a short time. Once he is on the rope, the student tightrope walker must try to keep his balance and stay on it for a while. Once the right balance has been found, he has to move forward on this rope without falling and keep his balance. In mediumship, it's the same thing: find the right frequency, get used to it and maintain it to be able to move along it and speak with the spiritual world.

Clairvoyant people can capture a spirit's energy just by looking. They see the energy fields moving around them, whether or not this field is communicating with living beings. We are constantly surrounded by "the afterlife". Just like radio or television waves. We live in an environment of waves without knowing it, until the day we are able to apprehend them by means of a receptor. We can therefore look at a medium's spirit like an antenna and his body like a radio.

We shall now examine this term which can drive away even your closest friends, which has the power to make you look like a hopeless madman or even to turn you into the worst of charlatans, greedy for money and always with a trick up your sleeve. This term which, on the other hand, draws other people to you, people who will take you for someone with extraordinary powers.

The term *medium* applies to any person who communicates with a non-incarnated being. Any other ESP has nothing to do with a deceased person, but with his own spirit. In this type of ESP, the term "medium" is not at all valid. Once again, I remind you that mediumship has nothing to do with fortune-telling, because fortune-telling is done with one's own mind. "Medium" simply means "between two worlds".

To communicate between these two worlds, the medium places themselves into an altered state of consciousness which can be described as a sort of excitement. It is in this state that they are best able to receive information telepathically. This excitement, as with joy, stage fright, or enchantment, consists of rapid vibrations. Once the medium is in this altered state of consciousness, they extend their field and ask the spirit of the deceased to approach so that the medium's field can read that of the spirit. They then translate the information received "to the client".

The spiritual world evolves at a higher frequency than ours. To be able to enter into contact with this high frequency, the medium must accelerate their vibration and the spiritual world has to slow down its own. Communication takes place somewhere between the two frequencies. Any information that is transmitted by the spiritual world is received telepathically and transcribed by the medium. Despite its irrefutable proof, mental mediumship will never be an exact science. Let us try and understand why:

The deceased's spirit sends its information via telepathy. This information is received through the channels described in the chapter on sensitivity. The channels used to receive information are clairsentience, clairvoyance, clairaudience, clairolfactance, clairgustance, and claircognizance (ESP). The translation to the intellect is done in a subjective manner, in other words in the medium's head.

The clear-senses

Clairsentience

This is the most frequent form of clear-sense. It is used by anyone, medium or not. Any person can feel things that are not perceived by the five ordinary senses: the presence of someone behind him while standing in line; walking into a room and getting the impression that there has been an argument; or having the gut feeling that indicates that a project or a person is beneficial. Clear-feeling, as it is also called, is the most uncomfortable sense. The information goes through the body. The person may have a stomachache, feel tremendous sadness or, on the contrary, great joy.

It is important to establish a certain discipline, an instantaneous reaction that allows us to tell ourselves that this feeling does not belong to us, that it isn't ours, and to get rid of it immediately. I know a lot of people who hang on to these feelings for hours or days, and who suffer because of them. People who have little experience and who perform energy therapy, or those who become personally involved in a therapy, are particularly vulnerable. People who manage their feelings well can receive very precise information. A lady medium that I know well does not see the spirit: she feels it. She becomes the dead person. If she is in the presence of an elderly man who walks with a cane and is somewhat overweight, this medium becomes masculine, heavy, feels pain when she walks, grows old, and feels a cane in her hand. As soon as she cuts off communication with the deceased, all of these physical characteristics disappear. Clairsentience passes through the energetic center, the "Manipura", which is located at the level of the solar plexus.

Clairaudience

This clear-sense manifests itself through hearing, as its name implies. It is a clear-sense that is rare and is very often objective. When this clear-sense is used, a sound is not actually heard. It is more like a soundless voice or a whisper. Through this sense, names, surnames, or partial utterances in another language can be perceived. Among my acquaintances, two or three mediums can even manage to give the names and addresses of the deceased, or of his entourage. Astonishingly enough, when this clear-sense activates in me, I hear the spirits in my right ear which is half deaf! Clairaudience thus has nothing to do with the physical ear itself or the sense of hearing. To develop it, the medium must concentrate on what is happening behind or below the ear: sometimes the whisper almost comes from the back of your neck. It is quite probable that the chakra involved is "Vishuddhi", the throat chakra.

Clairvoyance

This is the best-known of the clear-senses. Many people would like to develop it and focus on it alone. Many students are so concentrated on what can happen through the "third eye" that they neglect or frankly ignore their other clear-senses. The advantage in clairvoyance – even if it is the most subjective tool among the clear-senses – is being able to access extremely precise details about the deceased's appearance or his living environment, for example. It functions objectively for some mediums, allowing them to see auras or energy flows in a room or outdoors. For most mediums, clairvoyance is subjective. The image that is stored in the medium's memory is taken "from the file" in his memory and used to construct a description of a person or a place. The brain learns to extract the image that is closest to the information that appears on the energy particle sent by the deceased. It is for this reason, among others, that the medium can describe the deceased in a detailed and adequate manner. When he sees a picture of the deceased person he has described, the medium will be able to distinguish the differences between his mental representation, the image that his brain has constructed, and the deceased as he actually was. Sometimes the terms used in the description may cause misunderstandings: where one medium might say "fat", another might say "a little plump". Clairvoyance mobilizes a lot of energy in your head. In fact, its center is the "Ajna", located in the middle of the head, at the top of the spine.

Using Ajna can cause headaches and other physical problems. We will be examining these effects in more detail in the chapter on "Side effects". Once and for all: the sixth chakra, "Ajna", is not a third eye! Two of the main chakras are called Trikuti and Bhrikuti, and are emanations of "Ajna", on the forehead. In the West, we call these the third eye, while in India they are simply referred to as "Guru Chakras". But the sixth chakra, the "Ajna", *is not located on the forehead!*

Claircognizance

This is a magnificent sense and certainly the most difficult to identify. Information enters through "Sahasrara", the crown chakra, at the top of the head. It suddenly appears, without us knowing how it got there. It is very difficult to separate your own thoughts from claircognizance. Is this information in me, or did I perceive it from somewhere else? The message is there. It takes a lot of training to learn to distinguish between your own thoughts and claircognizant perception. This sense provides no images, no feelings, no sounds, nothing, just information. We also receive inspiration through this sense.

Clairgustance
This clear-sense involves taste. The medium suddenly gets a taste in his mouth, the impression he is eating a sweet, an orange, medicine, anything. This tells him the deceased liked certain things or ate certain foods.

Clairolfactance
This clear-sense involves smell. An odor tickles the medium's nostrils. He may smell motor oil or farm odors and thus know that the deceased was a garage mechanic or farmer, baker or chemist. General meditation in view of developing the clear-senses can also help develop clairolfactance and clairgustance.

In my shape I am born
Small and soft
In my shape I grow
Changing and tough
In my shape I die
And crumble
In my shape I return
With an ear-to-ear smile
And the sun in my heart

In mental mediumship, there is constant interaction between two beings that are in contact with each other. When communicating with a deceased person, the medium will have a high to very high brain frequency. Inversely, when he is in a trance or a state of spiritual healing, his cerebral frequency will be slow or lower, which thus corresponds to a passive state. The terms "high" and "low" have no qualitative meaning. They are related to the medium's inner state.

However the information enters and whatever the clear-sense used, it is essential that once the mediumship task is completed, the doors are closed and the antennae used for perception are drawn in. It is absolutely necessary to come back to a normal, grounded life and get back into the daily routine. As soon as I come out of my cabinet, I don't see any other spirit or any other aura. When I eat my soup, I eat my soup; I don't want to see which deceased grandmother is in the same room. If I perceive any energetic movements by deceased persons or other energies, I do not pick them up, I no longer interact. My antennae, my access doors, are voluntarily closed, that's all. This appropriate attitude is difficult to adopt at first. You are so happy and so enthusiastic about having described the beauty of the afterlife that you find it hard to let go. The same is true of *healing*. When I discovered my healing talents I wanted to heal everyone in the streets of my town of Neuchâtel every time I went for a walk. I was becoming a "charitable sponge" and was returning home completely wrung out. I soon stopped that. Open up when it's time to work and close when you are done. Act as you would with any other job: before the time, it's not the time, and after the time, it's no longer the time.

Possible sources of confusion

Once you have found the right frequency to communicate with the spiritual world, you still have to practice. As I explained earlier, it isn't enough to receive information, it is also necessary to determine its source.

A sensitive person will know how to clearly grasp the energetic difference between students who are doing readings and communicating with the deceased when working directly with the person sitting in front of them, i.e. using an interactive frequency, and students who are doing healing work or in a trance, i.e. using a passive frequency.

Making the distinction between communication through mediumship and psychic reading is a real challenge. Indeed, the medium who does not accurately direct his energy and his reading on the deceased person's field can deviate into the client's aura, in which all of his life and all his deceased are memorized.

Another source of confusion may arise when the deceased mentions a living person and makes remarks about them or wishes to send greetings. This can shock the client: they have come to talk to a deceased person, and hear, for example, the description of their still-living mother! This may well lead them to think that their mother has just died! Of course, if the medium refocuses on the deceased's energy field, this misunderstanding can be quickly corrected. But it is still better to avoid it.

The medium is simply an interpreter, and ambassador of the spirit world. His attitude and his interior state determine whether it is possible to interpret the contact.

If the medium has doubts before commencing the task he will automatically set up barriers. His negative attitude will make communication very difficult and even laborious. The medium who is enthusiastic about being this channel and who is happy to be this magnificent bridge between two dimensions will reach out to contact with vibrant joy. He will automatically be at the right frequency. When my students have doubts, I ask them to be as relaxed as possible and to imagine they are going to pick up a lottery win. This immediately affects the results of the communication.

In mental mediumship, the medium must provide proof that allows the client to recognize the deceased person who has come to speak with them. It is assuredly in this aspect that the greatest difficulty lies. Thus, before communicating a message from a deceased mother, for example, the serious medium must focus on providing a certain amount of convincing evidence relative to the identity of the person: the mother's physical appearance, her life in general, how she died, the place she lived in, and other pertinent information. It is only when the client has recognized the deceased that the medium can give the message, the reason why the deceased has come to speak.

If the medium already cannot clearly identify the speaker, how can the person for whom the message is intended believe what the deceased is trying to communicate? In this exercise, the client's attitude also plays an important role. For example, in Italy, all you need to say is, "There is a lady with me..." and the client immediately exclaims, "Maammmaaa!" and promptly volunteers all the information the medium is supposed to provide. In Iceland, even given the most factual proof possible, the client will reply, with his arms folded over his chest, "Mmm, hmmm, yeah..." These examples show that there are clients who come in very good faith and those who come in very bad faith. It is also a question of mentality. Other clients absolutely insist on speaking to a specific deceased person. If the grandfather comes to visit and not the mother they wanted to speak with, these clients may provide negative answers or pretend not to recognize the one communicating. But strangely enough, as soon as the hoped-for mother appears they suddenly remember all that was said about the grandfather. These attitudes require the medium to exercise great control over his energy in order to not lose the frequency and be able to honor the wishes of the spiritual world. We cannot call up a spirit! We can only see what is within our energy field when we open it up to work.

Some clients may be surprised by the simplicity of the message. Very often, it's a message of love or comfort. Of course, any medium can invent these words, even if the description of the deceased, given previously, was accurate or if the communicator has commented on events in the client's life which took place after the death of the deceased or things that happened a few days earlier. Factual evidence might be as follows: "I love your new earrings," or "It was about time you washed the hall carpet." In my clinic, I once did a reading during which a deceased couple came to speak to their son. The father said, "It's time you cut the grass." The son had promised his neighbor he would do it for him but had not done so. The mother said, "It's time you went to check the water damage," because the warehouse where the material was stored had been flooded two weeks earlier, and he had not yet gone back. With this kind of factual evidence that the client can confirm, it is easier to believe in the affectionate and encouraging messages that deceased loved ones wish to send.

Some sources of information are unfortunately among the primary reasons to doubt the deceased is truly present. There are six possible sources of information:

1. Projection by the medium: information that the medium invents or interprets incorrectly.

2. Interpretation by the medium of the client's gestures and expressions.

3. Information that the medium reads in the client's aura. This in itself is already a sensitive action, but not one that comes from the desired source.

4. What the medium reads in the Universal Memory, often referred to as the akashic records.

5. Information that comes from the spirit world, not from the expected spirit but from a guide or another deceased family member.

6. The deceased who appears for the client.

Number six is the only desired source of information. What the client expects is the deceased!

The first thing the medium has to do when carrying out this task is to clearly and honestly determine whether his energy field changes as the deceased approaches. Feeling the field change is much easier for mediums with well-developed clairsentience. For clairvoyants, this change is much more difficult to determine.

If the clairvoyant sees objectively, he has irrefutable proof because it is not created in his memory. If he sees subjectively, like the majority of mediums, he will have to construct and develop the link. A medium must know as little as possible about his client and the person who has come with a message from the spirit world. In this way, the information provided by the medium is truly provided by the deceased, not by the medium's imagination or by the client's aura. However, this can be disconcerting for the client: he may have to do some research or ask other family members, if there still are any.

Providing unquestionable evidence is very difficult. Nevertheless, giving this type of proof is the basis of any serious work. A medium who does his work conscientiously never asks for a photo or other information about the deceased person. Promising to be able to contact a specific deceased person is a fraud – it's a lie! The medium simply greets the person who appears in his field on behalf of his client. I have so often seen clients or students who wanted so badly to contact a specific person who did not appear, for various reasons. That is the spirit world's free will! A deceased person can elect to appear or not! If not, it may be because he or she has not yet completed his or her transition to the light, is not interested in returning, or knows that his appearance would not be in the client's best interests. For example, a deceased husband may not appear because if he did it would be more difficult for his wife to overcome her grief. When doing a reading for a number of people at the same time, several spirits may appear but because the medium is already busy with another one, they will not be recognized. In reality, the deceased so ardently hoped for by the client does indeed appear very often. On several occasions I have seen, and also received the information from the spirit world, that when the living become obsessed with a deceased person or his or her presence, these spirits withdraw because this situation is unhealthy for the client. By unhealthy, I mean that this obsession makes the individual less accountable for their life as they expect too many answers or signs from the afterlife. I know mothers who believe they are connected to or in constant contact with their deceased children. Others feel the same about one of their parents. In the long run, this obsession with a particular deceased person may lead to psychoses. It is a fact that we are visited often, but not permanently, seven days/week, 24 hours/day. This obsession with being constantly connected to the spiritual world does not only involve the deceased, but also the guides. The guides, those beings who accompany us so often, are a fascinating topic which I will develop in the next chapter.

To illustrate a situation in which the client wants very badly to see a deceased person about whom he often thinks, I would very much like to describe a reading that I had with a friend:

Before asking to have this mediumship session with me, my friend had been thinking a lot about her deceased nephew. She wondered if she could contact him through me. As soon as she had that idea, the light in her lamp flickered. My friend took this as a sign from her nephew: she could indeed contact him through me.

That very evening, when I went to see her, we went for a walk in a park and we sat down on a bench under some trees. She just asked me to establish a connection without telling me who the person was or why. I was sure it was her deceased husband. He had died recently. I therefore said my opening prayer, extended my field and asked the deceased to approach and come into my aura so that I could interpret for him.

To my great astonishment, the information I was receiving was not at all what I expected. I did not perceive her husband, but rather a young man in his thirties, athletic and elegant, with short brown hair. He had a yacht and a fast, expensive car. When I gave this information to my friend, she encouraged me to go on, because the information was meaningful to her. I continued my communication, describing two houses: a new one that the deceased had helped build and an older one with thick walls. The houses were on high ground. They overlooked a forest and a valley. I received the name "Luigi" and saw that this man had light-colored eyes. However, the young man who had appeared when I established the communication had brown eyes. An image of a candle or a light, behind a glass or a vase, flickered before my eyes. As I continued to see information by working with the link that I had with this deceased man, I understood he had died suddenly. I did not see any blood, even if I received the word "motorcycle". I therefore simply mentioned he had died rapidly. With this information, I asked my friend to tell me what it meant. She told me it was her nephew and that all the information I had given was correct. She confirmed that this man had died instantly in a motorcycle accident when he was 35, with no external injuries, in the forest I had seen. He indeed looked as I had described, and had a boat and a Maserati. Luigi, the first name that had been revealed to me, was his grandfather's first name, and the grandfather had had light-colored eyes!

Once this information had been acknowledged, I went back to communicating with this young man. He began to describe his mother, who was still alive. He described her current state of health, as well as other pertinent details about her. He told me that his mother did not believe in life after death. With my help, he asked his aunt to insist on this point. He really wanted to help her. He told his aunt to write down everything I told her. This was not the first time a deceased person had asked such a thing: it gives disbelievers time to assimilate the information from the spiritual world, on the one hand, and to imagine that there is a life after death, on the other. A person's intelligence leads him to know that such a wealth of correct information, with no mistakes, coming from a stranger, *is not something that can be invented!*

This nephew gave me a lot of information about his mother and his life. At the end, he commented happily about my friend's life. To finish the reading, I asked my friend if she had any questions. Without hesitating, my friend said she didn't have any. She wanted to know how to help her sister. The deceased nephew had given her all the indications she needed to do that. Once again, the spirit world shows us that not only it is alive, but it is also aware of our destinies and, above all, it is world of information.

After having thanked the young man for visiting and for the information he had provided, I closed my field. As I was intrigued about the light behind the glass, I asked my friend about it. Amused, she explained that at her home, they had built a glass case, with a sort of torch inside, in memory of the deceased. Each time someone opens the door the torch switches on automatically.

The reading I have described above helps us to understand the accuracy of a subjective reading and how it functions. Remember that in a subjective reading, the spiritual world accesses our memory bank. It's more that our brain retrieves from our memory that which is closest to the information inscribed on the energy particle sent by the deceased. I had described the light inside the glass correctly. Not THAT specific light, but something similar. THAT light could not have been in my brain. I saw a boat, but not HIS yacht. I saw a car but could not, in this case, determine what make it was, even though that can happen.

Mental mediumship works this way: "My spirit perceives information. My brain has to learn to translate it for my intellect, in order to be able to provide information that is as close as possible to the information that was telepathically perceived," whatever the clear-sense employed!

Chapter 11

Guides

**I was brooding, without work,
No money and broken dreams
When my guide whispered to me:
"Ripe, shiny fruit
Is desired and eaten.
The fruit on the ground
Is trampled
Yet from it trees grow..."**

Through my travels, my experiences in a variety of cultures, my teachers, and my students from different countries and faiths, I have tried to "grasp" this vast subject. It is clear to me, as I suppose it is for every reader, that nothing that can be read or heard can ever replace personal experience.

In order to analyze the topic of "guides", it is worthwhile to try to understand the possible sources or definitions of the word. This assumes, of course, the acceptance of the concept that another form of intelligence exists beyond the physical world.

1. For most people, a guide is a being whose intelligence, knowledge and spirituality are more evolved than ours. Its reason for being is apparently unconditional love and support in our rise to a higher level of awareness.

2. Guides may be deceased loved ones: parents, friends met in our present life or that we knew in the spiritual world before we were incarnated. Nevertheless, what we generally call a guide has a vibration and an awareness that is greater than that of an "ordinary deceased person".

3. One of our guides is our higher consciousness, the Self. This category includes the traces of people we may have been in past lives and from whom our energy field has memorized past knowledge.

4. The divine power or what is called the "Great Spirit", as a direct source, which takes on a form chosen by our mind and which is often closely linked to our beliefs and cultures.

5. Our illusion, psychosis, which is so close to genuine perception. This is nevertheless a product of our mind, of our dissociation and our hysterical trances. [See the corresponding chapter.] This sort of production is often mistaken as a guide, a being that is so blindingly brilliant.

Cultures and beliefs

Cultures and beliefs can influence the image that we have of our guides. How can you explain why the Buddhist mentions Bodhisattva, the Christian talks about Guardian Angels and the Virgin Mary, the Hindu calls on Shiva and the Jew speaks of Abraham? Are we entitled to some guides according to our beliefs or does our mind produce images according to the dogma that governs it?

Icelandic culture and beliefs provide a good illustration of the way and the extent to which subtle perceptions can be influenced. In Reykjavik, in the Construction Department, the government offices have an official delegate in charge of elves. This employee asks them if a planned road or building will upset their homes. In Iceland, there are roads that go around the presumed habitat of elves and pixies instead of being laid out in a straight line. Five percent of the people in Iceland say they have seen elves or some other fantasy creature. Almost 70% of the population believes they exist. There is also a lobby for the protection of these little beings. I myself have seen two "nature spirits" in their concrete form but I have never worked with any. Many people in Iceland give accounts describing their lives with these beings. Do we first have to believe in the existence of pixies and elves to be able to obtain their help or is it the other way around? Does it become possible to perceive them because the culture in which we are living teaches us about them?

I would like to distinguish between dogmas and religions, on the one hand, and beliefs and ESP on the other.

Obviously, meeting people who are attached to dogmas results in stereotypical accounts. As for the non-dogmatic beliefs, the celestial beings appear to them in ways that are much more varied. I think I have understood that the two groups may have a genuine access to higher intelligence. However, these beings are going to take on appearances that we can accept, one that our minds can manage. Maurice Barbanell himself [see the chapter on Trance] says that he is not sure if his guide "Silver Birch" really was a Native North American. If he appears that way, it is because this appearance is "acceptable" to Maurice.

We can rightly ask ourselves to what extent these guides are individualities and where collective awareness, the "Great Spirit", begins. This awareness is available to anyone who is seeking to uplift himself or herself. It apparently takes the exact form that our mental and spiritual abilities are able to understand and accept.

Ego and mind

The ego and the mind can therefore play an important role. I can address this subject serenely as I myself have seen these two aspects of the human personality. That of the projections into phenomena and that of the incredibly powerful and indescribable beauty in the encounters with beings of unconditional love.

In my clinic, I have seen several patients who were suffering from serious psychoses. They believed, for example, that their guide was a famous person. Others vomit all their actions and responsibilities onto their guides. Unfortunately, no light being will ever decide or live their lives for them. A light being never predicts the future.

I have seen many an ego boast that their guide was more powerful than their neighbor's guardian angel. Others insist that they "work" only with masters because the angels are worthless in comparison! These same people are not even capable of describing a deceased person, whose energy is supposedly "denser" than that of a guide with respect to his degree of evolution and are thus much easier to perceive. An excessive ego is just as dangerous as a lack of self-confidence.

A side note regarding the correct understanding of the notion of "density" as it is used throughout this work: Although the concept of density will later be illustrated using the property of physical density, the former should not be confused with the latter! Whenever we refer to the concept of density, we refer to the vibrational frequency and the color of the particles involved which can be perceived through the clear-sense of clairvoyance. A higher density then implies a lower vibrational frequency and a gray tone which may even reach into black; conversely, a lower density implies a higher vibrational frequency and an increasingly brightly shining golden color. A decreasing degree of density is generally linked to an increasing degree of spiritual development.

No matter what, no living guru or celestial guide can make us their disciple. We choose to make them our masters. It's the only way to take part in their glory. It's up to us to decide to benefit from it!

If we have guides, we just need to trust them. If they are there, it's because they have chosen us. They know us down to our smallest details, with our strong points but especially our challenges! The ego does not make it easy to communicate with our guides, and even less so with the spiritual world. For example, if you are obsessed with the fantasy of having a bald, muscular Shaolin monk as a guide, how can a celestial doctor assist you in your treatments?

With a few rare exceptions, I have always refused to describe guides to my clients, even if I am capable of seeing them very clearly.

The goal is to avoid conditioning to a defined image. A strongly-defined image would perhaps close the door to other celestial beings, as I have just shown in the example with the monk. I firmly believe that we have a "Guardian Angel" from our birth until we return. I also have a great deal of proof that we are surrounded by groups of entities. In these groups, "individuals" or "apparitions" change with respect to our activities, our degree of evolution and, obviously, with respect to our resonance. By resonance, I mean the quality of our field or our mind at a specific moment.

The choice of how to use these natural abilities of our mind is what allows us to develop our spirituality with respect to the application of personal qualities and values. This allows us to associate with good causes and to be part of those who, humbly, help to create a society that is healthier and more aware.

I have seen Angels and guides; I've shaken a soft, warm human hand that came out of the void. I have had the honor of experiencing many materializations of celestial perfumes in the palms of my hands during my treatments.

Omnipresence or stunning precision

Regarding the omnipresence or absence of our guides or our loved ones, we can let ourselves believe that the intelligence of the spiritual world is worthy of trust and that they know, be they guides or deceased, when to appear to us.

To conclude this chapter on guides: whether it is a guide or a deceased person – provided the latter has made the transition into the light – they know what is happening. They hear our sobs or our laughter. The Spirit that is behind such beauty must really be magnificent! This world can be immensely heartless and cruel. Knowing that the parable of love is not a fable, but a truth, makes existing so much more beautiful and serene!

I will never forget the day when, in tears, sitting on my bed, everything seemed bleak to me and I was brooding. It all looked black, and I was alone. Suddenly, just behind my right ear, the one that is nearly deaf, I heard the Beatles song *With a Little Help from My Friends*. I didn't even have a radio in my room. The song could be clearly heard. It filled me up more than anything. My guides were there, with me, for me. I was jumping with joy for this comfort; I wasn't alone, but surrounded with love. Even today I can't thank them enough. I encourage you to reach out to them…

Have faith, you are loved, and be sure to keep it.
If it happened to me, it can happen to everyone.
Let faith be with you, but also reason…

Chapter 12

The usefulness of mediumship

A woman I did not know came to see me at my clinic. She explained that at night she dreamed of the deceased and that they spoke to her. She thought she was going mad. A few days earlier, a spirit had told her to meet at my clinic. When she came in, I saw a young man with black hair come in with her. As I am unable to decide who will appear from the afterlife to communicate with my client, I greeted the one from the spirit world who had appeared for her. Please remember that I do not make any invocations; I place myself in this welcoming state from the outset and observe whoever wishes to appear for the client through my field. Since I always work in the light, the message-bearer also comes from the light and is well-intentioned.

When I opened my field to the spiritual world on behalf of my client, I noticed that the young man was her deceased son. The woman's mother, who had died when the woman was only three years old, also appeared for a brief moment. The woman was not very familiar with her, but enough to be able to identify her. During the greater part of the reading, the dominant presence was that of a man. I described him by mentioning his appearance, his hair, a bit of his character, and two or three things he liked. It turned out that this was the woman's father, but she only told me this after the reading. It was he who had asked her to meet him at my clinic. Thanks to this reading, she knew she had not gone mad. She understood that during her sleep, in this modified state of awareness, she was accessing the spirit world.

This example may seem spectacular to the reader. It is often precisely the simplest evidence that reassures and brings peace.

It is very important that the medium have the courage to give the information as accurately as possible. It may seem quite logical, but it can be a real challenge because the information received may seem absurd and outside of any logical context. With regard to the courage needed to verbalize far-fetched information, I can give you a very good example. A couple had come to see me in order to communicate with their deceased son. Having described the deceased and given factual elements about him, all of which were acknowledged by the couple, the woman wanted to ask her son a question through me. Without promising anything, I did so. Her question was about a book she had written. She wanted to know if she was going to present it at the Paris Book Fair. My first reply was to tell her that when she mentioned Paris, I saw the Eiffel Tower. It was thus difficult for me to know if the information was coming from her son or from my own mind and I told her this. The woman encouraged me to go on. At her words, I went back to the connection with the boy, and asked him his mother's question. He did not reply. But suddenly, I was covered with soap bubbles. I told the lady I had no answer to her question; and that the elements I was receiving could only insult her intelligence. She insisted that I tell her what I had received anyway. I told her I was covered in soap bubbles. She dropped her pen – I'll never forget that. The spouses looked at each other with big round eyes and she cried, "My book is called *Bulles de Savon* [soap bubbles]!"

What seems absurd to one person can be the ultimate proof, the missing link, to another. It is critical that mediums express what they think they see, that they take the risk of looking ridiculous or silly, or of just being off the subject.

In spite of the image it may raise, the mediumship task of obtaining proof and information is a concrete one. It is real. It especially proves the existence of the spirit world and of life after death.

The following story will help us to further understand just how useful it can be to have contact and communication with the deceased, how the burden of grief can evaporate, and how healing peace can be.

My parents spoke with me after their deaths

The following is an extract from an article published in the Swiss magazine *Femina*, November 2008:

"Having arrived at the hospital too late to say goodbye to her dying mother, Clara contacted her through a medium. Below is her account of a troubling experience.

'Last year, in June, my mother had to be hospitalized when she became seriously ill. After a month, her condition seemed to be more or less stable. My husband and I were thinking we should give up on our plans for a holiday in Brittany. I called one of the doctors who were taking care of my mother to tell him we felt unsure about leaving for ten days or so. He reassured us, "You needn't worry about leaving, and your mother will spend Christmas with you." So we left, leaving it to my sister to stay with our mother.

Eight days later at 7:00am, my sister phoned. My mother's health had taken a turn for the worse, and she advised us to come back as quickly as possible. We tidied the house, gave back the keys, and packed up as fast as we could to go back home to Le Locle. When we got to the Jura foothills, it was 9:00pm. We stopped by the house to shower and have a coffee before rushing to the hospital… and it was horrible.

Mama had died just a minute earlier. I blamed myself terribly for not having been able to say goodbye. Why, at such a time, did I have to think first about having a shower and a coffee? I felt guilty, I was really hurting. We had just barely missed each other! The months went by. I spoke to my mother, but she didn't answer me.

And then, one day in February, I came across a TV program in which a medium, Hannes Jacob, was talking about life after death and the possibility of communicating with deceased persons. What this man was saying was very sensible and concrete, and he did not seem to be an eccentric. I thought it would be worth going to see him because I felt that my mother perhaps still had things to tell me. But I wanted to get my mother's opinion. I sent her an unspoken request to show me a sure sign that meant she agreed I should make an appointment in Neuchâtel with the medium. I got one. One day in May when I was coming home, I saw that the light was on in the bathroom, whereas I remembered perfectly having switched it off when I left. The light! It was clearly the sign from my mother, I was sure.

So I went to see the medium. He explained that my mother would contact me if she wanted to, and if so she would appear through him.

That's what happened. Mama came to see me. She appeared to the medium, who asked her to give him information that would identify her. She showed him a pearl necklace and some handbags. My mother adored pearls and handbags. In fact when we were cleaning out her belongings, I can't tell you how many bags we found! At one point, the medium told me, "There is a scar on her face." He also described her hairstyle. And a dress she especially liked. It was true. The medium described her very well, though he had never seen a photo of her.

My mother let me know she was fine, that she was serene and that she had found her father whom she loved very much. The medium saw her as happy. Mama also said that it would please her if my sister or I would sometimes wear her favorite dress, a dark silk one with a flower pattern. It was the dress she wore when she was young and slim, and one which she had refused to give away. Mother also added that she would be present when my niece had her baby. And yet, she could not have known my niece was expecting a baby because the latter had become pregnant after my mother died! I was also struck by another thing she said: "I was there when you cleaned the windows." Indeed, a few days before, I had washed the panes in the windows in my little pottery shop, and I had suddenly felt sad. I had started to cry because I felt Mama's presence. I got confirmation she was nearby at that moment. The medium said she had a big smile on her face. I wanted to ask if she did not regret that I wasn't the daughter she might have wanted, but the medium told me this wasn't necessary since "up there" only love counts. "You loved her and that's what she remembers."

To my great surprise, my father also appeared. I wasn't expecting that at all. He identified himself by describing the red armchair next to the window, where he often sat near the end of his life to watch television, when he was ill. It was true. I was not on good terms with him. We had had a rocky relationship, and his drinking problem did not make for an ideal family life. Papa said to the medium: "Tell her I understood a lot of things too late. I'm sorry. Tell my daughters that I love them. I'm happy Clara came. I waited a long time for her. I thank her." I was crying. I was so moved... I was even more touched because my father died in 1983, when he was 51. And there, in three sentences, he said everything he had not said in his whole life. What a present! It's crazy how much you understand afterwards.

He loved us, but didn't know how to say it. We weren't used to saying how we felt. It also struck me that, according to the medium's description, my mother and father appeared the same as they were before they became ill. The medium said, "That's common, you know; these people like to show themselves at their best." Finally, I went to visit my parents' grave. I thanked them for coming and I felt like the family had been reunited. When I told all this to my sister and my niece, they cried too, and we hugged each other. Before, I often used to quarrel with my sister. But before she died, Mama told us, "If I leave, you must remain friends." That's how it is today.'"

Chapter 13

Healing

**I give myself to You
So that the best will happen
I give myself to You
For their greatest good
I give myself to You
So You may do your work
I give myself to You
So that your light may fill those who
Ask
I let go
For it's their role
To keep it**

Healing... what a term!

Where healing is concerned, it is easy to get lost in philosophical ideas. These discussions often include, as a starting point, the fact that removing a symptom does not mean the person is healed.

With a wink, I'll just quote Dethlefsen and Dahlke who provided an ironic illustration of allopathic medicine in the following example:

A gentleman takes his car to the mechanic.
– "Sir, my low oil pressure light is blinking!"
– "Let me fix that," says the mechanic.
He removes the bulb and says to the client:
– "Look, your light isn't blinking any more..."

The discussion on healing tends to run along the same line.

Removing something harmful does not necessarily mean "healing".

To start with, it must be accepted that most physical afflictions are either psychosomatic or are the physical body's reactions to a sick spirit. For example, stress is one cause of stomach ulcers. These ulcers can be treated with a simple operation. Yet the patient is still not relieved of his stress. That's why the term "healing" is delicate and often incorrectly used. In every single case, no physical or mental disorder can coexist with a healthy energy. These concepts are totally incompatible. The energy is necessarily affected.

One of the criticisms that are often heard is that the positive result of healing is due to the placebo effect. This is also the argument put forward by some of the "healers" I came across in the Philippines who did not really practice healing but who cheated instead. They said, "I cheat because it's enough for a person to start believing and then they heal themselves." One such healer told me that there are ways to learn how to fake psychic operations. There are even places where chicken offal is sold and used to make people think human tissues have been removed. Such practices do serious damage to the honest healers in that country!

Faith in your healing is obviously useful. It will enhance the client's positive thinking. Not believing in your own healing is more problematic. Many people hang onto their illnesses. Where chronic illness is concerned, they are used to holding onto it, like a traveling companion. If a person who has migraines no longer has them, who will feel sorry for them and what will they have to complain about? In the case of more serious chronic illnesses, if they were to go away, the person would have to go back to work, because the invalidity insurance would no longer have any reason to compensate them.

Certain "healers" claim that illnesses are karmic and that there is nothing that can be done. Some people use this affirmation to hang on tighter to their illnesses. Even if it were karmic, that karma can stop at this very moment, with the current treatment, now! Jonathan mentions this in his accounts at the end of the book.

I once treated a woman who had been suffering for years from fibromyalgia and who was in terrible pain from head to foot. Her doctor had sent her to me. After the fourth consultation, she became very angry, spitting a flood of hateful words at me about the pain she felt in her palate. I then understood that except for this pain in her mouth, all the other pains had been gone for a week. Do you see how such attitudes that focus on the negative points, on what is wrong, instead of marveling at having recovered a better quality of life after so long, will never lead to a healthy being? A real and deep awareness of such mental patterns, associated with self-improvement assisted by a psychologist if necessary, can help this kind of person to have a better outlook on life. If we take beauty in, we will live it!

Experiments in energy transmission

Two flower pots: I energized the one on the right, but not the other on the left. The grass is not experiencing a placebo effect because it obviously does not believe in me.

To carry out this experiment, the same number of seeds was planted. The pots were watered at the same time with the same amount of water.

I did not energize the porous terracotta pot on the left, in which the grass should have grown better. I did energize the white, totally nonporous enamel pot on the right.

After a few weeks, the difference was significant: the grass in the enamel pot, which had been energized, had flourished. Why should it be surprising that the energized pot contains stronger sprouts, when you know that some people, and not just yogis in India, can live on only Prana, or in other words, on energy alone?

Pranism

People who live on only energy are called *Breatharians*, or *Pranists* (from *Pranism*, or *Prana*, also known as "Universal energy"). I myself have met some of these people. The German newspaper *Der Spiegel* ran an article on the yogi Prahlad Jani, who is the subject of Austrian filmmaker Peter-Arthur Straubinger's *In The Beginning There Was Light*. Jani is a Hindu yogi who claims he has not eaten for 60 years and who only drinks liquids occasionally. He agreed to be placed in quarantine in a hospital for ten days under medical surveillance, during which he underwent a battery of physical examinations and blood tests. During this experiment, he neither ate nor drank. He did not urinate either. His bladder produced urine but it was as if it were reabsorbed internally. Of course, not eating for ten days is not a problem, but not drinking…!

There are Pranists in Europe also. One example at the beginning of the last century was the German stigmatist and healer Therese von Konnersreuth, who ate only a single communion wafer per week. In the 15th century, according to the legend about him, the Swiss ascetic Nicholas of Flüe lived on only communion wafers for 19 years.

Modern-day Pranists include the highly publicized Dr. Michael Werner, who was born in 1949 in Germany and now lives near Basel. He has been the director of a pharmaceutical research institute for 20 years and gives lectures on Pranic nourishment. He has also written a book on the topic. Indeed, since January 2001, Michael Werner has eaten no solid food.

A professor in French-speaking Switzerland has gone through the Pranic initiation process, which every person who wants to live exclusively on Prana must follow. This professor has eaten nothing for five years and drinks very little. Social life soon became an issue, because not eating is disturbing to colleagues, friends and family. To avoid any criticism, many people who have gone through the process and no longer eat do not mention it in order to preserve their social life, like this professor who does not wish to be named.

In Israel, Ray Maor, who also lives only on Prana, is a well-documented case. Indeed, he was challenged by a national television channel to neither eat nor drink for eight days while being constantly monitored by cameras. In the documentary, which is available on the Internet, the journalist admits to being highly skeptical about Pranic nourishment. He claims this is the most unusual case he has ever covered. The idea that it is possible to get one's sustenance from an energy that exists in the air was just another scam, in his opinion. For this experiment, Ray Maor was followed regularly by the renowned Dr. Ilan Kitsis of the Sourasky Medical Center in Tel Aviv. The first meeting between a spiritual person such as Ray and a Western doctor was not without tension and skepticism. This experiment in *Inedia* (the Latin word for *fasting*) could not be carried out without this medical "constraint" in order to ensure Ray Maor's health was not affected.

Like any other serious physician, Dr. Kitsis predicted that an experiment involving eight days without water would have foreseeable physical consequences: sunken eyes, dry mouth and throat, the onset of labored breathing, and lowered blood pressure since the heart rate would also slow. Ray would have altered awareness and clouded thinking as the cerebral blood pressure would diminish. But that wasn't all! His kidneys would fail and Ray might have a heart attack. In fact, the surest result of no fluid intake for one week is death. Dr. Kitsis explained the symptoms of cellular dehydration: as the cells need water to function, they draw it from outside, from the blood, in order to be able to regenerate and maintain their internal sodium and potassium levels. They then release the excess water back into the blood. When a cell cannot ensure this exchange of water with the organism – as in the case of a deficiency such as dehydration – it collapses and dies, to put it simply. If a massive number of cells were to die, the entire organism dies. The level of creatine (product of the degradation of the muscle cells) in the blood and urine increases. When this exceeds acceptable values, the kidney fails and can only partly filter the fluids that reach it.

Dr. Kitsis therefore expected to find signs of dehydration in Ray's blood and urine tests, along with total or partial functional distress in the kidneys and liver. All of this just to prove that Prana, or energy, was just sham, in his opinion. Moreover, he thought that with renewed water intake, Ray might have a cerebral edema and die. Indeed, the brain cells are the most sensitive to dehydration: they are the first to lose water, and a sudden and large intake that exceeds their absorption capacity will cause brain swelling and death. Despite this medical prognosis, which was indeed quite pessimistic, the experiment that was to show whether energy really had the nutritional potential that "these visionaries" claimed began.

Throughout the experiment and with each blood test, Dr. Kitsis could not believe his eyes when he read the results of Ray's blood work. The creatine level had only gone up one-tenth of one percent during the experiment, and was completely normal for a man of his build and age. The results of his blood tests were excellent! At the end of the week, Ray looked weak and was pale and feeling cold. But he succeeded in the experiment! A week without drinking, under the watchful eyes of the cameras and Dr. Kitsis.

The doctor congratulated him publicly. He admitted that the positive results of the analyses were beyond medical understanding. He even acknowledged being a little jealous of Ray Maor's incomprehensible success. He didn't just take his hat off to Ray, he also bowed to him.

I applaud Dr. Kitsis for not having denied the scientific evidence and for having publicly supported Ray Maor. If only more scientists would do likewise, by analyzing and commending such experiments instead of stroking their own egos and squashing their piles behind a lectern just to avoid being challenged and having to shift their paradigm! The world would advance so much more quickly!

Some Internet articles state that the Ray Maor experiment was suspended due to his mental state. But this is not true! Ray Maor won this televised challenge, and all you have to do in order to verify this is to watch the documentary to the end. Today, Ray Maor introduces entire groups of interested people to Pranism, by offering retreats lasting approximately eight days and taking place in various countries.

I have participated in one of these retreats myself – a long time after my own Pranic initiation which I will discuss below. In my experience, the retreat was of somewhat minimalistic character (especially considering its rather hefty price tag, $2400 for eight days without any food, of course, but piled up in a room without daylight like sardines in a can) and the fact that supervision should have been more inclusive of all participants and seamless at all times. Still I am glad that such retreats now exist and allow those who are ready to expand their consciousness in a very profound way. From my point of view, the content being presented during the retreat did not include any new knowledge, concepts or tools, but I found considerable value in the way these different elements were brought together, in order to allow new connections to be made. In short, I believe such Pranic retreats, wherever they are held, to be the ideal occasion to work on one's own values and to dissolve any old behavioral patterns that don't hold any value for oneself any longer, as a way to reboot one's life. A tiny but fitting anecdote: To the surprise of many, a 15-year-old boy was among our group's participants. This teenager participated in the entire retreat with the rest of us adults and felt great the entire time. A physiological issue with his sternum caused him to have more difficulty breathing than the average person, effectively reducing his lungs' capacity and limiting the amount of energy available to him. From what I have heard from his parents sometime after the retreat, he had changed significantly when he came home: A newfound will and drive to work on himself, to do physical exercise on a regular basis – not only *despite* his physical limitation, but to *overcome* it consciously – and a much more constructive attitude towards life in general.

Let's take a strictly Cartesian, purely rational and even economic point of view: what are some of the most striking benefits of Pranism? Let's look at some benefits of a Pranic life:

The first and most obvious consequence of practicing Pranism is that you don't need to eat anymore. What is your monthly food budget? Take a calculator and do your own quick estimation. Don't forget to include food eaten at home, at work, out and about and in restaurants. What is your total amount? You now have that much more money in your bank account each month. You may also add to it whatever bills you pay your dentist every year – because after all, if you don't eat you most probably won't get any cavities.

The second most important aspect probably is the enormous amount of additional free time you gain. There is almost no more shopping to do, no more cooking and no more cleaning dishes; but most of all, Pranists usually require only four to five hours of sleep per night! Some people use the additional time to generate more income, by adding a second job or to play more sports, others to indulge in their hobby or to start that one project they have always dreamed about. This has an obvious knock-on effect on your level of happiness, because you live your life more actively and can make more things happen. And not only do Pranists need *that* little sleep; they also wake up naturally and get up without the slightest effort, because to them, it's like they're "switched on" within a matter of seconds after opening their eyes in the morning. And they also benefit from a level of energy that is wholly steady throughout their entire day.

If you are among the health-conscious, the following discussion will be of interest to you. Not eating also means you are prevented from ingesting any carcinogenic substances or food, such as fried potato products, red meat or sugar, and of course any toxins that are added to all sorts of processed food products that are sold to us in huge quantities in our supermarkets. Add to this the toxins stemming from the pollution of our food chain, which is the result of the general pollution of our planet. As a Pranist, you automatically avoid any and all food-related pollution, no matter what its origin is. When you avoid food, you also avoid unconsciously maintaining any problematic eating patterns, such as consuming unhealthy food or unhealthy amounts of substances like sugar, salt or fat. As a result, you also strongly decrease your risk of heart and blood circulation diseases. Our body features natural cleaning mechanisms. In the case of the liver which attempts to filter approximately 1.4 liters of blood every minute, some of the extracted wastes and toxic matter that may remain in the liver over extended periods of time may be cleansed by regularly applying a so-called "liver flush" procedure. A Pranist's liver, however, will never even carry any remains of wastes or toxic matter to begin with, since the bloodstream is never being polluted by any toxins originating from food. Pranism allows for a happy liver that never reaches its cleaning capacity limits and thus offers you the cleanest possible blood quality. It is obvious that clean blood leads to optimal health for all organs that are supplied with it, as it will no longer lead to any disease-inducing deposits of toxins throughout the body. Your brain will be among the first to celebrate and offer you increased mental capacities as a gift in return. And in its center sits the pineal gland which plays a crucial role for your connection to the subtle realms and the spiritual world. Keeping your bloodstream completely clean by living a Pranic lifestyle will accelerate and maximize the de-calcification of your pineal gland and thus increase its strength. You will find yourself with a higher vibratory rate, a stronger light body, sharpened senses and clear-senses, a more significant connection with your higher self and your spiritual guides, resulting in a stronger ability to manifest your true essence. We are convinced that Pranism can reveal to you your innate healing capacities and other hidden capacities and gifts, or increase them if you already work as a healer. And although we currently do not yet have a complete list of pathologies or diseases which Pranism is certain to eliminate in those who practice it, we are convinced that it will improve general health for humankind in a very significant manner. As a small anecdote: During a channeling session, Jonathan, the entity that speaks through me in trance, has advised one of my students who suffered from severe fibromyalgia to practice Pranism in order to get rid of the disease. She followed his instructions and since then has been nearly free of fibromyalgia.

Pranism is not equal to fasting. Furthermore, wanting to lose weight should not be the reason to do it. Whereas fasting is a process that remains limited in time and would result in death if this limit was not respected, Pranism has the decisive advantage that it can be practiced without any time limit, throughout an entire life, and will not result in death, as long as its rather simple set of conditions or rules is respected. The main point I need to stress is that Pranism isn't equal to not eating; Pranism means eating all the time – but differently; it means nourishing oneself with light or energy.

As a matter of fact, Pranists not only lose any notion of the feeling of hunger, they also do not experience any mental or physical energetic fluctuations throughout the day: Since their digestive system remains passive (and as a result saves them lots of energy), they are no longer subject to the blood sugar-insulin cycles which are caused by food intake and ultimately result in after-meal slumps or a reduced level of energy and potentially – as a result – in cravings for more sugar or other stimulants. For Pranists, this also means that there are no more nutrition-related mood swings throughout the day and no more "need" for stimulants of (at best) questionable health benefit such as coffee, nicotine or other so-called "energy drinks". But not only are such slumps and periods of sleepiness avoided, mental fog is dissolved as well, and mental clarity is thus increased.

Depending on your personal situation, your well-being may increase in even more ways: imagine your life without flatulence, without constipation, without diarrhea, without stomachaches or burning sensations in the stomach area and without the need to belch. And quite obviously, you don't need to go to the toilet. When you practice Pranism, you automatically reach and maintain your perfect body weight; any excessive body fat, which until now may have weighed you down either physically or psychologically – thanks to culturally anchored beauty standards – will evaporate naturally and not return. Being naturally slim usually increases self-confidence, but it will definitely leave you feeling lighter and better in a very physical and tangible way.

Hunger is the false and limiting belief of humankind's dependency on food. It is a prison implanted into all modern cultures, fully endorsed by the current state of science and thus entirely accepted by the majority of human beings. As long as we experience the sensation of hunger and believe we require food for our survival, we can be manipulated into doing things we would normally not do. As soon as our belief system has integrated the fact that food is nothing more than an option, we are free.

Eliminating one of the most important limiting beliefs humankind is still subjecting itself to – the belief of addiction to food – teaches you an extremely powerful lesson. It proves to you based on your own body that you are capable of so much more than what you were taught. You realize in the most profound way that you can change your belief system which is the rule set that defines your reality, be it material or immaterial. This in turn changes your life entirely. You have manifested what most members of society currently still choose to call "a miracle".

Pranism will contribute significantly to leading humankind to a higher state of consciousness – a necessary condition for its survival and evolution. As a Pranist or Breatharian, you directly contribute to the profound transformation of our own species.

But on a personal level, challenging the ordinary with the extraordinary is difficult and dangerous to do. It raises too many fears: fear of having to reconsider a lifetime of erroneous thinking, fear of being ridiculed by peers, fear of being socially and professionally sidelined, as was the talented Carl Jung by a narrow-minded Sigmund Freud for having had the effrontery to be interested in metaphysics.

I was greatly encouraged by the documentary on the Ray Maor experiment. In fact, when I watched it, I was in southern India and was being initiated into Pranic nourishment, all alone and quite isolated.

I myself was not hungry at any time. In fact, I was not thirsty either and only occasionally missed the taste of certain flavors. The first week without water was very difficult for me. The fourth day, I saw myself dying. I was alone and lying on my bed, unable to even get up any more. That is when I saw my spirit leave my body and I was able, from above, to contemplate my body lying on a forest floor, while physically I was on my bed, in a rented studio. I didn't understand what was happening to me, but I remember letting go. I can't tell if I went to sleep or if I fainted. Several hours went by – it's impossible for me to say how many; it could have been one hour or three. I came to myself peacefully, filled with a new serenity and very happy. Then I felt the first very cold drop on my palate, at the Lalana spot, the throat chakra situated between Vishuddhi and Bindu. I was nevertheless hot, because in that season the temperature can go up to 37°C (98.6°F). The nights are cooler, but still hot. Where could that drop, so cold, so rich and so incredibly refreshing, have come from? I received several; as I learned later, they are called "Amrita", i.e. "divine nectar". Without my faith and extreme conviction, without my long periods of concentration and meditation, but especially without the spiritual world, I would never have survived this lack of water! It's not without risk. I am not encouraging you to imitate my experiment. According to the World Health Organization, who has established that a person can only survive for three days without water, I was supposed to have died twice already, after one week without water! How did I survive? I did not eat anything for a month. Yet, beginning on the 23rd day, my weight stabilized at what it had been in my early twenties, in other words, ten kilos less than when I left for India. How could my weight remain stable without my having eaten any food?

If I compare the experiments carried out by the yogi, Ray Maor and myself, it is surprising to note that the yogi did not urinate even once, whereas Ray Maor and I did.

Apparently people have died during the 21-day initiation to Pranic nourishment. These deaths are due, as far as we know, to the way water is taken in again after going without. As mentioned above, too much water absorbed by the organism too quickly can cause brain swelling. Nevertheless, at least 10,000 people have gone through the process with proper accompaniment – unlike me, alone in the far reaches of India – and have survived without any problems. After the process, these people said they recovered a healthier and more spiritual life. As for myself, I am no longer able to eat meat at all. My morning meditation, which lasts between 75 and 90 minutes, is deeper and better focused. My daily life is much more balanced, but above all much, much more productive. As I have chosen to eat again for social reasons, what seems challenging to me relates to the desire for certain things, which is slowly returning, whereas during my month's fasting it was nonexistent. I find that I presently react with less tolerance to human ignorance and have something of a "don't mess with me" attitude; but I hope that will go away again. The best and most beautiful thing is the peace that has remained. The connection with and gratitude towards the spiritual world are much more intense. Since I discovered Amrita, I have a deeper understanding of the Biblical passage in which Samson prayed to God not to let him die of thirst. This passage can be seen in the less-revised versions of the Bible, in the Book of Judges 15:19:

> But God clave an hollow place in the jaw, and there came water thereout, and when he had drunk, his spirit came again, and he revived…

I am possessed of a new freedom. This freedom is, in fact, associated with this peace. I now know that I can live without any material things and that I can feed myself very well with only the divine essence. I do not need anything other than light. Since it is omnipresent, I can not only live happily but also do my work in it and with it.

To finish, since a plant knows how to use light to feed itself, through the process of photosynthesis, why couldn't any living organism also do so? I have included the above paragraphs in this book to prove, through the experiments of the people involved as well as my own, that we are energy; we are information. Our intentions build what we are or will become. Matter is only a creation of the spirit. In a similar manner, the intention, during a treatment, to cleanse and to transmit healing energy – this intention is expressed so that it will be executed in the best interests of the patient!

Readers, I beg you! Open your horizons to other sides, to other paradigms. Give your body the chance to be healed through spiritual healing. How marvelous it is to realize what our mind can do! We are all divine beings; it is only our awareness that is more or less developed.

One energy, different techniques

Energy transmission has different approaches with a variety of techniques and treatments. The technique which interests us here is spiritual healing, in which the energy from the spiritual world is channeled by the medium in order to make the client well. Spiritual healing is one of the branches of mediumship.

Whatever the technique chosen – Therapeutic Touch, Reiki, or any other approach, the therapist draws energy from the Source. That can be the earth, the universal energy, God or

I am almost normally conscious, but I am preparing to carry out a treatment. My physical energy, shown in red in the first two photos, is still very present. [Interpretation by Sébastien, the artist who took these photos.]

I am going deeper into myself. Only a very small amount of physical energy is left. [Interpretation by Sébastien, the artist who took these photos.]

Only the spirit energy is left, shown in blue. [Interpretation by Sébastien, the artist who took these photos.]

something else, depending on the therapist's beliefs. Drawing energy from the Source allows the therapist to channel it and pass it on, without using up his or her own energy. It is useless to debate on which technique to choose: all pasta is cooked in water... the difference is only in the sauce...

The Kirlian photos above show three different states of consciousness. These photos are those of my fingers on the machine.

We are an energy field. It is only a partial reflection of our physical body. This field can be accelerated and slowed. It can be moved, built, guided in flows or used to reinforce existing flows. If we do not consider this field in priority and try to understand and grasp it we will never reach our full potential, either on the physical level or – and even less so – on the spiritual one.

Awareness of and consideration for the elements of which

we are all made is an aspect that is often neglected [see the section "Medical and energetic side effects"]. A great many pathological cases are due to a lack of one of these elements or its imbalance. Where psychiatric disorders are concerned, I have never seen any case, and I mean not a single one, in which there wasn't too much air and thus not enough grounding.

We are all made up of the four following elements:

- Earth: This element enables physical manifestations. It is responsible for organization, health, the vital forces, safety, perseverance, stability and our grounding. A lack of earth causes depression, weakness, incoherence, lack of perseverance and above all chronic fatigue. An excess of earth leads to a stubborn, brooding and greedy personality.
- Water: This element represents our emotions. A lack of water leads to a lack of feeling and a cold attitude. An excess of water causes too much emotional sensitivity, and leads to a hypersensitive, paranoid personality that takes refuge in an imaginary world.
- Fire: This element represents our fears and courage. A lack of fire will lead to lack of willpower, a loss of vitality, and a sluggish personality that is limp and fearful. An excess of fire will lead to a hyperactive, destructive, uncontrolled, violent and furious personality.
- Air: This element represents a lively mind, logical thought, mental strength, humor and intellect. A lack of air leads to irrationality, intellectual stupidity, a dull or uncreative personality. An excess of air causes hyperactivity, arrogance, forgetfulness, distraction, and can lead to psychoses due to a chronic lack of earth.

Spiritual healing works on both levels. The first is easy to understand: "When you lack energy, you are like a car without petrol. All you need to do is fill the tank to get started again." The healer simply influences the energy field to be treated by supplying fresh energy.

The second level is a little more complex to grasp. Here the action is carried out by the spirit beings. The healer must therefore be able to get ready to open the connection to the spiritual world and build up enough energy for these beings to be able to access it and act. Building and managing this kind of field is a learned ability. It takes time. It takes practice. It takes meditation. Even after training, it must be understood that healing is sometimes possible, other times not. It is important to learn to get out of the mind, to render it inactive. When it is in this inactive state, the ECG shows that the brainwaves are theta or delta, which is a very passive state, like in sleep or in certain illnesses.

The healer must absolutely not mistake themselves for a doctor. They have not studied medicine or acquired medical knowledge. It is therefore strictly forbidden to diagnose and even more so to prescribe anything whatsoever. A healer must encourage the patient to consult an allopathic physician if they are asked to deal with a serious illness or a pathology they are not familiar with. The only possible solution is to work hand in hand with allopathic physicians. Moreover, in general, complementary practices are not contradictory ones.

Some doctors send me patients while forbidding me to tell anyone that they do so. Many of these patients have seen their condition improve or have gotten well after treatment in my clinic. Despite the positive results, many patients do not dare tell their physician they are consulting a spiritual healer. This is a sad attitude but also very revealing with respect to the societal conditioning to which we are subjected.

The danger for a healer is at the level of their personal investment. This can have two forms:

1. Pity: The healer wants to heal their patient so much that they become emotionally involved because they are moved by the patient's case. The healer no longer feels compassion – which is a neutral emotion – but pity.
2. Ego: A healer treats an influential patient or someone they care greatly about and whom they want very much to heal in order to feed their own ego.

In both cases, the healer's energy is linked to the patient's. This is not wanted either by the patient or by the spirit world. The latter can no longer perform the work that is requested, and the energy will be biased. To illustrate the healer's implication I like to compare it to a "ham omelet": the hen has participated by providing the egg, but the pig has gotten involved! The hen goes on living in better health whereas the pig...

The right tool, to avoid getting involved as a healer, is the intention that the treatment provided is in the best interests of the patient and not through the healer's will. As mentioned above, it can be in the patient's best interests to understand why he is having ulcers rather than just fixing them. Or in understanding the reason for which a person is suffering from chronic illness, rather than just easing it with painkillers... There are many examples. It is the patient's higher awareness that enables him to let go of an illness or to hang on to it. Of course, the ego can harm the patient by holding in the bad. It's like sitting on an uncomfortable chair and realizing it is uncomfortable but remaining seated nevertheless. It's unpleasant but we are familiar with it, and who knows whether we will have a chair if we get up? It's often fear of change that makes a patient hang on to his illness. As taught in India, the ego does not have a negative connotation like it does in Europe. Jonathan also speaks of this. In India, "ego" simply means "identity". For us, this fear of change exists, as well as that false belief that we will lose our identity, so we certainly must not get over a chronic illness, which, because it is known, defines us.

Channeling and guiding energy can be easily learned. To prepare for spiritual healing it is recommended to first calm and control your body at the same time as your mind by breathing. First do "Anapana" breathing and then spinal breathing to be well centered. To learn these breathing techniques, I suggest that you read the chapter and exercises devoted to meditation.

Since energy is the tool of my trade, I seat myself in a ray of light that falls on me and envelops me. This light beam is also my simplest and fastest protection:

Where there is light, there is no shadow!

Once my mind is at peace, I imagine breathing in from my fontanel, at the top of my head. With each breath, I draw energy from the light beam into my core. Most people's core energy is in the heart chakra or on the sternum. My core is going to build itself automatically. Like a small sun that begins to grow, spreading through me, in the same way as a large sun. This extension not only enables the flow to travel through my arms and exit from my hands but also prevents me from using up all my own energy. And best of all, I receive energy for myself. Isn't that magnificent? I help my patients and myself at the same time!

In spiritual healing, to position our hands, we let ourselves be directed by our intuition and our guides. There are, however, some well-defined procedures such as Therapeutic Touch (TT). In this technique the steps to follow and the required placements of the hands are defined according to a specific protocol. TT was invented and promoted by Dr. Dolores Krieger, an American physician, and her therapeutic partner Dora Kunz. TT is taught and performed in many countries, especially in hospitals. The full protocol is presented in the "exercises" chapter of this book. There has been a great deal of scientific research done on TT, and it is very promising and encouraging. In my classes as well as in my clinic, I relate TT to spiritual healing. In this way I get two birds with one stone.

Letting go

Learning to let go is not as simple as it may seem. When you feel sympathy for someone, you want them to get well. This wish is a mistake, as I have already said, as it gets the therapist involved. If a patient does not heal, the therapist may feel let down and inadequate. We cannot determine whether a patient will heal. We can only do our best. The most difficult thing, perhaps, is to be able to distance ourselves after having performed a "miracle".

I have had that experience and I learned a very impressive lesson:

Once, on a trip to India, I was on the terraces above the Tirumala Temple. On my left were some stairs with wide steps that led to the temple. I was sitting almost at the top and contemplating this spiritual place while doing my pranayamas. To my left, I could see a young couple who were helping a woman in her sixties down the long staircase. She was one of the faithful who had come to pray and was wearing a white robe like some nuns and had shaved her head. She was in great pain, which was visible from afar. Her back was so bent you could have used it as a tea table. She was walking sideways because she was incapable of walking straight to go down the stairs. I don't know what hit me, whether my guide pushed me or I was overcome with my faith, but I got up and went towards the little group. I gestured towards the woman, almost ordered her to sit down, and said, "I can help you." I was surprised myself at how spontaneous that sounded: I never promise results when I offer to help. Perhaps because I was wearing a white robe too, they did not ask any questions. The young people helped the woman to sit and I sat down beside her. I said, "I'm Mahān; this will take a little while." When I placed my hand on her lower back, I did not feel anything different to the therapy that I always have performed. The only nuance was that after about ten minutes, my arm and my hand began to shake so hard that I let them shake. The treatment ended with a sort of pat on the same area. I understood they were speculating to each other that I must be an American. I said nothing else and left, smiling, to go back down the stairs. I was walking on the terrace towards the temple and turned around. I couldn't believe my eyes! This woman whom I had just treated was going down the stairs, her back straight, one hand on the rail, of course, but straight and with ease as though she had never had the slightest problem. When I wanted to approach her, a very loud voice interrupted and said, "No, now you have to let go!" I turned back around and nearly ran away so they would not catch up with me. I never saw them again. At the time I was shaken and hurt to not have been able to speak with them after this incredible miracle. But the joy of having experienced this and of earning the confidence and honor of the spirit world was so tremendous. My shock at having to let go was one of the most important lessons in my career as a healer. Perhaps it is because of it that I am in good health, because I don't get involved. I don't lose my own energy during the treatments and I don't waste any afterwards. When I have finished my closing prayer for all my patients, I no longer relate.

Tirumala Temple, India

Chapter 14

Distance healing

In principle, distance healing follows the same procedure as spiritual healing. Energy is also built up through the same breathing exercises. Sending out distance healing requires a higher level of concentration because the patient is absent. It is easier for the therapist's mind to deviate like it can also do during meditation. Energy may be sent through the hands, the heart chakra or the third eye. In a similar manner to spiritual healing, the energy is sent to the patient, trusting in the higher awareness to send it to the right place, the one that is the most beneficial. The key phrase for any distance healing is: "May this energy be used for his (or her) highest good!" With this intention, the energy does its work and goes where it is required.

The TT protocol can be carried out at a distance. All that is necessary is to visualize in your mind how the hands are placed on the patient's body as required by the protocol. There are many doctors' reports on the patients I have treated at a distance available for any interested scientist. The results are clear: distance healing works! I encourage everyone to help and support their loved ones in times of need. There is no risk. You just have to include the intention: "May this be for his (or her) highest good." In this way, therapist and patient are both protected, just as in a normal treatment procedure.

Experiment in distance healing

In this experiment, we connected and synchronized a test subject who was located in another room of the hospital. This person was simply required to remain seated on a chair for about two and a half hours. He could relax but not go to sleep. In an isolated room, I was to perform distance healing on this test subject. He did not know when I was going to do so. It was the doctor who gave me the signal to begin and end the treatment, via a microphone. The result was astonishing: not only did the test subject's brain frequencies change and slow while I was performing the distance healing, but the most amazing thing was that as soon as I received the signal to stop, the subject's brain reacted within a second and returned to its initial rhythm. A reaction within the same second over a two-and-a-half hour session is no coincidence! One doctor nevertheless had the ridiculous idea that this reaction was due to a military fighter plane flying over the hospital at the same moment. This shows to what lengths the medical world will take their desperate attempts to deny certain facts.

These are the results we obtained during the experiment on distance healing:

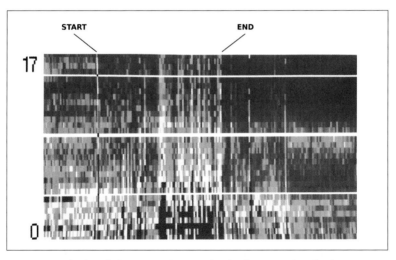

Analysis of the test subject's brain frequencies during distance healing.

At the beginning of the treatment, the variations were very slight. Then, as the treatment progressed, two slower frequencies appeared (shown in violet on the graph). When the treatment ended, the test subject's brain returned to a state similar to that before the treatment began.

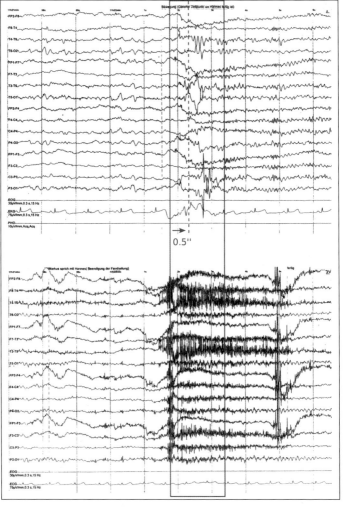

Synchronized EEGs recorded during distance healing. The patient's graph is pictured above and therapist Hannes Jacob's is below it. The instant the two brains synchronize appears in red. One-half second after the doctor gave the order to cease the distance healing, the patient's brain reacted. The patient's reaction appeared within the same second as the end of the treatment.

During my experiments at the *Institut für Kommunikation und Gehirnforschung* (Communications and Brain Research Institute) in Stuttgart, I worked with a patient in the care of Dr. A. Amsel, psychiatrist in Bern and head of forensic psychiatry. Dr. Amsel also sees patients in her private office.

Her patient was suffering from chronic depression with suicidal tendencies. She did not know at what time during her four months of treatment I would be working with her. Dr. Amsel had obtained her agreement in principle. I worked twice with this woman, once before I went to a meditation retreat and again after my return. There was no difference between the EEGs taken before I went into retreat and after my return. Both experiments showed that my brain frequencies were delta frequencies, as in all the recorded treatments.

The doctor's report, in which she includes her patient's comments, is very surprising:

After the first treatment: "I was participating at the time in a group art therapy class. I wasn't happy with either the venue or the group. But this morning I went and I was happy!"

After the second treatment: "I was at a friend's house having breakfast with the family. I was very surprised that morning to realize that I wasn't just in a good mood, but that I was encouraging the others to chat with questions and stories, which is not usually something I like doing and all the more so in the morning."

According to the doctor, after the two distance healing sessions, there was an abrupt and medically incomprehensible change in the patient's attitude. The first distance healing session resulted in this patient feeling happy. The second resulted in increased humor and a decrease in her depressive behavior.

Chapter 15

Scientific approaches

As fascinating as it is, this topic is no less a difficult one. It is a great joy to see that more and more doctors are striving to understand sensitivity. The prejudices that arise in some minds at the word "medium", and especially the fear it provokes in a great many members of the medical profession, have stifled all but a limited interest in actually doing scientific experiments. But things are progressively changing. In my experience, I have learned that it isn't possible to just go hire equipment such as a tomography machine to do MRIs. First you have to go before an ethics committee who analyze and assess the research project. This procedure can take a very long time and end up with a negative response after all, if there is one...

One of the greatest fears some doctors have lies in the realization that throughout a lifetime of work they still haven't seen the truth. This fear is deeply rooted. They are also anxious that they might be sidelined by their peers. A number of doctors confessed they did not reveal their interest in my methods or whether they had participated in my research. Others simply disappeared into thin air after successful experiments, because they were afraid of the consequences. On the one hand they feared the possible repercussions from their professional colleagues, and on the other they were afraid that proof of life after death would change their approach completely. For example, a psychiatrist not only will have to acknowledge that we are first and foremost spirits incarnated into bodies, but also and above all that this spirit continues to exist after physical death and, moreover, can be perceived by his patients. If the spirit became a scientific fact, psychiatry as such would have to review the way it diagnoses disorders and prescribes treatments.

It is a shame and an insult to all intelligence to deny the reality of the spirit. Fortunately, there are daring doctors that have become involved in recognizing this reality, such as Dr. Elisabeth Kübler-Ross, Dr. Raymond Moody or Dr. Jean-Jacques Charbonier, to name only a few. These pioneers have brought forth evidence of the continuity of life after death. We must thank all the scientists who have had the courage to invest themselves in this undeniable truth. There are millions of people who have had out-of-body and near-death experiences. These people have given details about what was happening in the room or hospital they were in when they were outside of their bodies, during their clinical deaths.

There are other areas in which irrefutable proof of life after death can be found or at least the existence of the spirit that we are. In contacts through mental mediumship they are clearly evident, as they also are during a psychic reading. Appearances in physical mediumship provide undeniable proof of life after death.

There is no political will to restore the truth of survival after death. This reality should be taught as early as kindergarten. It should be presented as a natural science, not just during catechism classes, from a religious point of view! Imagine the extra peace the population would feel. What a relief to be able to rejoice in that peace and that love which is waiting for us, at least in the afterlife!

Another certain and reliable source attesting to life after death is children. How many children see spirits? How many talk about them? How many describe them? Unfortunately, far too often, these children are not taken seriously.

Let's look more closely at what happens in the brain, in order to better understand its relationship with our psychic abilities.

The frequencies in our brain

- **Gamma:** 30-100 Hz. These frequencies have not been experimented or analyzed very often, because up to now technology has not been able to pinpoint them due to their rapid frequency. A gamma state indicates intense cerebral activity, as in creative processes or when solving problems that arise during moments of intense concentration or focus. Many gammas may enrich or reinforce sensory experiences, which may explain Olivia Boa's objective vision, for example, because her EEG clearly shows gamma waves in the occipital area, where sight is centered. It is a proven fact that at certain stages of meditation, the gamma waves appear in the right temporal lobe and are related to beatific states.

- **Beta:** 13-30 Hz. Normal state of consciousness and awareness; everyday consciousness.

- **Alpha:** 8-12 Hz. A state of sleepiness, hypnosis or light meditation and visualization. These waves allow for subtle contact as in ESP or with a deceased person.

- **Theta:** 4-7 Hz. A slow, passive cerebral state. Dreaming or meditation phase. In mediumship, this corresponds to light trance, spoken trance or spiritual healing. These waves can also be seen in the case of certain neurological illnesses.

- **Delta:** 1-4 Hz. These frequencies are a sign of severe pathologies such as "Grand mal" epilepsy, stroke or some types of coma. These waves can also appear in normal individuals who are deeply asleep. They are also visible in monks who are highly trained in meditation (according to accounts by Matthieu Ricard). In mediumship, they appear during deep trance or trance healing.

NIRS – Near InfraRed Spectroscopy experiments

These experiments were carried out in order to better understand what happens in the brain during modified consciousness states. They allow us to compare rapid states such as ESP and mediumship with passive states such as healing and trance.

Verification of the mental normality and psychic health of an experimental subject is essential prior to undertaking any experiments. To this end, I was subjected to the following procedure:

1. Two minutes of psychokinesis: moving a beverage can without touching it
2. Two minutes reading a newspaper out loud
3. Five minutes of psychic reading for an unknown person
4. Three-minute Q&A session with factual questions such as days of the week and simple math
5. Seven minutes of mediumistic reading
6. Five minutes of "normal" rest
7. Ten minutes of spiritual healing
8. Ten minutes of spoken trance

This procedure was repeated twice.

Scientific validation cannot be established unless the experience is structured according to a very strict protocol that ensures it can be reproduced. The experiments that I am going to present meet these criteria, whether they involve contacts with the deceased, psychic readings, spiritual healing or trance.

During the scientific protocol, the electrodes were placed on my head according to the following layout:

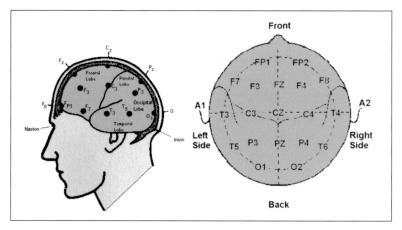

Placement of the 10-20 electrodes on Hannes Jacob: lateral view (left) and top view (right), during the NIRS (Near InfraRed Spectroscopy) experiment.

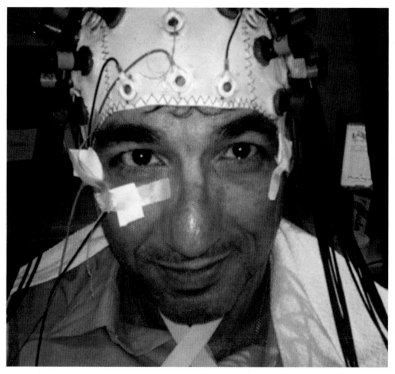

NIRS electrodes on Hannes Jacob.

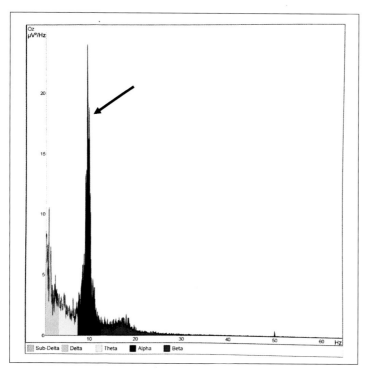

Frequency analysis for Hannes Jacob in a normal state.

The EEG (electroencephalogram) was recorded while my brain was at rest, with my eyes closed. The black area represents a basic cerebral rhythm that is predominately alpha. There is little presence of the theta and delta frequencies shown in orange and yellow. This EEG is altogether representative of a person in a normal relaxed state with his eyes closed.

After this resting exercise, I did two psychic readings of five minutes each, followed by two mediumistic readings of seven minutes each. For these readings, two psychologists from the medical staff – whom I did not know – were made available to me.

During the psychic readings, the NIRS activation sample indicated a right lateralization. A stable hemodynamic response appeared, in particular in the region of the right temporal lobe.

121

This hemodynamic response was particularly obvious during the reading in which the positive response rate was close to 100%. In other words, all the elements of the reading for the unknown person were correct.

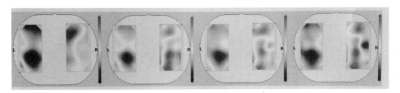

Obvious irrigation of Hannes Jacob's right temporal lobe, in red.

While in contact with the deceased on behalf of these psychologists, I was connected to electroencephalogram machines as well as to the NIRS. We obtained the surprising proof that from the start of the mediumistic reading, the right frontal cortex – especially the right temporal lobe – was irrigated with hemoglobin. For information, the right temporal lobe is implicated in the creative and spatial processes while the left temporal lobe is implicated in the speech- and language-related processes. Throughout the experiment, there was little to no irrigation of the left temporal lobe. This disparity in irrigation was also visible for all the psychic readings such as reading recent memory or the aura. The right temporal lobe is therefore our primary tool for perception and physical translation; this tool begins to function as soon as the antennae in our energy field pick up information. It must be noted that in a simple guessing game, this lobe is not irrigated.

The illustration below represents my brain during mental mediumship while doing a reading. The red areas indicate the oxygenated areas of the brain, which are the regions that are working.

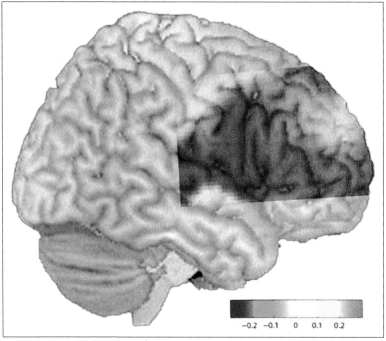

-0.2 -0.1 0 0.1 0.2

Irrigation of Hannes Jacob's brain during a mediumistic reading.

According to the activation samples, during the various mediumistic and psychic readings on the different volunteers, I tallied up correct statements at a success rate of almost 100%. The accuracy of this information was confirmed by two certified psychologists from the University of Tübingen, by a psychiatrist, Dr. François Moll, and by two psychologists who were present when I did the readings. Dr. Moll not only suggested carrying out the NIRS experiments, he is also a practitioner who considers his patients as beings with a spirit and does not reduce them to their sole neurological and endocrinal systems. This very human approach is part of the reason for his success and allowed him to treat one of the psychologists that participated in the test, who was very upset by the accuracy of the reading I did for her. Being confronted with truths that her system of beliefs refused to admit up until that point was certainly a shock to her. Fortunately Dr. Moll was able to find the words to reassure her. Before collaborating with me, he had come to test my mediumistic work in my clinic. He was delighted with the session; the description of his late father was accurate, and the latter had given a message for his grandson by name. As Dr. Moll knows that his grandson does not have a name that could be easily invented, this left him with no doubt about the accuracy and veracity of my work.

Thus we have here a type of doctor – and moreover, a psychiatrist – who is ready to expand and question his knowledge. Alas, for many colleagues, it is not at all obvious they can accept such truths. I once met a psychiatry professor, at a conference. This man was well-known and often mentioned in the media and wished to remain anonymous. He was very interested and invited me to talk over dinner. In the middle of our discussion, he felt the need to know "exactly how this works." A spirit then appeared in my field as if he had been expected for some time. I immediately understood it was one of the professor's deceased colleagues and described this colleague to him: physical appearance, character, age at the time of death and the heart attack that had killed him. Everything was perfectly accurate. The professor was visibly astonished and repeated, several times, that studies in this field would be undertaken. On the other hand, he did not wish me to mention his interest to another of his colleagues who had also attended the conference several days previously. After the last handshake, this professor never answered any of my messages or phone calls. Once again, for some the confrontation is too strong. Imagine you are an eminent professor and have been teaching and publishing papers for many years. Suddenly your truths are radically challenged and you realize that what you have been teaching about human function is incomplete, if not erroneous… Worse yet, you are a psychiatrist and you are used to placing a lot of people in a psychiatric ward for schizophrenia.

These people are shut away, cut off from their senses because they are put under strong sedation, forever labeled as psychotic and have little hope of shedding that label one day.

We can understand that it takes a lot of courage for this kind of practitioner to review his diagnoses and paradigms when he has overcome the stupefaction he feels at this new information. Inside, he may be going through a major crisis as he understands that his entire career has been based on inaccurate concepts. Such courage is that of the true scientist, the researcher who is ready to give up all of his old theories when they prove outdated. These people are few and far between, so once again, let's applaud the pioneers and the courageous.

Creative, focused processes, but also and above all access to memory content, take place in the right lobe of the brain. This is very logical since subjective perceptions depend on memory! These results play a key role in the explanation of the "Hannes Jacob Syndrome" presented in the relevant chapter.

It is not only during psychic and mediumistic readings that the right lobe is irrigated. Psychokinesis, such as bending a spoon or moving a can of soda without touching it, among other things, solely through the movement of energy, also clearly reveals the irrigation of the right temporal lobe. The left lobe stays empty!

To move a soda can, it is simply necessary to link your energy to the energy let off by the can, and then slowly move your hands. The can will then follow the movement. It is not the draft from the hand movement that moves the can. If that were so, anyone could move a can, which is absolutely not true. Given these results, let's compare what happens in the brain during spiritual healing or trance.

Experiment in spiritual healing, slow frequencies

This experiment was carried out using an EEG machine and was done in different hospitals and neurological clinics. This research focuses on the examination of the cerebral states at slow frequencies, spiritual healing states, trances and trance healing. The goal of the experiment was to measure the extent to which my brain waves slowed when I was working. The results were similar to those of experiments carried out on Buddhist monks during deep meditation: my brain's activity dropped in a few seconds from an alpha or beta frequency to theta and finally to delta, the slowest cerebral frequency. In each trial and at every clinic, the results were the same. We thus better understand the link between this passive state which has been reached so strenuously through training and is used in treatments, and its objectification through cerebral analysis.

I have shown the illustrations on the following page to a neurologist, without telling him that it was my brain or telling him about the experiment. When he read these results, he concluded they must have been due to an epileptic seizure of the "grand mal" type. Later, he was sincerely astonished. Theta waves and especially delta waves are visible in particular during a state of deep sleep or in severe pathologies such as strokes, epileptic seizures, and some forms of coma. The classical neurologist does not understand how a healthy person can reach states this deep in such a short time, and on command to boot!

These two EEGs show clear differences between the alpha waves, on the left (between 8 and 12 Hz, or simply put, eight to twelve peaks per second) produced in a person who is starting to fall asleep or in a meditative visualization state, and the delta waves, on the right (between 2.5 and 3 Hz, in other words between two and one-half and three peaks per second), produced during deep sleep or in the presence of a serious illness. But this isn't the case – I am in a state of spiritual healing.

While I was doing the two spiritual healings with two different people, a combined EEG-NIRS measurement was taken. The seven-minute spiritual healing phase was followed

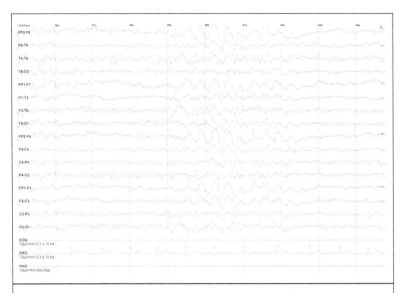

The vertical lines represent seconds and the zigzag curves are the frequencies measured in hertz (Hz). The three seconds in the middle each have three peaks, in other words, 3 Hz/second. They show the delta state.

Hannes Jacob wearing the cables connecting him to the EEG machine during an experiment in spiritual healing.

EEG alpha waves/EEG delta waves

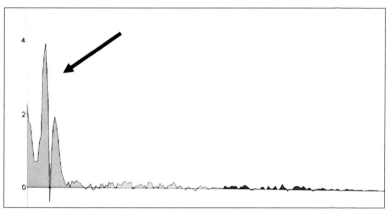

Measurement taken during spiritual healing. Only the delta frequency, the slowest, can be seen (in orange).

by a ten-minute spoken trance phase.

The results of the EEG measurement of the two spiritual healings shows a clear increase in the frontal delta waves in comparison to the EEG at rest.

The trance states are clearly distinct on the EEG samples. This corresponds to the central electrode placed on the frontal area. The delta zone is shown in orange. We can see that there is no activity in the frontal region.

Spiritual healing thus indeed occurs during passive cerebral frequencies. This is the complete opposite of the active interaction that takes place during mental mediumship. No matter who the healer is, he must learn to let go of his mind and his desires. He has to open the way for this very beneficial flow. It is via the passive cerebral frequencies that the spiritual world can access the patient. In this way the energy is not tainted by the healer's thoughts. No patient wants to receive the imprint of his healer. He wants to receive the purest energy possible!

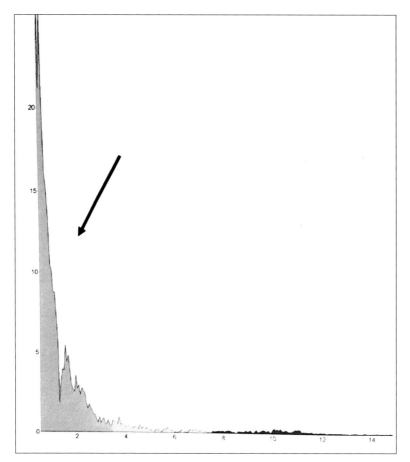

During a trance (in orange): the delta waves are greatly accentuated.

When they saw the results of the spoken trance the doctors were highly astonished. The question they were never able to answer popped up by itself: How could I speak in a sensible way for several minutes when the frequency in the frontal region of my brain was in delta waves and thus this region was not irrigated by blood, in other words, it was "empty"? How can someone have a coherent discussion for several minutes, while the cerebral region linked to organization and thought was in a state usually considered as "coma-like"?

We should remember Olivia Boa's observations. They confirm that the intellectual region is cut off and barely active during spiritual healing or trance. The planning and reasoning zones of the personality are scarcely active, if not shut down completely. The Supplementary Motor Area (SMA) – the zone in which thought is elaborated and which is involved in the planning of complex movements – is "switched off".

Thus the mystery remains unsolved, and the question remains...

Chapter 16

Kriya massage

Kriya massage is a technique that is generally carried out in a trance, or at least in a light trance, depending on the experience of the medium that does the massage.

Kriya massage is a physical application of the pranayamas that are explained in the chapters on meditation at the end of this book. This technique has a dual advantage: it focuses on and relieves muscle tension, but above all, Kriya massage is a fantastic tool for stimulating the patient's energy and getting it to flow. Given that the dense particles (fear, anger, etc.) are found in the lower spinal region, this technique allows these particles to be released and displaced and then to be dissolved. Thus the patient not only enjoys significant corporal relaxation but also and especially an increase in his or her vibratory field. Since the dense particles dissolve, the duality that is present in the person being massaged loses its strength, negative karma can be evacuated and above all the person will experience a profound sense of peace.

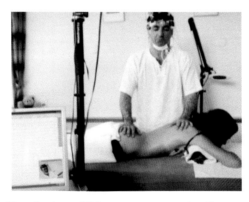

Data recording during a Kriya massage, under the supervision of Dr. Ralph Hassink, head of pediatric neurology in Bienne.

When we were joined by Dr. Ralph Hassink, pediatric neurologist and department head in Bienne, he commented with surprise on the results of the EEG. The reason for which he was interested in parapsychology and phenomena, which have not been scientifically explained, is easy to understand. He explained that as a doctor in his field he was of course interested in how the brain works. *"Yes,"* he said, *"we know a lot of things but there is also a lot we don't know. Where treatments for children are concerned, new discoveries can play an important role. That's why I am obviously interested and why I try to contribute to this research."*

"With Hannes Jacob, we can see at the neurological level that changes take place when he carries out various types of mediumistic tasks. These phenomena can be indicators for future validation. One astonishing fact concerns his Rapid Eye Movement (REM), which is the term that is used to describe a phenomenon that takes place in the dream phase during sleep. The question that therefore arises is: how is it that Mr. Jacob presents these characteristic signs of sleep when he is standing and doing a massage?! The day I can do my administrative job while sleeping, I will thank Heaven!" he laughed with a wink.

While studying the EEG as we were being filmed for a documentary on this phenomenon, Dr. Hassink explained the model that is shown here. The different sequences, as he called them, are clearly visible. He showed everyone present the screen that displayed rhythms of four and eight seconds, where: *"Hannes Jacob's brain produced very slow theta and delta waves. He himself seemed to be lost in a void. These waves speed up, and then slow down again, and so on."* He explained that in a healthy person, they correspond to waves that occur during sleep or outside of a waking state. *"Mr. Jacob produces them particularly in the right temporal lobe and occasionally in the central and frontal regions. It is amazing to observe how calm some regions of his brain become. Muscular activity has nearly disappeared and even the heartbeat is in harmony with the EEG. When the EEG becomes lower the heart beats more slowly and at the same rhythm it speeds up again. All of this can be seen in these EEGs, like the slightest clearing of the throat, it's really very precise. We are just as amazed to note that when Mr. Jacob has finished, everything is normal again, which means that the waves move to alpha and then beta once the experiment is over."*

Dr. Hassink continued by saying that when a concept for a treatment is established for a complex case, that is, a patient with many pathologies and needs, it is important to identify other health professionals who work in the allopathic and complementary medical fields. *"This is done by taking into account the fact that patients are often avid consumers, both at the allopathic and medicinal levels and those of complementary treatments. It must not be forgotten that a medium will, of course, be 'consumed' for their ability as soon as the patient is in need. That's the way it is. Sorting out the therapeutic team is inevitable. It is applicable to the multiple medical prescriptions that are not really justified, as well as to the distinction between genuine healers and charlatans or mediums. If more doctors took an interest in these subjects, there would be more potential for cooperation in order to find people who are serious in what they do. I only work with serious people, who consent to share their knowledge, and also two very important things: they must agree to ask themselves questions about certain events and also to acknowledge their limits. This is true for both sides! Doctors and/or therapists in alternative medicine who are interested in proving the efficacy of their work and want to support research, people like Hannes Jacob who are not afraid to expose themselves and seriously contribute to this research, must be honored. Nevertheless, proof remains the deciding factor. By this I mean that you mustn't think that Mr. Jacob just walked in here. I have known him since previous studies."*

"I am thinking in particular about the case of that 14-year-old boy with multiple disabilities, the most severe that exist and with an epilepsy that was not responding to treatment. We tried several times to increase the dosage of his antiepileptic medicine, Valproate, from 70 to 90 mg/kg. These increased doses never led to any improvement. On the other hand, by combining his treatment with Hannes Jacob's

distance healing, the nocturnal seizures diminished to the point where the patient is now getting more regular sleep. He has even got a few full nights' sleep, which has consequently improved his daytime condition! His condition has not only clearly improved, but has remained that way."

"There was another young man, 23 years old, who was also seriously disabled including with epilepsy and who was suffering from chronic constipation. Despite regular and consequential doses of paraffin oil, Practo-Clyss and Duphalac, the patient's general condition was considerably weakened due to this constipation. This even had an adverse effect on his epilepsy. Once again, Mr. Jacob's energy treatment helped to significantly reduce the constipation. We followed Mr. Jacob's advice to better hydrate the patient. Not only were we able to completely cease administering the paraffin oil, we were also able to reduce the doses of Practo-Clyss by half! The patient recovered an improved quality of life!"

"It is fair enough to ask questions about these treatments, how they work and what they do. The patients did not know about the distance healing, because their disabilities would not allow them to understand this kind of treatment, so any placebo effect must be excluded. Moreover, Hannes Jacob never saw these patients. He never even got near them. All he knew was their name and their room number. So there you have it. I don't know exactly what Mr. Jacob does or how he receives information, and so on, and I would not try to provide an interpretation. However, I can read and see that something is indeed taking place, and it can be proved."

"These cases are the best demonstration that an allopathic approach alone cannot be the only method used, and neither can alternative therapies. They are a whole, like one hand in the other, with each discipline accompanying the other."

"To come back to the Kriya massage trials, I have to admit I am very happy because we have a real result. These brain waves are well known to science. We know that Buddhist monks in deep meditative states produce similar EEG models. The case of Hannes Jacob is very *comparable to that. What I will never be able to judge is whether or not there is a difference in the two techniques to get there."*

"In any case, today we can clearly see that these different modified consciousness states can be found in the EEG. They also correspond to what Mr. Jacob has explained or interpreted when performing his treatments. We can only hope that other scientists will support these approaches in order to elucidate some of these mysteries."

"And just by the way, Mr. Jacob removed my intolerance to apples in only a few minutes. I can now eat them without my throat scratching, closing and causing me difficulties in breathing. I enjoy apples again."

Chapter 17

Anatomy and its connection to energy

To be able to have an understanding of the health impacts in terms of sensitivity and mediumship, we have to briefly explain a few notions of energy transmission, anatomy and pathology.

Let's begin with a journey to the center of our brain in order to see how it relates to sensitivity.

The cerebral cortex fills the top of the skull. It is split down the middle into two hemispheres. Each hemisphere is connected to the other by a network of nerve fibers, the axons. This network of fibers is called the "corpus callosum". In this way, each hemisphere controls one side of the body. The left side of the cerebral cortex controls the right side of the body, and the right side of the cerebral cortex controls the left side of the body.

The right hemisphere is generally responsible for spatial perception, synthesis of ideas and appreciation for art and music. The left side is associated with language, hearing, and analytical processes such as resolving math problems as well as integrating and synthesizing between intuition and rationality. In most people, the functions of the left brain are dominant.

In mediumship and psychic readings it is, in fact, the right temporal lobe that receives the information.

The hypothalamus at the top of the brainstem is directly connected to the thalamus. It is part of the limbic system and is active in our emotional states and our reactions. It's here that the emotional response to happiness, sadness and anger is generated. It is often inhibited by the centers of the upper brain (cortex). The cerebral reward and punishment zones (pleasure and pain) are also located in the hypothalamus. It is interesting to note that the center of pleasure is much larger than the center of pain.

The hypothalamus is also the center of the autonomous

nervous system and the sympathetic and parasympathetic systems. These two systems are associated with the control and regulation of all the organs in the body from the heart to the eyes, from the lungs for breathing to the muscles, stomach, digestive tract, intestines, liver, adrenal glands and skin, including the rectum and sexual organs.

The pituitary gland is the maestro of the endocrine system. It works closely with the hypothalamus which manages the autonomous nervous system. The hypothalamus is also the bridge between the autonomous nervous system and the endocrine system as well as being the hub for reception and feedback from the endocrine glands in the body and the center of thermoregulation. The endocrine glands complete the nervous system. They regulate the sympathetic and parasympathetic nerves in particular. Together, these nerves make up a single neuro-endocrine system that integrates and coordinates the body's metabolic activities. This system controls the body's ability to adapt to changes in internal and external conditions. The two systems work hand in hand. The glands do not function independently; each gland interacts with and modifies the influence of the other glands. Thus any disruption of the endocrine system or of a particular gland, especially the pituitary gland, can have a negative effect on the overall health of the body.

Most people have heard of the pineal gland. It is a little gland the size of a pea that is located at the top of the spine, in the center of the head at the level of the ears. Technically, it is located between the two cerebral hemispheres and above the cerebellum. In yoga, as well as in other spiritual practices through the ages, both in the East and in the West, this gland is said to be the link, the antenna, that allows access to the highest vibrations. When it is stimulated or awakened, evolution towards more subtle models then commences.

It is important to note that the eyes are connected directly to the pineal gland, through the sympathetic nervous system.

In yoga or other mystical practices the world over, this gland is considered as the physical equivalent to the third eye, the intuitive eye of waking consciousness. It is known that an excess of fluoride calcifies the pineal gland. There are natural ways to prevent this and thus increase our extrasensory perception, especially by consuming raw cocoa, cider vinegar, green leafy vegetables, or boron, the oligoelement that is present in vegetables such as beets (preferably organic ones). Not only does it detoxify and cleanse the gland, but it also eliminates the fluoride.

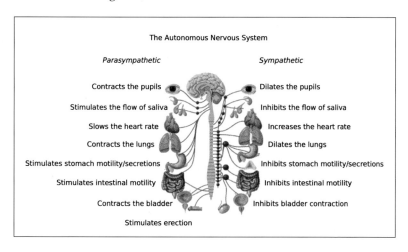

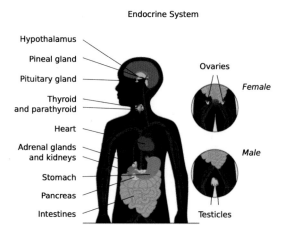

Ida and Pingala represented by two serpents climbing up the
column Sushumna.

The symbolism of Sushumna, Ida and Pingala

Ida and Pingala are more than symbolic values. These are two
concrete and vital channels.

Ida and Pingala are called "nadis" which is the Sanskrit word
for "flow". In this context, the flow can be physical, nervous,
psychic, mental or that of consciousness. Understanding
Ida and Pingala is normally limited to physical, nervous and
energetic aspects of the human structure. Ida is associated with
the parasympathetic system, Pingala to the sympathetic system.

Ida and Pingala have the same origin: the Mooladhara chakra
in the perineum. Ida is linked to the left nostril and Pingala to
the right. They cross the spine and continue along their paths,
finally meeting at the Ajna chakra at the top of the spine above
the palate. They mirror each other. If both paths are balanced,
the Kundalini can rise.

The central axis of Ida and Pingala is the Sushumna nadi
that represents the spine. Sushumna begins at the Mooladhara
chakra, passes along the spinal marrow through each of the

spinal chakras one after the other, to finally stop at Sahasrara, the crown chakra. This is the main channel.

These three paths are also known as Ganges (Ida), the Yamuna (Pingala) and the Saraswati (Sushumna) according to the names of these three Indian rivers.

It does exist
Because I saw it
The serpent in its nest
Curled in my loins
Strong enough to truly frighten
Gentle like a musician's flute
My breath rocks it
Will coax it gently out
Like the ivy climbing on the roof
So we can touch together
Heaven's light

Physical implications

Ida corresponds to the flow of breath from the left nostril and Pingala to the flow of breath from the right nostril. The two alternating respiratory flows are directly associated with the functions of the sympathetic and parasympathetic systems which regulate and maintain balance in the various bodily functions.

They are antagonistic: if one dominates, the other is subordinate. One system tends to conserve energy while the other tends to spend it. One tends to prepare the body for external action and the other tends to rest it and internalize the energy. In general the sympathetic nervous system accelerates the vital processes such as heartbeat, breathing rhythm and regulation of body temperature. On the other hand, the parasympathetic nervous system slows these functions and thus conserves the body's energy supply. These systems work night and day to regulate flow of blood from the heart, blood pressure and the speed at which all the bodily organs function or regenerate.

Why is the balance between Ida and Pingala so important in meditative techniques? The answer is simple: these functions are on the path of Sushumna. Ida and Pingala both belong to time. They represent, respectively, the interior psychic world and the exterior world, which are both dependent on time. Meditation is based on timelessness, which is why Ida and Pingala should be balanced. In fact, the Kundalini, the base energy, is capable of climbing up Sushumna. We then enter the kingdom of eternity. The Kundalini is often symbolized by a snake. It is also described by the expression "dwells in the pit". In the Sanskrit version of the Holy Book, it is said that the Kundalini devours time:

One was to control the sun (Pingala) and the other the moon (Ida) because they are the day and night of time; the secret is that Sushumna (the path of Kundalini) is the time-eater.

**I am the age
that you read in my eyes
my body
is as old as the earth
my soul
as eternity**

Meditative practices can contribute to resolving duality. The balance between Ida and Pingala plays a role in resolution. This was magnificently illustrated in the following story by Satyananda Saraswati:

Two birds, one black and one white, were attached to a stake, each one with a cord. They tried constantly to free themselves by flying up. But it was impossible to flee because they were held back with the cord. Finally they were worn out. Then they fell asleep at the base of the stake.

These two birds represent Ida and Pingala. They correspond to the flow of breath, respectively in the left and right nostrils.

This image shows us all of the importance and the benefits that can be obtained from meditation. Whether it is done by breathing alternatively through the nostrils or through spinal respiration, it is not only a question of spiritual awareness, but also an extremely important tool for our physical health!

Let's learn more now about breathing by looking more closely at the different respiratory techniques:

Ujjayi

Learning to do Ujjayi, which is called "ocean breathing", is recommended in order to experience greater calm and reduce inner stress. To do this type of breathing, close your throat slightly to slow it. This method of breathing sounds like a wave or ocean movement. Breathe through both nostrils at the same time. Ujjayi can be done at the same time as different pranayamas, during the asanas or postures and while doing abdominal respiration. The Ujjayi technique amplifies the effects of these exercises. Breathing in and out are identical and in harmony without having to strain. The breaths get longer automatically. When breathing out, simply relax and all the air will flow backwards, i.e. from the top to the bottom.

During Kriyas, Ujjayi and Kechari are not incompatible and can be activated at the same time.

Kriya

Kriya means "action". Kriya Yoga uses these breathing practices.

You do not remain fixed in one place, as is the case for example with Anapana, but you are performing inner movement. You activate energy and make it flow. This activity is beneficial to some parts of the body including the nervous and endocrine systems, since the two collaborate.

To practice Kriya Yoga, it is necessary to perfect the breathing and discover the chakras, their emanations and passages.

Once these places have been clarified and integrated into our conscience, the movement of the energy begins in various directions and passages, especially around the body and inside the spine. This affects the sympathetic Pingala, the parasympathetic Ida and the Sushumna, and has a positive influence on our physical and energetic health.

Kechari Mudra

Kechari means "flying through empty space". This mudra directs the flow of Ida, Pingala and Sushumna in the Ajna and Bindu chakras. It is also called the king of mudras, or the yogi shortcut, because it is capable of accelerating illumination. The medium that does not care about illumination would still benefit from applying it during the pranayama exercises, because irrigating Bindu is not only for that – it is also for expanding clairvoyance as well as obtaining the positive effects mentioned above. The person doing this mudra rolls his tongue back in order to touch his palate with the tip of his tongue, going as far back into the throat as is comfortably possible.

Bindu

At the physical level, activating Bindu helps fight depression, burnout syndrome, anxiety, and nervousness. The Bindu chakra is very important in Pranism. Besides the fact that it controls thirst and hunger, it also helps get out of the habit of eating unhealthy food. Bindu produces Amrita, the sacred nectar of immortality.

The following prayer is very often lifted to beg for these virtues:

Take us from ignorance to reality
Take us from darkness to light
Take us from death to immortality

Manipura (chakra number 3, at the solar plexus) encloses the sun and Bindu the moon. Normally the precious Amrita nectar flows directly from Bindu into the sun and burns. By reversing the flow with specific pranayamas, we stimulate longevity and the spiritual awakening of a limitless conscience. The transformation itself takes place in Vishuddhi (5th chakra) through which the flow circulates between Manipura and Bindu.

Bindu is closely associated with the pineal gland. Indeed, this gland metabolizes melatonin and serotonin, which are both activated by light, thus by Prana. The light boosts the secretion of these hormones. As we know that pure energy is luminous, the calculation can be quickly made: breathe energy in for a healthier and happier life!

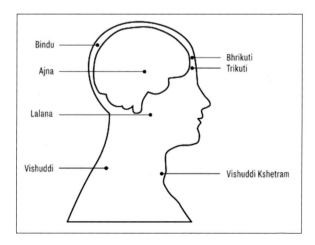

Medical and energetic side effects

**The worst thing isn't
That we are missing out on life.
The worst is
That we know it.**

People who are deeply involved in esotericism do not want to devote their lives mainly to matter, though matter is responsible for the health of the body and mind. Hyperfocusing on spiritual aspects causes an imbalance at the level of the elements (earth, water, fire and air). Like the mind, sensitivity belongs to the "air" element. An excessive amount of this element over a long period will inevitably lead to a deficit in the "earth" element and thus a lack of grounding. With too much air, living in the present becomes as impossible as vitalizing yourself through grounding. The first signs of a lack of grounding are chronic fatigue. In the long term, disorders similar to those seen in most psychiatric patients appear.

At the energy level, the balanced oval shape of the energy field that surrounds the entire body takes on the shape of a light bulb. This disproportionate dilatation of the upper chakras can lead to "explosive" manifestations of the lower energies – the ancestral Kundalini energy. These "explosions" can be compared to volcanic eruptions. They appear as anger or psychotic states. At the physical level, insomnia, hair loss, nausea or even headaches may occur. This excess energy in the head upsets the pineal gland, as well as the pituitary gland, and finally the hypothalamus.

This is how activities involving mediumship, psychic readings, trance, or trance healing can bring about serious problems at the level of both the endocrine system and the nervous system.

Even if the intention and goal of some meditation techniques is to clear the energy system in the lower spine and dissolve the dense particles that are stored there, it needs to be done in a gentle and constant manner. Remember that these particles hold our ego, our hates and our fears, our desires, all our greed and all our aversions. It is dangerous to take the risk of seeing these particles free themselves in violent spasms instead of in a regular series of adapted movements.

The above-mentioned disorders can have a domino effect on the organism, nervous system and endocrine system. One sign of this imbalance that is apparent in a considerable number of professional mediums is regular weight gain. Their bodies become flaccid and even obese. In fact they are constantly stressed. Over many years of research and inquiries of professional mediums, I found that at least 70% were diabetic!

Thyroid imbalance leads either to hyperthyroidism with disorders that can be as serious as anorexia in some cases, or hypothyroidism with considerable weight gain, slowed movement, chronic fatigue or even depression.

The adrenal glands secrete cortisol, adrenalin, and noradrenalin. These are hormones and neurotransmitters associated with the autonomous nervous system. Overproduction of cortisol increases the blood sugar level and the physiological reaction is an increase of insulin. Insulin facilitates cellular assimilation of sugar. To lower the blood sugar level, the insulin causes the sugar to migrate to the cells.

The saturation of the cells facilitates the production of fatty tissue and the person gains weight.

In the male reproductive system, sexual disorders may appear: premature ejaculation for some, erectile dysfunction for others. Given that the endocrine system works with the nervous system and that the sympathetic and parasympathetic systems are behind this process, if there is an imbalance, these disorders may occur.

In women, a lowered libido may be observed. In the female reproductive system, an imbalance at the level of the ovaries may lead not only to hormone secretion but also to infertility or the development of a favorable terrain for cysts. As there is a lack of energetic irrigation, the immune system is weakened and this opens the way for such conditions. Irregular menstrual cycles with possible endometriosis (lumps in the uterine mucosa that cause bleeding) that may appear on the ovaries or bladder.

Someone who works regularly with high energy frequencies and powerful energies such as those of spiritual healing and in particular trance healing must take special precautions to ensure proper hydration. This is much more critical than for a person who does not work in these types of frequencies. For good energy flow, it is essential that the body is well hydrated! According to Dr. Faridun Batmanghelidj (*Your Body's Many Cries for Water*), dehydration may lead to diabetes, headaches, migraines, back pain, high blood pressure, vascular dementia or even Alzheimer's disease.

An excess of cortisol in the body may lead to a state of permanent stress and this subject deserves special attention. The usual sources of stress that must be managed, such as stress caused by changes in your professional or personal life, illness-induced stress, or stress caused by the environment, family or phobia, are already present in sufficient numbers for everyone. It is a known fact that a sensitive person reacts much more intensely to these different factors. Indeed, activities involving the perception of subtle information expose a sensitive person more intensely to the various sources of stress. The "stress" factor, when associated with dehydration and the physical imbalances described above, is therefore dangerous. Stress leads to high cholesterol levels, digestive problems, an increase in stomach acidity, allergies, immune disorders, increased sugar production (for greater energy), and metabolic increase (thus faster heartbeat and breathing). Stress can cause local inflammation (redness, swelling, heat or pain) and faster blood coagulation, which means a higher risk of thrombosis. Any or all of these combined causes the sufferer to become "hypersensitive" and consequently more and more difficult to live with in the eyes of family and friends: he or she reacts too strongly to the least inconvenience and is more and more

"touchy". In short, he or she exhibits the perfect behavior that can lead to isolation...

When dealing with powerful and rapid energy during psychic readings or contact with the deceased, the medium feels a sort of vitalization, rush or shock. When the medium comes out of this frequency and sense of unity, a feeling of emptiness settles in alongside the exhaustion. This is often compensated by eating, which generally involves sugary snacks and not fruit and vegetables. Sugar is then assimilated to a reward and sweet snacks become "comfort food". The medium tries in this way to overcome a state that is mildly depressive or at least melancholic. Eating a lot of sugary foods obviously leads to weight gain in association with depression, its unwanted companion.

It is important that the medical and energetic side effects are known and discussed in the world of mediumship. Too few mediums talk about them. If the energy rules are respected, this sort of work has no physical side effects.

Please take this advice to heart: look after your body, because it is your vehicle. It takes you where you want to serve, where you will be an ambassador of the spiritual world, where you will bring solace to people in distress. If only for this reason, it is worth taking care of your health. As an added advantage, your loved ones will enjoy your healthy presence much longer!

Chapter 18

Hannes Jacob Syndrome – Sensitive disorder

Who am I?
What's happening to me?
I'm sure I am right
Why can't anyone see what I see?
Who am I?
What's happening to me?
Don't you hear anything, then?
I can't blame you
I've gone beyond my senses.
My eyes are all around my head
And other places too
Who am I?
What's happening to me?
I'm shivering at every breeze.
My body feels like Fiberglass
I'm invaded by my senses
All at the same time
My brain feels like pulp
Or is it yours?
Divine, where are you?
The mirage leads me astray
The city that I see
Isn't there at all
Although it's its reflection
It really exists
Healthy earth
I miss your roots
Welcome me
As ashes if it must be

For sensitives that I would qualify as disturbed, I have been able to observe a particular disorder. Based on these observations, I have written a paper entitled *Hannes Jacob Syndrome/Sensitive disorder*. Dr. Laura Martignon from the Max Planck Institute and the late Dr. Ulla Mitzdorfer, both professors at the University of Ludwigsburg, endorsed my work so that I could submit my paper under Open Access (scientific publications). Thus the community of interested doctors, professors, and scientists can not only access my original postulate, but also develop a procedure to validate my hypothesis.

A person who has gone for too long without grounding will suffer the medical and energetic side effects described in the previous chapter. Lack of grounding also causes psychotic episodes, or even chronic psychoses. It is not surprising that psychiatry classifies a person who sees things or hears voices as "schizophrenic". Yet, just because a patient hears things that make no sense, or which are not related to the present time or events, does not make them a schizophrenic. He or she may simply suffer from sensitive disorder! My experience with the spiritual world has confirmed many times that a so-called "schizophrenic" can in fact be a sensitive who lacks grounding and is in a permanent state of excessive air.

Long-term unchanneled sensitivity can lead to a psychotic state! The way we diagnose in this case must change, or at least be broader, in order to be able to distinguish between clinical schizophrenia and sensitive disorder! Without going into detail, here are some suggestions for reflection with respect to certain criteria that are used to diagnose schizophrenia. Those who are interested can consult the reference manual *DSM-5* (*Diagnostic and Statistical Manual of Mental Disorders*, American Psychiatric Association, 2013). It should be noted that the subtypes of schizophrenia no longer appear in the updated version of the *DSM-5*; however, for enhanced understanding they will be mentioned here.

Schizophrenia appears in various clinical charts, either with a predominance of so-called "negative" symptoms or that of so-called "positive" symptoms. These two categories of symptoms are also present in sensitive disorders. Indeed, mediumship uses rapid frequencies to establish and maintain contact with the deceased. Once the session is over, the medium may feel mentally and physically tired, as if he were drained of his energy. Regular practice of mediumship brings the medium great joy, excitement and enthusiasm. He or she takes pleasure in moving within these rapid frequencies and experiences a certain amount of euphoria. Coming out of this leads to a state that can be compared to depression. Thus, the medium that is unaware of this risk can start to become dependent and trigger a cycle that alternates between a state of euphoria and one of depression. I have already mentioned that sugary foods can become palliatives which give one the illusion of returning to a "high" energy level. Alcohol and cannabis are also used as substitutes. During the depressive phases, the medium may neglect themselves, their personal hygiene and their housekeeping. They suffer from generalized apathy and discouragement. Some hypersensitives then decide to cut themselves off completely from their surrounding environments, isolating themselves and carefully avoiding any interaction with others. Since an individual cannot retract his sensitive antennae, he constantly perceives the stimuli around him. This situation becomes unmanageable and he prefers to go into isolation. In extreme cases, this isolation becomes a way to function in society outside of his work as a medium. The person protects himself so completely that he loses all notion of the impact his words or behaviors have on other people. He no longer sees the consequences on those who associate with him. From the outside, the medium appears cold, emotionless, lacking in empathy, hard and even cruel. This toughness of character can obviously hurt those with whom he is in contact.

These negative symptoms have been described in the "simple" subtype of schizophrenia (active coldness, lack of interest, apathy, depression, chronic fatigue, etc.) and are relatively unknown to the general public. The following symptoms, called "positive", which are notably described in two types of schizophrenia, are found most frequently in sensitive disorder: hallucinations (auditory, visual, coenesthetic, etc.) and delirious ideas (persecution, paranoia, special mission, special rank, etc.) are characteristic of so-called "paranoid" schizophrenia, while drug abuse is frequent in schizophrenia of the "heboidophrenic" type and in the sensitive can be the result of an intense desire to know God or of some unidentified inner call that he cannot satisfy. Regarding hallucinations, one must also consider the complexity of the definition of the term. A person who only uses his five senses will consider anything he does not perceive through them to be a hallucination. Thus, for example, a mirage will be qualified as a hallucination even though it is simply the reflection of an existing object that our vision places in the wrong perspective: a faraway object will be seen as being closer due to an optical phenomenon of refraction of the light rays in the atmosphere. Must this be considered as a hallucination when we are actually talking about a visual distortion of reality? If I see a city in a mirage, I can briefly describe some of the elements, like contours, whether or not it has a tall tower, a wall, etc. If I see a deceased person wherein my frequency is not correctly established, I may describe a big nose or I may see a particular hairstyle for a short instant. There may be mistakes in the rest of the description, but that does not make it a hallucination. To describe the city properly, without the phenomenon of distortion, I have to be in front of it, close up. In a similar manner, to describe a deceased person and be sure I am not hallucinating, I have to establish the right frequency and maintain it. Let's suppose that my psychiatrist's late mother is present during our session. As long as my connection, my link to her has not been correctly established and my subjective vision does not allow me to provide a correct description, my psychiatrist will continue to accuse me of hallucinating. I will have trouble proving her presence to him. The energetic field of an individual with sensitive disorder is vast and scattered. It is therefore logical that his perception of spirits or any other wave that goes through him will have images and words that come to him as incoherent fragments. Any thought, sound or noise travels and can be picked up at random.

Below are a few hypotheses or ideas that can be used when evaluating or interviewing a person with symptoms of schizophrenia. They can be used to compare real schizophrenia with a sensitive disorder.

First, in sensitive disorder it is very rare that auditory hallucinations include commands, injunctions, or demands in a voice that is unfamiliar to the person. On the other hand, the sensitive will regularly receive bits of messages that are scattered and disorderly but inoffensive. Since he will not know where they are coming from, his family, and eventually he himself, will believe he has gone insane. In a limited number of cases, someone who is familiar with the afterworld can believe that these messages are sent by a guide or a deceased person. In schizophrenia, the voice or voices heard often order the person to accomplish something. They command him to do things, to act in a certain way. The time element comes into play; in the sensitive the phenomena are constant and regularly occur, while in schizophrenia the episodes are characterized more as intermittent phases. Regarding visual phenomena, it is difficult to differentiate a person afflicted with sensitive disorder from a schizophrenic as both can sometimes be capable of objective vision.

Secondly, a person with sensitive disorder can recall, and literally relive, scenes from past lives since the information on each abhorrent or greedy thought is stored in our system.

These scenes come back to the surface in a repeated and incoherent way. If the life in question is linked to a trauma, the memory of these images may become obsessive and repeated.

Thirdly, in cases of sensitive disorder there can be a dialogue about the phenomena that were experienced. Often at the outset the person is not aware that what is happening to him cannot be objectively understood by the people around him. But from the moment a tolerant and open discussion is undertaken, there can be an exchange. In this way the individual in question can better understand the situation. In schizophrenia, it is more difficult, even impossible, to have such a discussion, especially during an acute decompensation phase.

After diagnosis, treatment with drugs is usually implemented targeting the receptors to the dopamine neurotransmitter. Induced sedation is carried out on both the schizophrenic and the person with sensitive disorder. As a result the symptoms cease, particularly the so-called "positive" ones.

An ESP is measured in the brain as described and evidenced by the NIRS, especially in the right temporal lobe, with the same observations each time! In the future, psychiatry will have to compare the irrigated cerebral areas, or cerebral paths, in patients declared as schizophrenic with those of a sensitive! In this way thousands of people would be freed of a damning and erroneous diagnosis. They can simply be treated through grounding and channeling their energy. This allows some people to reduce their intake of prescribed medications and, finally, to stop taking them completely. If you have psychiatrist friends, be brave enough to talk to them about this!

If your doctor has diagnosed you as schizophrenic and you have doubts about this diagnosis, we ask you to contact us and register for a pilot project that is currently being prepared and which should, we hope, clarify your condition and your symptoms. A few psychiatrists send patients to my clinic so that I can assess whether they are detecting actual phenomena or suffering from psychosis. Thought, or any sort of information, travels in the form of a particle or energetic field that I can often read. Either the energy particle emanates from the client's mind or it is brought to him and enters into his field. It is therefore possible to determine whether the person is having real perceptions (information entering his field) or if they are producing them (information exiting their field to the outside). Similarly, any contact with a deceased person can be seen by a clairvoyant, who will confirm or negate it.

To summarize: sensitivity can be seriously harmful to your health! If your energies are unbalanced, your endocrine and autonomous nervous systems will no longer work in harmony. The most severe consequence of this imbalance is the onset of psychotic disorders similar to schizophrenia! Esotericism is a good thing – as long as you follow its rules.

Chapter 19

Adequate meditation

**There is no road to there
Because it's not a place
Heaven
Is inside you
And that is why
It is so far away**

Each type of meditation has its own access and usefulness. I distinguish between the techniques that support our physical and psychic health, those that train our various sensitive practices, and lastly, those that assist us in our spiritual development. Of course, some meditation techniques allow us to do more than one at the same time.

All of the forms of meditation presented below will be described in greater detail in the last chapter. You can read them aloud and record them for later practice.

After you have understood the various aspects of the different types of sensitivity, it is time to approach them in an adequate manner and learn to live in harmony with them. The stakes are far too important. Considering what has been said previously, it is quite clear that mental mediumship, spiritual healing, trance and trance healing should not be avoided but must be carried out conscientiously and with confidence.

Meditation allows us to live in accordance with our sensitive abilities. It is the best tool for maintaining physical and psychic health. For those who are interested, meditation can even lead to enlightenment!

The most frequent excuse for not meditating, but also the one that is the easiest on the ego, is: "I can't meditate because I can't concentrate." Everyone has difficulties concentrating, except monks or hermits... and even then! The mind will wander here and there. Distraction, fatigue and doubt are the ego's most powerful weapons. No one can stay focused all the time. The longer the meditation retreat, the more the ego defends itself so as not to disappear. The calmer the surroundings, the greater the interior noise. In a way, we are all waste bins for all kinds of inscriptions. It is essential to empty them from time to time! I myself have experienced great struggles during my meditation retreats, even to thoughts of suicide. And yet I have been to some 40 retreats! Despite all of these stays, which lasted between seven and 32 days, in an isolated cell and in silence, I still have a plethora of shortcomings, though much fewer than before. In the end, that's the only thing that counts, the only reasonable comparative reference is my own evolution...

The more the dense particles dissolve, the stronger the emotions and pain that rise to the surface. Obviously! So what can be done? Trivialize them! Observe your depression, your anger, your hunger or your lust – whatever appears. Observe, but don't react! This is just your past that is coming to the surface. It's only your ego trying to distract you. Don't react; it won't last! Everything is ephemeral except for your essence. Don't let yourself be fooled by this small and ignorant part of your being. We are all made of shadow and light; this is the light that is overcoming – that's a promise. You will be different; you will be more at peace, less anxious and easier for your loved ones to live with, and they will thus also benefit from the results of your meditation. You will be able to focus better, serve better and live better. You will dissolve those dense particles. You will break the resonance with the unpleasant aspects. You will be able to resonate with peace, joy and love. Because, behind the veil, this is what we all are!

Grounding

With the exception of the pranayamas (spinal respirations) described below, grounding is the most important of all the exercises for a sensitive person! Grounding increases the presence of the earth element and helps us to live in the present moment. People who are going through emotional phases or mental overload should begin their day by grounding for about five minutes. Then, during the day, they can repeat the breathing exercises intended for grounding two or three times per hour for one or two breathing cycles depending on their mental or emotional state. Grounding can be done seated, standing or lying down.

To practice grounding, imagine you have roots under the soles of your feet. As soon as you see yourself anchored, visualize how you pull in the earth's energy through your roots each time you breathe in. Pull this energy into your center of energy, which is located, depending on your feelings, in the solar plexus or in the heart chakra. Each time you breathe in, visualize how your center lights up and spreads throughout your chest and then your whole body. Don't release this energy through the fontanel, at the top of your head, as this would reinforce the "air" element. Breathe in as far as your center while thinking, "I am grounding, I am in the present." When you breathe out, just relax. This is not only recommended for sensitives; it significantly calms depression, fights insomnia, and physically revitalizes your body.

I would like to urge my readers and students to take the following testimonial to heart, as its message does confirm my observations, is of great importance to and should be taken seriously by all sensitive people. It goes without saying that the risk of uncontrolled "outbreaks" of the so-called Kundalini energy is much higher for sensitives than it is for "normal" people, since in the former, the energetic movements within the spinal column are already naturally in movement and may thus lead more easily to an explosive rise of this energy.

U. from T., one of my patients, relays her own experience which still brings up strong emotions whenever she speaks about it:

"It happened during an energetic massage treatment – my Kundalini energy got activated so much that it shot upwards straight into my head, much like a volcano erupting, and left me in a state of great shock. This force caused an extremely strong heat wave to shoot through my body, which made me lose my mind. It lasted several days! I could neither eat nor sleep. I lost weight massively. I had very strong visions and suffered horrible pain that felt like burns, all over the body. I also felt as if I constantly floated one meter above the ground – this alone lasted for a good week. Physically, I became progressively weaker and mentally, I felt delusional (I want to note that I had never had any kind of psychological problem throughout my entire life). I then attempted to cool down by taking ice-cold baths, doing gardening work and grounding exercises. But my success remained only limited. Ultimately, a medical doctor who was familiar with this subject advised me to take Valium which she wrote me a prescription for. Within a few days and by keeping up the regular grounding exercises I was able to eat, sleep and to take up my various activities again. This entire experience ended up lasting almost a month, which – given such conditions – feels like eternity.

The obvious take-away from this experience is the following (and I can say this also because I know three other people who had this experience happen to them in a very similar manner): Be cautious with energetic techniques – consult only well-trained therapists. I believe I could have avoided this horrible experience had I started regularly practicing the grounding exercises from the very beginning."

Pranayamas

Concentrating on breathing and balancing the energies is a "must" for any medium. This meditation guarantees that the endocrine system will not be disturbed by the high energies and that the autonomous nervous system will be balanced. Pranayamas are the most efficient way to ensure balanced energetic density as well as a harmonious increase of your vibrational frequency.

Alternative breathing through the nostrils
(Nadi Shodana)

This breathing technique is used to balance the cerebral hemispheres and the autonomous nervous system. It helps to focus and concentrate. For mediums, it is very useful for increasing the abilities of the third eye, thus improving clairvoyance.

To do alternative breathing through the nostrils, sit down comfortably on a chair or in the lotus position. First focus on the area from above your upper lips to the opening of your nostrils (this Buddhist meditation technique is called "Anapana"). Maintain this focus for a few minutes in order to calm the mind. Then change to "Nadi Shodana" either by simple willpower and intent or by pressing one finger against the inactive nostril to close it. Breathe in and out through the left nostril only, then switch and breathe only through the right nostril. In the same firm and determined manner, move to the next phase: breathe in through the left nostril and out through the right, then breathe in through the right nostril and out through the left, and so on. The full exercise can last between five and ten minutes, depending on the amount of time you have and what your needs are. Aside from grounding, I don't know of any other exercise that is so beneficial in such a short time. It is an excellent exercise to do before meditating, whatever the form you practice.

Always begin and end with the left nostril because the left side is associated with Ida, one of the two serpents in Sushumna. Ida represents freshness.

Vipassana

Vipassana is the meditation technique by which the Buddha Siddhartha Gautama was enlightened (though I did not see it). Today, this technique is taught in universities under the name *"Mindfulness meditation"*. Its aim is to reduce stress and increase general well-being. This is a Buddhist technique for freeing ourselves from that which binds us. It brings real inner peace.

I really want to share what I received during a discussion with Jonathan on this topic:

You are birds in your cages! When you open your magnificent wings wide, you hit them on every bar, battering yourselves against them and hurting yourself. Under one wing, the word "desire" is written, under the other, "refusal"… You keep beating yourselves on the bars… until the day you are so exhausted that you can't even move a feather anymore. You sit, motionless. It will be in this calm moment with neither aversion nor greed that you will see that the bars are wide enough to let you get out of the cage just by slipping between them… Fold your wings; leave calmly, fully aware. You will fly free, with the wings of Anapana and Vipassana… Higher than ever.

Dr. Britta Hölzel of the University of Massachusetts has published some very interesting research on the benefits of the *"Mindfulness"* technique, i.e. Vipassana. This woman of German descent has not only managed to prove that stress-generated secretions are greatly reduced through this meditation, but has also shown that the brain is capable of reproducing cells and recovering its "health".

Matthieu Ricard, doctor of cellular genetics and Buddhist monk, interpreter to the Dalai Lama, is the author of a number of books on the positive effects of Vipassana, or "mindfulness". His monastic experience and the research he has carried out on other *bonzes* (Buddhist monks) has brought to light that their meditation techniques generate passive cerebral frequencies – i.e. delta waves – just like the healer who is able to detach from his mind during spiritual healing.

There are many monasteries and monastic centers offering guidance in Vipassana.

A selection for Thailand:

- "Dhipabhavan" in Koh Samui is highly recommended for beginners. The rhythm is not too strenuous for novices, who can register for seminaries of just seven days. Sleeping arrangements include a wooden plank and a wooden headrest. Even though the center is only 30 minutes from town, it is deep in the jungle and the area is stunningly beautiful. Payment is made in the form of a donation. [Information is available at www.dipabhavan.weebly. com.]
- The Suan Mokkh monastery in Chaiya/Surat Tani, under the guidance of the venerable Ajaan Po, is suitable for those who have more experience in meditation. Retreats are ten days long and are held once a month. Participants sleep on the floor with a wooden headrest. Payment is made in the form of a donation. Hot springs bubble up to form small magical ponds. [Information is available at www.suanmokkh-idh.org.]
- The Doi Suthep monastery is absolutely marvelous! Seminaries can be from four to 21 days long. This retreat is recommended mainly for those with advanced practice as there is very little guidance for beginners. The monks'

English is extremely limited and communication is very difficult. The structure is quite luxurious for a Thai monastery and participants sleep in individual cells on real beds. Payment is made in the form of a donation. [Information is available at www.fivethousandyears.org.]

A selection for Switzerland:

- Beatenberg Meditation Center: Seminars are from three to 20 days. Classical Vipassana is taught by Western instructors. The center is highly reputed for its professionalism and is nonsectarian. The rates are reasonable. [Information is available at www.karuna.ch.]

- In Kandersteg, the various seminaries are given by monks from several monasteries all over the world who work in rotation. Retreats are from three to five days long. Payment is made in the form of a donation. [Information is available at www.dhammapala.ch.]

- Vipassana Goenka, on Mont Soleil in the Jura. This center unfortunately promotes an obtuse and dogmatic viewpoint. True Buddhist monks have said they were very disappointed with this deformation. In fact, this establishment tolerates no meditation technique other than the one that it teaches. Healing practices or energy therapies are forbidden. I am mentioning this establishment because it operates not only in French-speaking Switzerland but also in France at the Dhamma Mahi center and elsewhere in the world. Instructors such as Philippe Fromont teach in various Goenka centers, and therefore one may come across the same dogmatic discrimination. The establishment itself is magnificent, well organized and very clean. This is why it is nevertheless an ideal place to focus on meditation: all the material aspects such as meals, housekeeping, and class hours are rigorously organized. All you need to do is to refrain from mentioning anything about your life or your private and professional activities and simply go to meditate. In this way the ten days of silence will go by very nicely and will be highly beneficial. Payment is made in the form of a donation. [Information is available at www.sumeru.dhamma.org.]

The meditation techniques presented herein are presented in greater detail at the end of the chapter on exercises. After each one, please ground yourself even if this is not expressly indicated. Grounding should be done as a matter of course. All the techniques mentioned below will open and expand the antennae of your perceptions. It is therefore essential that they be drawn back in once you have finished meditating.

Sitting in the power

Training the clear-senses is the beginning of all mediumship.

This meditation, which is to be followed by grounding, is for extending the psychic abilities – the different clear-senses. It is the most complete method for combined training of the clear-senses. The key to receiving all of the possible benefits of this meditation is not to imagine or project the various levels and layers but to simply have the intention to reach them.

"Sitting in the Power" is a form of meditation that was given in the 1990s by a well-known guide called "James". His medium was Mark Webb (UK).

The Great Spirit's Gardens

This meditation works first of all with the vitalizing and harmonizing colors. It allows us to increase the abilities of the principal layers of our aura. Finally, it provides the greatest possibility of giving way to the energy of the Great Spirit, in the image of the sponge in the ocean and the ocean in the sponge, which is a very efficient way of letting go.

Meditating with the Guides

This form of meditation leads to that magnificent meeting with the luminous beings that surround us and who work with us from the invisible world.

This meditation brings clarity with regard to distinguishing whether we are evolving in projections or even fantasies, or if our perceptions are actually real. It is therefore an essential one for all mediums.

Like the Great Spirit's Gardens and Sitting in the Power, this meditation can start with pranayamas.

Trance

This type of meditation guides us through the passive frequencies in which no interaction with the mind is desired. Without having learnt to let go, it is impossible to become a pure channel, either for speech or for healing! This technique is the opposite of working with the guides, which is an interactive method.

Chapter 20

Religions, dogmas and fears

When I get to the afterlife
I smoke shisha with Allah
Next to Buddha, leaning on his cushion
The Pope plays the harp; Jesus cleans fish
The Dalai Lama makes tea
We look down at Men
And how they behave
We're a little sad
But well
We know
How much these cultures
Are ephemeral, after all

I would so love it if the religions could establish a dialogue, so that men could become closer rather than fight. These combats and wars are so violently opposed to what is taught in the holy books.

Since I have been able to meet saints from various religions, who all touched me on the same level, I find it simply impossible to adhere to one religion in particular. Thus I am incapable of saying, "I am a Christian because I was brought up that way and I have met Jesus," or "I am Hindu because I have met Sri Yukteswar, the master of Paramahansa Yogananda." With respect to the practices that are intended to lead to spiritual elevation, I believe more in Theravada Buddhism in association with the pranayamas taught in the Kriya Yoga. In this approach, there is no veneration. The only thing that is important is to show respect for the monk who is teaching it, because he represents the Buddha who has gone beyond suffering. There is no veneration, because these monks do not believe that the Good Lord will be kinder to he who prays than to he who does not. It could be that someone does not pray because in his culture or in the education he has received, prayer is not done. Whatever the case, above all, the Buddhists believe in karma – i.e. in the inscription of our particles – and in the resonances they can have with the events that attract them. Absurd Catholic ideas such as "a child which has not been baptized will end up in limbo" are absolutely appalling. With all due respect to everyone, first of all, half of the planet has not been baptized, and secondly, limbo was closed on 20 April 2007 by the owner. I have no idea where those souls went to but there is probably quite a crowd.

In Vipassana, the only thing that counts is work on the self, and I know that this procedure is efficient. In fact, for me, it is very efficient. Working on oneself does not mean you cannot work in collaboration with the Saints or the Ascended Masters. It is necessary to invoke or pray to the Saints if we want them to collaborate with us. It is utopian to think that placing one's destiny in the hands of a Saint takes care of everything. Prayer is often a "hypocritical" thing as people make many requests for themselves. Very few among them pray for another person, or simply to give thanks for all the good they have received. He who prays only when he needs something... may well get it... But who knows if it will be good for him!? We pray according to our desire and not our wisdom!

My guides have clearly told me that they do not act upon the outcome of our lives unless they are invited to do so. This would be an intrusion on our free will and against celestial laws. The will of a living person to work with the Saints is a sign of faith, just like believing in God or in the Light.

The benefits of prayer on the sick have been shown. However, this is another approach, because we are not praying for a personal need, but for someone else's welfare, often a stranger's. Aside from the help which is asked of the Saint, prayer has a positive effect through the principle of positive thinking, as described in the book *The Secret*, by Rhonda Byrne, or in the NLP (neurolinguistic programming) techniques and in hypnosis.

The risk or the danger with NLP or other tools for positive thinking lies in replacing an aversion with a desire, or one desire with another one, or wishing for something that is not necessarily in our best interests. With this type of replacement nothing is resolved, and nothing is healed.

It is easy to see, and we know it through psychic readings, that any thought is registered and that we are a repository, sometimes even a real trash bin, for all the thoughts emitted. Our vibration reflects the average of all our thoughts. Since we are this average of our thoughts, we might as well make them positive ones through prayer, in particular for someone else or to give thanks for the beauty in our lives. The best tool that I can recommend to empty our trash bin and dissolve our negative thoughts that are linked to greed or aversion – is meditation. Vipassana or pranayamas, among others, dissolve the dense inscriptions. I encourage you to practice the Kriya Yoga breathing techniques and Zazen in order to have less resonance with dangerous events. By doing these meditations and practicing these techniques, there will be less and less reason to pray for yourself and life will get better and better...

Some aspects of positive thinking make me smile. Indeed, I hear a lot of people who reserve their parking place with no problem; they are all proud and happy because it works and they get their parking place in this way. Yes, of course. But when it's a matter of finding a new apartment, a new job, a new partner or a new way of life, these people are not as perseverant about it. The reason is very simple: their minds do not include this kind of perspective for these areas, and they are lacking in the basic understanding of the procedure... The key is letting go, letting it happen, while knowing that what is desired, is achieved!

Religion is nevertheless a dogma established by humans. Or in other words, as Dan Brown writes in his book *Angels and Demons*, "Religion is imperfect because man is imperfect." This dogma is used to control the people and make the clergy rich. This is one of the reasons why Martin Luther was excommunicated. In fact, not the entirety of the Catholic hierarchy was represented in the Bible and a part of it rebelled against the Vatican, accusing the institution of fraud because of the payments it asked the people to make in exchange for the indulgences which promised to open the gates of Heaven for them. Faced with these facts, among others, Luther founded Protestantism. In India, there is a form of indulgences that is practiced even today. In the house in which Krishna was born, between Delhi and Agra, where the Taj Mahal was built, I was shown a list of wishes that could be granted if I paid for them. For a certain amount in rupees – though Krishna prefers dollars – I can, for example, go to Heaven; my dead parents can find peace in Heaven; my children will be successful at school or lead happy lives, etc. In the same way, with the Buddhists the bigger the temple offering, the better for my karma. This greatly impacts the population, half of whom are already so very poor. These people feed the monks as soon as they appear in front of the house, even if the family has almost nothing for themselves. Moreover, the higher the rank of the monk in question, the better that is for the donor's karma.

All religions are dogmatic and political, due to internal power struggles. To illustrate this, I would like you to name a religion that has or has had a woman as its leader. Are there any women who hold important positions in any religion? I haven't found any among the Buddhists. In India there are only private sects like Amma's. There is no trace of women leaders in Catholicism, except to do the housework; with the Orthodox, none; and none with the Jewish, either. In the end, it is among the Protestants and English spiritualists – thank God – that we find women pastors or ministers. What a joy! Is God perhaps a Protestant spiritualist?

The attacks which have targeted my school or me personally are always made by sects who are often Christian, such as the Jehovah's Witnesses, for example. I would just like to add here that it is senseless to try to quote the Bible word for word. There are thousands of different versions that have been rewritten several times over the millennia, and different sects and religions… However, it is interesting to note that despite the revisions, many parts remain similar or have been included as they were. The first criticism that is often addressed to me is that "it is written that you must not speak to the dead!"

In the Bible, THE dead is certainly he who has no faith in God, who does not believe in Jesus, representative of God on Earth! THE dead is thus a person who has no faith, which has nothing to do with Death in its physical form.

To illustrate the difference between the two, there are more than 40 passages on the subject in the Bible, from the Old Testament to the New (from Daniel 11:22 to the Book of John). John 3:16 explains the difference between a person who has no faith and physical death: "For God so loved the world that He gave His only begotten son, that he who believeth in Him shall not perish, but have eternal life." Or yet again, John 11:26: "He who believeth in me shall never die."

In all these passages, the term "the dead", i.e. the deceased, has nothing to do with physical death! We are alive, here and now, in this life and also after our physical death, provided we have faith. If, in this life, we are fit and healthy, but atheist, in the Biblical sense we will be considered as dead. It is all a question of attitude, belief in God, faith, and nothing else…

One of the Fathers of the Church and the wisest man of the era that dates back to about 180 CE was Origen of Alexandria

(185-254). His main work was *De Principiis*. He was a fervent activist and he believed in reincarnation. Head of the highly renowned School of Catechism in Alexandria, he knew all of the original Christian documents such as the Gospels and the letters of the Apostles, due to his privileged access to the Alexandria Library (which, it is said, was burned by a Christian fanatic, the patriarch Theophilus). There are many parallels between the works of Origen of Alexandria and the Hindu spiritual teaching "Bhagavad-Gîtâ". The latter describes the soul's path, from illusion and evil to the return to God, which takes place over several lifetimes.

During the various Catholic councils held between 381 and 553, what had been written and said about reincarnation was subsequently stricken from the Bible. Origen's teachings were definitively banned at the Constantinople Synod in 543, under Caesar Justinian and Pope Vigilius.

Fortunately, a few important passages referring to reincarnation were forgotten, such as the one describing the reincarnation of the prophet Elijah 900 years later as John the Baptist, for example. At the end of the Old Testament, Malachi says: "Look, I will send you the prophet Elijah," or again, when Jesus says, in the Book of Matthew, "for he who will accept him, it is Elijah who will come as John; let him who has ears listen."

I am not only mentioning these passages to add to the debate on reincarnation itself, but also to highlight the importance of accepting the reality of the spirit which travels and which may appear and converse after having left its charnel home, whether the spirit reincarnates or not.

Catholics, Orthodox or Protestants who know the Bible well and who have studied it closely tend to be much more accepting of mediumship. This acceptance or understanding is found in 1st Corinthians, chapter 12, verse 5 and seq.:

Now to each one the manifestation of the Spirit is given for the common good. To one there is given through the Spirit a message of wisdom, to another a message of knowledge by means of the same Spirit, to another faith by the same Spirit, to another gifts of healing by that one Spirit, to another miraculous powers, to another prophecy, to another distinguishing between spirits, to another speaking in different kinds of tongues...

In this single paragraph, we have absolutely everything that is done in mediumship: from healing to the different ways of contacting the spirits, as well as trance. Thank you, Jesus, and thank you, Paul, for having noted this, and thank you to all those who know how to read and accept their teachings!

Why don't we take these countless and magnificent metaphors that we find in the religious books as examples and encouragement to live a healthy life, full of love? Beyond dogma, the religions open the way to a truly spiritual life and can guide us to a constant interior peace. They preach love. Let's make it worth living. If we have the courage to follow a path such as this, the events and the evidence of the reality of the natural phenomenon will come to us. Be it the God of Jesus, Abraham, or Shiva in India, it does not matter. He loves all nature. We can find faults everywhere, but why concentrate on them rather than looking for the common points and developing them? We would all be so happy and complete if we reached out to each other!

Wandering spirits

Many people say they are afraid of spirits, trance or simply of the spiritual world. I myself have no reason to fear the afterlife. In my career, I have never been afraid.

Why should I be afraid of a deceased parent if they were dear to me in their lifetime? Why should any deceased person frighten me if I am not afraid of anyone I meet in town?

The natural phenomenon of survival after death is very clear, powerful and proven! When the physical body dies the soul leaves its envelope. This is a fact and has nothing to do with a religion or belief; it is our nature. I have seen the spirits of people who had died only a few days or even a few hours earlier and who were already beside me or in my clinic, concretely, with proof such as the description of the clothing the person was wearing when they died. At the time of death, the spirit reproduces an exact copy of the physical body, including its clothing. I have been able to describe the nightgown worn by a woman who had entered my clinic well before her daughter, my client, walked through the door. The elder woman had died two days before. When the physical body dies, the spirit leaves its charnel vehicle; this is a fact.

The only factor that may vary is the time a deceased person takes to transition to the light.

It is obvious that almost all the people who die will immediately transition into that light. When this is not the case, some spirits are as if they are "stuck". They are what are called wandering spirits. These wandering spirits only represent a fraction of all the deceased. It could be that after a sudden, violent and unexpected death, or after a suicide, a spirit remains "stuck" on our material plane for a while. Nevertheless, it is not a fatality.

The best proof that I have to illustrate this is the tragic story of Georges.

Georges, my symbolic blood brother, with whom I had mixed my blood as a child in a fraternal pact, committed suicide at the end of his teenage years, to the great astonishment of his family and friends. This boy has already come back several times to visit me from the afterlife, surrounded by a light that touched me deeply. These meetings are amazing every time! With his light, this boy could be a guide, he shines so brightly! He was also just as luminous in life. Georges was a pacifist, a good musician, very gentle, very refined and he therefore disagreed with the military service he was supposed to do. So he decided to kill himself. Yet, when he came to see me, he was in the light. For me, it is thus evident that he has not been "punished" for his act, as some religions or beliefs claim. Georges shone in his life and therefore he will reincarnate in that same light and not in the internal confusion in which he removed himself from it.

I think that as soon as we transition into the afterlife, we move into the light. It is rare for a soul to remain stuck here. The few souls that I have seen who stayed were beings that were extremely dense, either due to an extreme attachment or a very strong aversion. For these souls, the attachment or the aversion is so strong that they cannot perceive the beings in the brilliant afterlife. The attachment is so strong that only the perception of matter remains and that of what is subtle is lacking. These souls are unable to perceive the love and the light, which is why they remain stuck here in the earthly plane. This is in fact one of the rare points that I like in the film *The Sixth Sense* with Bruce Willis: the latter does not realize he is dead. I can accept that part of the film, because I have experienced it, or rather seen it in my practice.

In all so-called "haunted" houses that I have visited to clear them of wandering spirits, I can count on one hand those in which there really was a "stuck" spirit. In all the other houses there was no wandering spirit. Before going to cleanse a house that is supposedly haunted or to claim your house is haunted, I recommend that you consult the check-list for this type of case.

When children or teenagers live in a "haunted" house, there can be hyperactivity, anger, stress, etc. which releases kinetic energy (electromagnetic energy produced by the physical body). This energy can cause objects to move or burn out light bulbs and computers. People who are not very grounded are the first to cause computers to freeze up or explode and watches or household equipment to stop running. Once again, I would say that in the majority of cases it is the energy from the living that causes these phenomena which are usually blamed on poltergeists.

Cleansing and blessing a room or place

As a shaman uses white sage to cleanse a place, when I bless a room – before clearing out the old energies – I make the sign of the cross. The symbol of the cross is not just for Catholics. Personally, I believe in a Great Spirit and am convinced of the presence of the light in men, just as it was in Jesus, Krishna, and Buddha. Where angels and guides are concerned, the evidence is the same. All these shining beings that I have seen have convinced me that the sign of the cross covers all.

Cleansing is done in several ways. The first thought is to remember that light chases shadows away. Then, by moving from one room to another, you can smudge them with sage or burn incense and make signs such as the cross. The most important thing is your conviction in doing so. If you find a wandering spirit which has remained on the earthly plane, you have to initiate the dialogue and invite it to go to its loved ones in the light.

Check-list of questions to ask before going to cleanse a house (established by healing facilitator Margaret De-Petro, www.margaretdepetro.com).

- Call the person, but make sure your phone number does not appear. Do not give any personal information.
- Ask a series of questions:
  ○ Name and address
  ○ Does this person participate in any spiritual activities in a mediumship group? If yes, in what way?
- Have they seen anything on TV about the subject (spirits, haunted houses, or more generally about paranormal

activities)?

- Details about how the spirits make their presence known:
  - When did the "strange" phenomena take place for the first time?
  - How often do the phenomena occur?
  - What happens? What do you see? What do you feel? Do things move?
  - How many people have seen these phenomena, and who are they?
  - How long has the client lived in the house?
  - How many people live in the house?
  - How many young people live in the house or visit it regularly?

The two latter questions are particularly important because pre-teens and teenagers (between 13 and 19 years of age) can create thought forms, "poltergeists" that are generated by hormonal changes. Hyperactive children can also generate these phenomena.

  - Do any animals live in the house? If yes, how do they react to these manifestations?
- Could there be any problems with the:
  - Plumbing
  - Electrical installations
- Have the plumbing and/or electrical installations been inspected recently? Could there be a spring under the house?
- Have there been any seismic problems such as cracks?
- Does the client or someone else in the house have health issues?
  - If there are mental health issues: does the client need treatment from a specialist? Otherwise the practitioner may be getting into something that is over his head.
  - Is the client taking medicines that may cause side effects such as hallucinations, sight disorders, nightmares,

dizziness, confusion, depression, anxiety, etc., as might be the case in treatments using beta blockers, benzodiazepines, antihistamines, antidepressants, or in treatments for schizophrenia?

- Does the client smoke marijuana? If so, he might be paranoid. Marijuana can cause this side effect.
- Is there a suspicion of alcoholism? How much does the client drink?
- Has the client been using a Ouija board?
- Are there any sources of stress: exams, separation, divorce, or mourning?
  - Personal questions such as significant changes in work, finances, personal/family life.

These questions are used to *evaluate* the client's apartment or house. In this way, the medium knows what to expect if he decides to go cleanse this house or apartment.

Outside of the rare case of a wandering spirit, a house can hold a memory, which is quite different. In terms of vocabulary, there is a difference between a ghost, i.e. a memory, and a wandering spirit which is a soul that has not yet transitioned to the light. With a ghost, there is no possible interaction or dialogue; it is an empty cell. With a spirit we can have contact, as we already know.

We might find a ghost – in other words, an empty cell that is active and continues to move – where there has been repetitive movement. This is a place memory. When there is a ghost, something might have happened that was very powerful and intense. There can be ghosts in a prison cell, for example, in which the prisoner paced the floor. There can be memories in a house in which the inhabitant was often present and in which he took the same steps over a long period or was always seated in the same armchair. These events can be perceived by someone who is sensitive. There are many more place memories than actual spirits. I have seen this in my experience. Having said this, I am always surprised to note that throughout my career I have met so few wandering spirits. Yet I have visited a great many places and held many old objects in my hands. For the so-called wandering spirits – who are few and far between – that have not made their transition to the light, there is a technique that helps them move on: the "rescue circle", as it is "officially" called. This is generally done by a group of mediums who come together to produce a great amount of energy. The group thus helps the wandering spirit to move into the beam of light that frees it of its density and carries it to the right place, into the light with its loved ones and guides. The popular press makes much of "haunted" houses, as does folklore. With what I know and have been able to observe, this is easily explained: the living can cause phenomena that are erroneously blamed on the deceased and on the ghosts – the memories – that may impregnate the place.

There are indeed beneficial memories, places with a strong telluric influence and to which we can go to resource ourselves. Many churches, temples, and also places of meditation or private clinics are positively charged. "The Peace Stone", located 100 meters outside the Hôtel du Chasseron below Les Rasses in Sainte-Croix in French-speaking Switzerland, is a good example. Regularly, 32,000 to 36,000 Bovis units (unit of measurement of the vibration rate for a body, place or object) are measured here, which is very high. Ten to 15 minutes of concentration are enough to recharge your energies in this place. To resource oneself when fully aware in these charged places, all that is needed is to breathe in the energy through your feet for grounding, or through the fontanel to strengthen and develop the energy centers in the upper body. It is not recommended to do this for too long as it may cause dizziness or other disorders of the nervous system! To my knowledge, there is no risk for people who visit these sites just to picnic, without being aware and without linking to the energy. The Chasseron was discovered to be an energetic place only in the 1990s. It was thus not mentioned in the book *Hauts-lieux Cosmo-telluriques* by Blanche Merz. I nevertheless wish to recommend this work for its description of these numerous places and churches. I recently went there with a friend and her dog who was suffering from very painful dysplasia. The very same evening, this Bernese Mountain dog showed no signs of pain and was able to jump into the back of the car like a young puppy.

The evil eye

The further south you go on the planet, the more you see beliefs related to the evil eye. If, in Africa, a person says to another, "I'm going voodoo you," the latter will become very agitated. If you say the same thing to a Swiss-German accountant it will just make him smile with no further reaction. In fact, the mechanism of psychic attack depends on two triggers: belief and auto-suggestion. The person who believes a psychic attack can harm them will indeed start having symptoms. This type of auto-suggestive function is not only valid for psychic attacks, or negative thoughts, but also operates in the presence of prayer, i.e. positive thoughts. Repeating "I am in good health" to yourself will set off triggers at the physical level that will strengthen the immune system.

Imagine that a person takes a piece of paper and writes, "I am going to make so-and-so break his big toe," and sets a time frame in which this will happen. They must then seal the paper. After that period of time, if the person concerned really has broken his big toe, we can probably deduce that the thought had really traveled and that it was able to influence the victim's spirit. Even in such a situation, the voodoo is not entirely proven because the witch doctor may have had access to the future and was able to see that the person would break his toe anyway. He would then have simply used this information to make himself look important and get people to believe he had "supernatural powers".

Whenever there is a world championship football tournament, the African marabous and witch doctors perform voodoo on the opposing teams and cast spells on the game so their own teams will win. No African team has ever got farther than the quarter finals. The only time this ever happened was due to the genius of Cameroon's Roger Milla.

Above all, we need to understand what resonance is: nothing can happen to us unless there is a response to it within us. It's like a magnet: it's impossible to connect two magnets by the pole which causes them to repel each other. I really believe that we are made that way. Karma is organized in a similar way; how else could it be? It's about information and information has resonance and magnetism. If it isn't a person's karma to be assaulted, then they will never find themselves on the same side of the street with an individual who could assault them; there is no mutually attractive information. Karma happens because there is information and it has a response, a resonance. This is why voodoo only works through auto-suggestion. An event takes place only if there is information to call it. At the same time, all the information inscribed in a person exists to take them further in their development. In the end, nothing is negative, even if it is unpleasant.

Every time I go into my clinic and get ready for a healing or a mediumship session, I say a personal prayer. Then, before each patient arrives, I also say a silent prayer so that everything will go as well as possible for the person.

I am not affected by my patients' stories or by dense spirits, because shadow does not come into the light. This is a universal law. I think there is a universal physical law and a universal metaphysical law, otherwise everything on this planet would crumble and nothing would hold up. If the intention to work with the light is a sincere one, there can be no malevolence.

This is also true for someone who cannot control his or her thoughts and who lives in fear of a dark and evil afterlife. Take two connecting rooms, one lighted and the other dark. If you open the door, the dark room is illuminated, and not the other way around.

Dense spirits do exist. I have already seen some. Once when visiting an acquaintance, I was sitting at a table in a small kitchen and watching the door at the end of the room because I could see spirits that were clearly dense, like black smoke coming through the door. I asked my host what was behind it. He said it was the studio of his son who carried out satanic rituals. The next day, we went into this basement room as his son had gone to work. All the "satanic" symbols were there, the ones that frighten people. As I have never participated in satanic rituals and am not at all interested in this type of practice, I cannot really describe what happens in such moments. However, we are spirit and because of this we can speak to a spirit. I am convinced that someone who is interested in satanic rituals can converse with a little-developed spirit. The latter can, for example, incite the person to take drugs. This spirit will want to share the energy emitted by this drug-saturated body or lead the person to commit crimes that he will try to justify by natural laws and other aberrant ideas. There are evil spirits that resonate with people.

By praying to evil forces, it is not the Devil who appears, but simply spirits who want to annoy the living. These spirits are not very enlightened and have a density that is much greater than that of someone who has worked to improve himself and is enlightened. The density varies with respect to each person's level of development. My guide, Jonathan, provided the following through me: he explained that this notion could be better understood if it is compared to the physical density of matter. It is this physical property that differentiates matter: lead sinks in water, and wood floats on its surface. Water has a density that is greater than wood and lead has a density that is greater than water, so that is why the lead is on the bottom, the water is in the middle and the wood on top. The spirit is governed by a similar law, and depending on the actions or the densities, it is possible to float at different levels. Here again is resonance! It all comes back to this!

Since I do not know all the information contained in an evil spirit, I cannot say what mission such a person had on this earth. I could not judge it. I have had spirits beside me who had come to see my clients and with whom it was pleasant to work as I was closely connected to their energy, in symbiosis. Yet the client himself would tell me that the deceased had been very disrespectful with him. One thing I am certain of is that the transition into the light changes many people's attitudes because they find themselves still alive, whereas they had never believed in any afterlife. The deceased also have a much more general view of the living and understand much better why some people might have been disagreeable to them. They also better understand their own behavior during their lifetimes; their horizon has simply opened out and their view of things has become broader. This transition can bring about great change. Actions are inscribed and remain in resonance. They lead each person to take the necessary steps to discard these resonances, through meditation, for example. Nothing is eternal. A body is not eternal; a spirit is not eternal; the only thing that is eternal is our essence. The spirit which travels from body to body and which changes with every thought, is almost as ephemeral as the body itself.

The Ouija board

The "Ouija" board (phonetically, this is pronounced "oo-ee-dja") can be, in my opinion, a means of proving the intelligence of the spirit world, but it is above all an energy reinforcement tool. It is not recommended as a means of communicating with the afterlife.

Ouija board with the letters of the alphabet and the words "Yes" and "No".

The board is used in the following manner: the participants place their finger on a disc which can slide freely on the round wooden board, on the rim of which the letters of the alphabet have been drawn and, assisted by their energy, the spirit world moves the disc to write messages, philosophize or make requests.

Some time ago, I was to participate in a TV project which was to prove there is life after death. There were three of us: my friend Roland who did the writing and managed the board; Béa, a medium, and myself. We trained with blindfolds according to the "triple blind" method that is done thusly: the mediums

When the mediums' eyes have been blindfolded, the board is spun so that they will not know where the letters are.

A fourth person, in this case a journalist, holds the drawing in the energy so that the spirit world can write what is shown.

A third person notes down the letters indicated by the disc which is guided by the mediums' hands.

are blindfolded. The Ouija board is spun so that the mediums do not know the positions of the letters. Then the third person draws or writes something that the spirit world is supposed to reproduce with the help of the letters on the board and the blindfolded mediums.

We trained for 18 months, blindfolded, before the board gave us a coherent message. We then produced texts from the spirit world and described unfamiliar images in words. For this experiment, a fourth person held a drawing or photo above our heads, in the energy, so that we could not see it. The spirit world wrote what was in the photo on the board. When the documentary was being made, there were three correct responses from the spirit world about the drawings that were shown.

Two weeks after the end of this experiment, the board never said anything coherent again. My explanation for this is that the spirit world had made a team available for us, for the use of this tool solely during this experiment, in order to prove that there is life after death. That team appeared not to be available anymore to talk about pleasantries, to answer questions, or to ask for favors.

I attempted to use the Ouija board with one of our teachers at the time, to show the students what exists. In class, the demonstrations worked very well. When the class was over, communication was no longer possible when its use turned to personal discussion. These two cases corroborate my explanation, i.e. that the spirit world makes a team available to prove there is life after death, but certainly not for fun or for personal gain.

I consider the Ouija board, as much as the practice of table-turning, as a tool for practicing the use of the energy itself. For the tables to move or turn or for the Ouija board to turn, or sometimes write, a lot of energy is required from the medium. Moreover, it takes a lot of commitment, work, training, and rigor to maintain this energy. The board is good training to become familiar with the stronger energies, to learn to maintain them and finally to use them in healing. As previously mentioned, this is why the board is useful and not as a communication tool. The Ouija and the revolving tables are like an energetic weight room.

There are different reasons for the Ouija board's poor reputation.

One of these reasons stems from the ego or subconscious of the participant who can direct the disc and make it move from one letter to the next to produce the words he or she wants to see written. The answers to his or her questions are induced by his or her own ego. The spirit or the team from the spirit world thus has no access; they can do nothing because it is the participants who "impose" their own will. The visiting spirit is helpless. Therefore it is no surprise that the messages are distorted.

Another reason involves the goal of the session with the board. If the objective is to have fun or for the practitioner's personal gain, or to provide entertainment, usually after a few drinks, playful spirits are capable of intervening and providing erroneous or frightening information.

This reminds me of the story of some students who, during a ski holiday, fashioned a Ouija board. The visiting "spirit" told them the gondola lift was going to fall down. The next day, half the students walked back up the slopes all day, as they were afraid of taking the gondola because it might collapse. There was no lift accident, of course. There is also another anecdote about what can happen to well-trained mediums who are acting in good faith: the message mentioned that something serious was going to happen to a particular boy. The mediums called the police, but – fortunately – nothing happened in this case, either. We will never know if a playful spirit or the subconscious of one of the participants intervened during the sitting.

However, I think that not only playful spirits but also some participants' hysteria is responsible for a lot of things. On the other hand, I have never heard of such spirits intervening when the entire group is dedicated only to serving Heaven.

Chapter 21

Electric Voice Phenomena (EVP)

Electric Voice Phenomena (EVP) is also known as "instrumental transcommunication" or ITC. The Italians call it "Metafonia", but I don't know what term the Chinese use. To go further into detail, the difference is that ITC also includes phenomena that happen on a computer, for example, whereas EVP only includes voices that can be heard. I myself would regroup these various techniques under the term EVP.

This is a form of communication with the spirit world which uses tools such as a radio, recording instruments, a computer or a television set. The spirits also know how to live with the times!

The former Portuguese consul, Anabela Cardoso, now lives in Vigo, Spain, where she practices EVP professionally. My assistant Mélanie and I have had the opportunity to be invited by Anabela Cardoso to watch her EVP experiments and also to practice this form of communication with the afterlife. Anabela warned us that there was no guarantee that the EVP would work, and that we might be making a long trip in vain. Mélanie and I agreed to take the risk and try it in May 2014. We were very well received and immediately began work. The procedure we used in our first recordings was as follows: first, we spoke into the microphone and then stopped speaking to allow the tape to record for a few minutes. Then we spoke again, and so on, for about 20 minutes.

Then Anabela transferred the recording from the cassette to the hard disk on her computer to work with audio software to sort and filter our words. I would never have thought it would have taken so much time. Unfortunately, my hearing is so bad that I could not hear anything. The two women, however, both heard feminine voices, but unfortunately they were too soft to understand what they were saying. Somewhat frustrated, we nevertheless decided to do the same experiment the next day. After all, hadn't we come all this way to do that?

Anabela explained that she usually used another system. She is authorized to use an unused static frequency that is free of programming, with no words or music and which therefore produces a white noise. Every Thursday and Sunday without fail, she leaves her radio on at this frequency all night. The next day she transfers these hours of recordings to her computer and notes the displays on her screen that show stronger recordings and changes on the tape. In this way, she has collected a lot of messages, some of which are very clear! Anabela described her experiments and compiled the messages she received in her book *Electric Voices: Contact With Another Dimension*.

The next day, I insisted we take the time to meditate before recording and to open the session with a prayer and fill the room with energy so that communication could take place perhaps more easily.

While meditating, my guide came close and told me we had to clap our hands from time to time to make a noise, which they would be able to convert into words. This method made me think of the physical mediumship in which the spirits use nearby tissues and convert them into ectoplasm. Anabela agreed to proceed in this manner: say short phrases, each in turn, and between each, clap our hands loudly. When we listened to the recording, poor Mélanie became almost as deaf as I because she had put her head directly on the loudspeaker... But we got results! Four times, after one of our phrases or after a clap, we received words. The words were: "Hello," "Goodbye," and a fraction of a second after Mélanie had said, "Thank you," they replied, "You're welcome." Even if these are ordinary replies, it was strange that the actual voice of a deceased person should appear so spontaneously. We are used to what takes place via telepathy, but this method, so factual and tangible, does not leave you indifferent.

It was a very nice visit with Anabela, and we want to thank her again very much.

Anabela Cardoso

Anabela Cardoso's recording equipment

Recording in which the peaks are human voices and the thicker line to the right of them are the voices of the spirit world.

Accounts of EVP

There are many stories of spirits using electronic devices to communicate from the afterlife. They are touching, and once more prove there is a life after death. Our dearly departed like to give us a nod and send us messages of love, whatever the supporting media. Here are two accounts.

Professor Rolf Leu was a physics teacher in St. Gallen (Switzerland); he enjoyed chemistry and mathematics as well as literature and was also an expert in antique cars – he himself owned an old Mustang. He died on 25 February 2013. Six months later, his wife Tina was watching TV with her mother, when he winked at them from the afterlife. The women were watching a program which presented all makes of cars with young people showing them and having a grand time. During the program a man came into the picture as if he were part of the film. Seeing him, the two women both cried out at the same time. There was no doubt about it – it was their dearly departed Rolf! At that moment, the deceased was examining a Mustang that was being presented with great attention, and then he gave the biggest smile through the flat screen of the TV before dissolving in just a few seconds. He was able to use the pixels in this medium to reproduce his image. The two women then knew that their dear one was part of their lives forever. On another occasion, Tina Leu saw her husband in the reflection of the window of her winter garden, sitting on his chair reading a book as he always had.

The second account is from one of my long-time friends, whom I will call Giulia, with whom I had spoken of EVP. She told me her own experience:

Giulia had lost her husband tragically when he was 34. She was left alone with her ten-year-old son. A few months after he died, a friend of the family called her because her dead husband Franco had sent her a message. Giulia was skeptical but her curiosity led her to accept the invitation and her friend showed her the EVP.

On the tape that had been filtered and slowed, the recording was ready: "I am Franco and I am alive, I am at number 32, believe me, eh!" No one but Giulia knew that Franco's grave number was... 32!

Up to then, Giulia had believed that there was life after death and since then she is convinced of it!

Another time, she was listening to music that Franco had played and recorded when the ten-year-old boy came home. Her son asked her to turn off the music because it reminded him too much of his father. She did so and both began to cry over his death. At the same time, the TV switched on and off six or seven times, by itself. That was when Giulia decided to buy some recording equipment for herself. She received several clear messages, some very reasonable, others very funny.

Shortly afterwards, Giulia's cousin's home was burglarized. She told herself that the electronic (noise) gate which had cost so much and which was stored in the cousin's garage must have been stolen. That evening, Franco spoke into her recorder: "Ah no, they did not steal your gate!" And it was true, the equipment was still there. Another time, Giulia left her recorder on and was cleaning house and complaining out loud to herself in the middle of the staircase. In an amused and teasing voice, Franco said, "Whew, she certainly can complain when she does the ironing!"

Chapter 22

Trance

Edgar Cayce is to trance as Mozart is to music! He is better known as the "sleeping prophet" because he actually went to sleep. While "sleeping", he talked. He provided information about the remedy that could cure the person in need and even said where the appropriate medicine could be found. During trance, he could evoke future events or say philosophical things. Maurice Barbanell, whom I will present later, is another trance medium. There was also the case of the uneducated boy who went into spontaneous trances during which he spoke and commented on Bible verses. He was discovered by the German priest Johannes Greber in the early 1900s. Such people do exist but they are rare, with only a few per century in the entire world.

The term "trance" often causes misunderstandings. In fact, trance does not mean a deceased person is present or that there is an activity in relation to the afterlife. Trance is a state of consciousness that is caused by a repetitive movement that reduces the frequency of the brain waves: a marathon runner can go into a trance, just like someone who is playing or listening to a drum can go into a trance, or an autistic child who repeats the same gestures incessantly. Whirling dervishes or Sufi mystics who spin without stopping, repeating the movement again and again, will go into trances. This particular state does not mean that some being from the afterlife is present or that there is any input from the spirit world. When a medium goes into a trance, for example through a breathing technique, and if he can control his mind and his modified consciousness states enough, then he may invite someone from the spirit world to join him. The two spirits – the medium's incarnated spirit and the non-incarnated spirit of his guide – will connect and fuse. This state, this fusion, will make a voice available to the spirit world. In this state of trance, the medium will thus loan his body and voice to the spirit world so that it can speak through him.

Trance teaching methods began to change in the late 1990s or the year 2000. Before that, when I was learning, we sat in a silent circle. All week. Not one word; not ever. This method of teaching has been abandoned, maybe because of the speed and the impatience of our present evolution. Today instructors encourage the students to say at least one word or phrase from their first attempts at trance. The students have to agree to say what they perceive in an inspired manner so that in the coming years the trance can gradually take over. If I compare the training to which we were subjected, Moira Hawkins, Sally Barnes, Tim Abbott, Chris Denton and myself (to name only a few, but silence was basically the method used for all the mediums certified in the field of trance by the *Spiritualists' National Union* [SNU]), it must be admitted that today's training is clearly different. Chris did not begin trance until after he had been practicing inspired speaking for ten years. Even after that, it took him three more years until he could reach a deep trance. In the visualization he was using to go into a trance, he finally gathered the courage to jump into that deep black ravine that he saw and the next year he successfully reached that unconscious state of deep sleepwalking. I myself sat for six years, sometimes for weeks on end, from morning to night, without uttering a single sound. Just being there, building energy and learning to make my mind passive. You can therefore see how today's teaching is different. Nowadays, even if at the beginning only one percent of what is spoken comes from the spirit world versus 99% that comes from the student's mind, this can be considered a good start. With practice, as I have just said, this gap will narrow, until the spirit world expresses itself fully, in its own words, through the medium's voice. The question remains: what percentage shows that it is the words from the spirit world which are being expressed through the medium? In this process, it is the medium's memory that is used; the spirit world must be able to reach the greater part of this memory so that the medium can pronounce the spirit's words, like switches that each light up different bulbs.

The disadvantage of the method used when I was learning trance without saying a word is the discouragement. Many people are discouraged along the way and have stopped working with this frequency that is so magnificent. With the current teaching methods, since speech appears immediately, the student has concrete evidence in which to believe and can therefore follow their progression. All they need to do is to not let themselves be fooled or try to mislead a spectator about what comes from their own mind and not from the spirit world.

During trances that I have witnessed, for example in the Philippines, I have noticed that these mediums, these healers, all keep part of their body or mind aware. Not all of their being is in a trance: they remember what was said and what was done when they come out of their trance. Even if the medium's body shivers when the deceased enters or exits it, the medium is always aware of what has occurred. For me, compared to these Filipino mediums in terms of the type of trance, I admit I do not experience the same phenomena, except in healing where memory extraction is concerned, or during a specific therapy, but not during spoken trance. When I am in a speaking trance, I hear myself from afar, as if I were in another room or at the end of a tunnel. Even though I can hear myself talking, I remember almost none of what I said, or maybe, when I am falling asleep, I can again access some of the things that were said through me, which can be explained by the fact that every word was processed by my mind and is thus stored.

An energy unlike the others
In a trance, the energy is stronger than the energy in spiritual healing, because the connection is stronger and deeper. This can be seen in the following example:

A very well-built and powerful man was enrolled for about a year in my TT (Therapeutic Touch) and spiritual healing classes. This man, who was quite gifted, channeled energy very well. Given his capacities, I invited him to participate in my private trance circle. He accepted joyfully. One evening, he joined us. The group of six people was seated in a circle around me. The entire group put their minds in a trance to provide me with that energy in order to enable me to use it for my own trance and be a voice for the spirit world. When we took a break, the man I had invited was feeling unwell. He explained that he had a pacemaker which, for the first time, in a long time, had started to overload. He had to leave the group. Never, in his entire course in spiritual healing, had he had the least problem. Two weeks later he asked if he might come back to my trance circle to try again as he was very interested in our work.

We went through the same procedure with the same result: the pacemaker went awry again. After this latter attempt we concluded that the energy produced in a trance was too much for him.

One of the most frequent applications for trance is healing. The correct term is thus "trance healing", which is in fact a form of spiritual healing, in a more detached, relaxed and interiorized state that is deeper and often more intense.

Before I could even utter something as simple as "hello" or a basic phrase, it took me six years of sitting, just as it took Chris Denton 14 years and Bill Meadows 17 before being able to produce physical materializations (you will learn more about Bill in the chapter on physical mediumship). So, don't give up on your training, develop your patience and your patients or future students will thank you!

What I would like to show through the various examples below – the Filipino healers, my own experience, Chris Denton and the Brazilian, Medrado – is that we experience our trances in completely different ways and the mechanisms of these trances are different for each of us too, except for the will to unite with the spirit world and loan our body. There is thus no fixed procedure, no established standard. The only thing that is certain is that we are all in a modified consciousness state, a cerebral state with reduced waves, at least for a part of the brain. In medical or neurological terms, we are situated at the lower frequencies, in theta or delta.

To sum up, medicine helps establish the reality of these modified consciousness states. These states produce amazing miracles with the help of the spirit world. Trance is therefore a state used for speaking or philosophizing and for automatic writing. It is also very frequently used in healing, when it is called "trance healing", which in fact is done in a state that is more detached, even more relaxed, much more interiorized, deeper and often more powerful.

Chris Denton

Chris Denton
(chrispdenton@gmail.com)

With regard to trance, I have never seen any controls (which means the main guide who controls the medium when the latter is in a trance) as precise and as powerful as Chris Denton's. I have watched with my own eyes as Chris got up from his chair, his eyes closed and thus in a trance, walked about the room, went to fetch students who needed trance healing and brought them to his treatment bed. He placed the student on the therapy bed and treated them. Then he would take the student back to their seat. At the end of this session, which lasted an hour or an hour and a half, and at which I was present, Chris went back to his seat and sat down, as if it were the most natural thing in the world.

To go into a trance, Chris had to work with a completely different kind of visualization. In fact, in the beginning, when he was developing his trance, he would try every time to go down into a trance using the staircase technique because visualizing the lower steps causes the mind to relax and let go, but he could not manage it. In his vision, he always ended up on the edge of a huge cliff, which caused him to stop cold. This continued until the day he gathered up his courage and jumped off the cliff. Since that "leap", his trance has been perfect, and he remembers nothing when he comes out of it.

Chris Denton also practices speaking trance. The guide he loans his voice to is named Achmed. When he is doing trance healing, it is Dr. George Mortimer, who was a physician in London at the end of the 19th and early 20th centuries, which Chris Denton was able to confirm through research.

Chris is now 60 and lives in Guiseley, north of Leeds, in England. He only practices trance occasionally these days. His daily work has caught up with him, and leaves him no time. What a pity that one of the most talented mediums I have ever met in my career should put his gift aside. One day I asked Chris what the biggest event or joy in his mediumship was. For him, it was not the materializations, but his first trance healing with his guide Dr. Mortimer. He had treated a lady who was suffering from endometritis. Three days later the lady's doctor called him to say she was completely recovered from her illness. What moves this very modest and very humble man the most is being able to help others and not the spectacular side that appears on the stage, with all the attendant glory! This is so typical of his personality.

In my opinion the most moving moment when I was present during one of Chris Denton's trances was at the sitting in which his guide Achmed built up his energy so powerfully above Chris' head that I was able to see him myself in objective vision. When he appeared, I immediately drew the portrait of Achmed. When I went to eat, I left the drawing in my seat. When I came back to the room, a woman I did not know passed me and, walking by my seat, stopped when she saw my drawing and exclaimed, "Wow, it's Achmed!" So I was not the only one who had seen him.

It's interesting and even intriguing to know that Achmed, when he appeared publicly, said that in his former life he was at the service of the Suleimans, an Arab people who lived in the 1500s. Achmed was an executioner! When a student asked how an assassin could become a guide, he would answer him peacefully, "I never killed anyone on my own decision. In my time, it was an honorable profession and my prayer to Allah was to ask that my arm be precise and my blade steady in order to prevent any suffering to the condemned person." I never heard Achmed say anything but words of wisdom and peace, as well as very good lessons about mediumship. His very strong voice could intimidate some people, but his words never offended anyone.

Maurice Barbanell

We cannot talk about trance without mentioning Maurice Barbanell, who was a highly Cartesian English journalist. One evening, a sick colleague called him and asked him to replace him. He was to go and watch a spirit session. Mr. Barbanell went, without much enthusiasm, since he had already seen one and had become very bored. Trance was really not his cup of tea. The session began and, according to him, he fell asleep right away. The whole group laughed when he woke up and excused himself. What had actually happened was that he himself had gone into a deep trance and did not remember anything. He had loaned his voice to a guide who introduced himself as "Silver Birch" and said he was a Native American. Even today, no one knows whether this guide was really a Native American when he was alive, or if he simply chose to appear as one. Nevertheless, Native American guides are often seen in the field of healing, such as Red Cloud who worked with the late Estelle Roberts, or White Feather who works with me, and I know of many others.

Silver Birch

Maurice Barbanell

From that day on, Maurice became one of the best-known channels in England and several books with spiritual advice and philosophy were channeled and published. These books can still be found in bookshops, mainly in English. In England,

Maurice's books have become a must for any spiritualist. After his encounter with trance and with Silver Birch, Maurice Barbanell founded *Psychic News*, a weekly paper he directed for many years, until his journey to the afterlife.

For a long time, he never told anyone he was the voice of Silver Birch. Among the famous people who frequented the spiritualist circles were Sir Arthur Conan Doyle, the creator of Sherlock Holmes, and Winston Churchill. They contributed in a significant way to Maurice's reputation outside of the closed spiritualist circles.

José Medrado

José Medrado is a lawyer and still teaches law. But when he is in a trance he paints. In his first trances, he became familiar with deceased artists, very famous ones in fact, who take control. He himself admits his first drawings were terrible, because he did not know how to paint at all. Today, his paintings are true works of art, done in just a few minutes. As I have had the opportunity to see him work when he is in a trance, I found his technique very impressive. During the greater part of his work, he keeps his eyes closed. He mixes all the pigments with the oil, often with very quick gestures. He never lets a color dry between two applications. The famous painters reproduce their own work through him, or sometimes studies of works. When the paintings are finished, they sign them. Rumor has it that only Picasso refuses to sign... unless he is satisfied with the reproduction.

The paintings, which are done in public and take between three and seven minutes in general, look very different from those done in a studio. Medrado can work for long hours on a painting in his studio, and they really look like photographs. Medrado says he does not remember what has happened when he comes out of his trance.

This lawyer has set up a magnificent foundation in Brazil where he appears before huge crowds. In his foundation, poor people get free medical treatment and education and there is even a small orphanage. His foundation is funded by the income from the sale of his paintings, which he auctions right after his demonstrations. His work can be seen at cidadedaluz.com.br.

One of José Medrado's works, which he painted when he was in a trance.

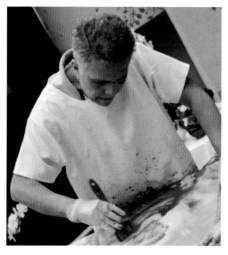

José Medrado at work while in a trance.

A painting by José Medrado, which is in my clinic, done in 5 minutes and 32 seconds.

Nechung the Savior

The most well-known or "official" trance is doubtless that of the Tibetan monk who put himself into a trance with the "Nechung" oracle. "Nechung" is the name of a monastery in Tibet. During this trance, the monk gave the precise route that allowed the Dalai Lama to escape from the Chinese. Nechung told him, "Go, go! Tonight!" and then drew the map on a piece of paper. The medium who channeled the escape route of the Dalai Lama was the abbot of that monastery. After the Tibetan government went into exile, the monastery was rebuilt in Dharamshala, India, not far from the residence of the current Dalai Lama. The medium that lives there holds the rank of vice-minister. He is regularly consulted during the New Year's holidays and also at any other time on specific questions or for his predictions about the future.

Since 4 September 1987, the medium who channels Nechung is Thubten Ngodup, who was born in 1957 in Phari, Tibet. He is the seventeenth official "channel". He succeeded Lobsang

Jigmé, who officiated from 1945 until his death in 1984 in India. In 1947, Lobsang predicted the crisis that would take place with the arrival of the communist Chinese regime. In 1959, it was he who advised the fourteenth Dalai Lama to leave Tibet. Since the monk Ngodup is the seventeenth person to hold this position, it is easy to imagine how old Nechung is.

Thanks to him, the Dalai Lama is still alive, because he was able to flee and avoid being captured by the Chinese. The monk connects with the deity "Nechung" and gives advice. Here is what the Dalai Lama said about this in 2002:

For hundreds of years now, it has been traditional for the Dalai Lama and the government to consult Nechung during the New Year's festivals. Additionally, he may indeed be called upon at other times if either have specific questions. I myself speak with him several times a year. This may sound far-fetched to twentieth century Western readers... But I do so for the simple reason that as I look back over the many occasions when I have asked questions of the oracle, on each one of them time has proved that his answer was correct... Surprising as it may seem, the oracle's replies to questions are rarely vague. As in the case of my escape from Lhasa, he is often very specific.

Dalai Lama, 2002

Thubten Ngodup in preparation for his trance and the Nechung oracle.

How do you know?

Determining what part of the content of a philosophical statement made during a trance really comes from the spirit world is not easy. It is thus understandable that there is so much more badmouthing about the work that is done in the area of spoken trance than about any other area of mediumship.

The narrow world of professional mediumship itself is already one in which many rumors and an incredible amount of jealousy abound. In the microcosm of trance, we hold the all-time record for malicious gossip! I have heard the confessions of seven trance mediums that are well-known in the field. Each one criticized the trance of this or that other medium, calling them fake or simulated. I have indeed seen innumerable trance mediums and attended many such sessions in which I was not always persuaded that the contact was properly interpreted according to the wishes of the spirit world. A good actor can easily imitate a trance state. Only a clairvoyant can say if there is at least an energetic bridge between the medium and the spirit. Even if this bridge is effective and the link to the spirit world is thus ensured, we still do not know what percentage of the words that are uttered actually come from the spirit world. The only confirmation remains the spoken word or the results if the work involves trance healing, and the apports of course, if it involves physical mediumship. Another indicator which reveals that a medium is simulating is the temperature in the room, which can vary by several degrees. Jonathan and his group have often done experiments in my little temple in Neuchâtel. During these experiences, the participants went from shivering from the cold to perspiring in the heat.

As a Cartesian man, I cannot help playing the Devil's advocate and questioning my own trance, so that I will not be accused of cheating. When examining my trance, two things have convinced me that it was not some sort of psychosis, but was really a genuine contact.

The first thing took place as follows: one evening, during a trance circle in England, it was my turn to go into a trance. This was the first time that "White Feather", my Native American guide, spoke through me. When he left and I wanted to come out of my trance, I returned to normal consciousness insofar as my head was concerned but I no longer felt my body and could not move a finger. Ian, the highly experienced English medium who was leading the circle, calmly told me that I had come out of my deep state of modified consciousness too quickly. All that was necessary was for me to go back into a trance and come out of it more slowly. I followed his instructions and everything returned to normal. The second thing that tells me my trance is not psychotic is that all of the people who have heard me speak English during my trance assure me (repeatedly) that my accent in English is different when I am in a trance compared to my usual accent. Though I speak English fluently, I would in no way be able to imitate another accent; I am already content just to be able to express myself in this language.

During my first years of practice, my speech during a trance was very hesitant and rather rough, not at all like normal speech. Indeed, although the connection was there, I did not know how to control the energy in a stable way. It was only with years of regular training that the sentences flowed more easily and it became possible to speak for longer periods.

Automatic writing

A trance state is also used for automatic writing and inspired writing (which is different from automatic writing because it only requires the person to be in a light trance).

Automatic writing takes place when a spirit from the spirit world has such control over the medium that he can move his physical body and the medium's hand writes by itself. Automatic writing can only happen during a trance in which the connection is very intense and the spirit world can truly control the medium's physical body. It has been seen that the writing produced by the medium when writing automatically resembles that of the deceased.

These days, when talking about and describing inspired writing, the American word *channeling* is used. The medium is in contact with the deceased – at least, we hope he is – and he will write what he thinks he has understood from the deceased. Yes, inspired people often exist. But the speech or writing is still that of the medium. It is in this trance state that we see the most mistakes or simulations by the medium, because there is only a slight possibility of empirical confirmation given that at the cerebral level the medium will not be situated in theta or delta waves, nor will he be in mediumistic contact as he would be with a deceased person. In this state, there are indeed impostors, though this is generally not the case.

In a trance, as with other mediumistic perceptions, it is important to understand that the spirit world is going to use the medium's memory to generate coherent speech or writing. The spirit world will not be able to express things that are not already present in my memory. It will not be able to speak in a language I don't know, because that vocabulary has not been previously learned. The spirit world cannot talk about scientific subjects that are not inscribed in my being. It can only use what is already there and assemble it, in a way, in order to be able to express itself through me. That is why trance is part of mental mediumship.

I have never met a medium who could speak a language he or she did not know. On the other hand, I have heard about this type of trance. As far as I know, this can only happen in during a very deep trance, i.e. when the medium is fully unconscious. Chris Denton remembers absolutely nothing but that does not mean he feels incorporated, i.e., that a deceased person has taken over his body.

When I am in a trance, I prefer not to be alone with someone

I do not know. As there are long moments which I do not remember when I come out of the trance, I would not tolerate it if someone were to attribute certain statements to me if I did not know whether I expressed myself in that way. Words can be used or twisted to the client's advantage, in whatever way he wants and however it benefits him.

Going into a trance

The way to reach a trance state is always the same: there has to be a repetitive element and the will to let go. Marathon runners, as I have already mentioned, and children who play with toys in a repetitive way can reach these states – a sort of waking dream, in which the mind is very little or no longer involved. The repetitive rhythm will send the brain into a trance.

Above all, in the case of a trance during which there is contact with a deceased person or guide, there has to be the will to want to connect. But it is also necessary to find the method – which is specific to every person – that will assist in leaving the normal cerebral mode.

One way that works for many people – outside of shamanic drumming or other repetitive techniques – is to observe your breathing; that is, to go inside yourself. As in every psychic discipline, you have to go inside yourself and reach your core. For most people, the core is located at the heart chakra. The center is where you find your peace, that relaxation that is needed to go into a trance. By observing, in a highly focused manner, the rhythm of your breathing, your thoracic rocking, the repetitive movement is created. From there, while you are observing your breathing, you can add some visualizations. Some people will work with staircases that go down inside them, like a sort of hypnosis by counting the steps. Visualizing yourself going down these steps brings about the necessary repetition and allows you to let go more and more, to let go more and more, and to let go even more, step by step in the staircase technique, while observing your breathing. You will find another way to go into a trance in the exercises in the chapter on "Meditations".

Hysterical trance

I have often been troubled by the behavior of some mediums during their trances. In fact, I have seen mediums act like children, mimicking them and imitating their voices. Such behavior is disturbing and is likely to be part of what are called "hysterical trances". We know that when a spirit communicates, its field connects with ours to use our memory and our vocal cords. Whether it is a child or an adult makes no difference, because it is the medium's voice that is used throughout a telepathic process that makes use of a physical organ such as the vocal cords. There is thus no reason at all why the voice we hear should be the deceased's. Moreover, whether child or adult, a spirit has lived many previous lives. It is therefore senseless to believe that the information received from a spirit comes exclusively from his immediate past. Even if the trance were achieved through total incorporation, the tool used is still the medium's larynx. The only exception lies in physical mediumship, in which the spiritual world creates a voice box out of ectoplasm in order to produce a direct voice. In this way, the voice from the latest life can be reproduced, like the voice of little Mary when she appeared to Bill Meadows, which I describe in the chapter on physical mediumship. Of course the medium can reproduce the deceased's or the guide's attitudes, if the connection is very strong, but this has nothing to do with the theatrics we see all too often. My professor was present during a hysterical trance in which the medium got down on his hands and knees and was growling like a bear! Even in EVP, an animal's message is transcribed in words in a language that can be understood by the medium, and not in barks or growls, because the mechanism is telepathic. The information is written on an energy particle!

In trance, believing you are possessed by your guide or by a spirit and changing your physical attitude and your voice to make the audience think it is the guide or the deceased is similar to the hysterical behavior described above. Suppose the medium is persuaded his or her guide is a Shaolin monk. It does not matter if it is true or not. The medium is putting pressure on themselves just by believing they have to put on a Shaolin performance to impress the audience. Incorporated trance is not the subject here, but if the monk really had incorporated himself, the medium would have known how to do Kung Fu and speak Chinese. During a normal trance connection, these Chinese characteristics would not appear or if they did it would only be very slightly. My professor was present during the incorporated trance of an elderly man whose legs were usually very weak. In his trance, he was actually able to do a somersault!

Some patients display hysterical or psychotic behavior but it is not related to a state of trance. I myself have had experience with this sort of behavior in a patient. She had worked with several therapists, using colors, NLP (neurolinguistic programming) and other techniques. Finally, not knowing what else to do for this lady, one of the therapists sent her to me. Her problem was this: every time she came into contact with energy, she would writhe, like in the pictures of diabolical possession worthy of a Hollywood studio. As soon as I touched her, the writhing began; I saw clearly that this was not due to outside energy but that it actually came from within her. When she came for the next consultation, I placed my hands on her as if I were channeling healing energy, though I had not established my connection – like a "placebo", in a way.

My client was not aware of my approach. Though I did not transmit any healing energy to her from the spirit world, she was twisting with convulsions. At the end of the treatment, we exchanged pleasantries as ordinary as talking about the weather and talked a little about her home country. All the time we were talking I left my hand on her knee, similar to a gesture of affection but sending her all the energy I could. There was no problem, no writhing – just a quiet chat like two old friends in a café. When I explained to her what I had just done, she was very surprised. From that day on, I was able to place my hands on her like everyone else and no other strange gesture or behavior was seen. This lady had been suffering from psychotic behavior, but was not going into hysterical trance.

To better have an idea of what hysterical trance is and understand the progression which may mislead the medium, I will present a psychological model of hysterical trance. This state is not a side effect of mediumship because as soon as the trance is over the medium is no longer concerned by the facts presented. This form of dissociation is not continuous according to what I have observed. It is active only during trance.

In these graphics, I am only discussing trance, even though some everyday dissociative states are similar to these models:

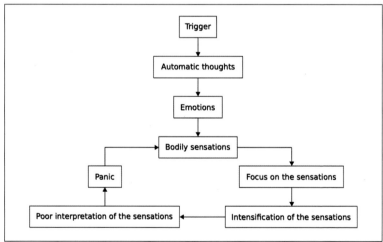

It must be understood that hope is a form of anticipation and that it generates the same physiological reactions as fear. Fear is healthy, because it signals danger; but in this particular case, fear is of course useless. It is simply due to excitement, just like anger or any other intense emotional state.

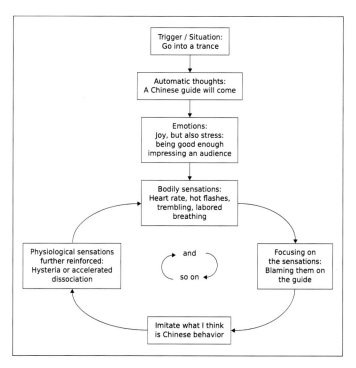

These steps are interactive; if one changes, the others do as well. The learning procedure, whether it is right or wrong, builds future experience. In a similar way, the present experience stems from past experience, such as childhood, memories or reminders. This sum of past experiences and learning will imprint its information on future experiences.

When looking at these graphs in the context of a trance, the mere fact of telling a novice which guide is speaking through him or her can trigger the mechanism described and thus have a dangerous influence on the novice. Simply sitting for a trance can also trigger the same process if the student has high expectations of who may appear as a guide. One element that triggers hysterical trance is stress or pressure, especially if the trance is to take place before an audience. The novice will put so much pressure on themselves that the physiological stress pattern will settle in by itself.

These psychological processes are set in motion if, during a trance, stages are skipped or if the person remains in his mind. These processes must not be generalized and patience is necessary. Trance is such a marvelous and useful tool! Imagine yourself becoming the actual word of the Holy Spirit... Making sacrifices and being the Devil's advocate in order not to be fooled are so worthwhile. What a miracle, in a way, to be capable of giving this voice to the wise ones! What a blessing to bring their true words to the ears of those who are seeking! There is no other discipline in which the guide who loves you will be as close to you. You will never be so close; you will be as one in this wisdom and this love. If your prayer is to serve, you will have those who serve by your side; if your prayer is to give love, then the spark of the light will spread among those who will listen to you and be healed. Don't bury your head in the sand like an ostrich; invest of yourself. You will never be alone in your quest...

Chapter 23

Extraction of Pathological Information (EPI)

Since the end of 2012, another form of trance has become part of my practice. During my trances, the spirit world extracts harmful memories from our bodies' energy system where they are stored in the form of information. I have come to call this healing method, of which to my knowledge I currently am the only proponent, *Extraction of Pathological Information (EPI)*. I have, however, recently started teaching it at *fréquences*, the school for healing I founded in 2005.

It took a long time before I was able to carry out one of these interventions. It started during one of my study trips among the healers in the Philippines. I was attending a spoken trance by the healer Esther Bravo. Suddenly, in that little chapel high up in the mountains, the medium, who says she connects with Moses in her trance, spoke to me, saying, "You have been chosen by the spirit world to perform surgeries like the healers do here; you will do good on your continent; we will come to you soon." Everyone in the audience, and especially me, was very moved, of course, and I waited impatiently. But it was not until a year later, just before going to bed, when I saw, next to me, a man dressed as a surgeon, in light blue scrubs, with a surgical cap on his head and mask over his mouth and nose. Without speaking, he made me understand that he was the sign these "operations" would commence. I saw this doctor objectively, with my eyes open, as a 3D hologram at a distance of one meter from me. When the surgeon had given me the message, he dissolved. *I was very excited and enthusiastic*: at last the "operations" were going to begin! And then... nothing! Nothing!

One very astonishing thing was that when this surgeon appeared to me, I was not in a state of mind that could have created such an image, since I was brushing my teeth while watching TV.

Finally, after four years, at the end of a Kriya massage during which I had worked in a light trance, the process got started in a most sudden and unexpected way. As I was placing some paper towels over the client's stomach to wipe off the oil, I saw a spot on the paper. How could a new sheet of paper have a spot on it? I took it off and I no longer saw any spot on the paper towel. I put it back and again a grayish spot appeared. Stunned, I placed my hand on the area from which the spot came, and it immediately began to shake and scratch. With my third eye, I saw the skin open up like a wound. Under my scratching fingers, indefinable tissues and liquids flushed out of the wound; I could see them with my third eye along with many other images that passed in front of my eyes. Suddenly everything stopped and a light shone from the wound. It was only for a few seconds, or one or two minutes in all.

Why did I have to wait five years for the ability to perform *Extraction of Pathological Information (EPI)* to develop? I can only speculate, but I was certainly not ready before then.

Since that day and that treatment, it has become an almost daily practice. I am only "taken" by the spirit world on my right side, even if I can feel that the spirit guide is very close beside me. I can open my eyes during the intervention, which I cannot do in a trance. And the only thing that may feel uncomfortable after a day filled with EPI appointments are my knees, as I will have spent the entire day standing; applying the EPI healing method leads to no loss of energy whatsoever. Whether I am treating eczema, menstrual pain, chronic or other forms of pain, chronic migraines, phobia, asthma, epilepsy, multiple sclerosis, fibromyalgia, restless leg syndrome, arthrosis, arthritis, spondyloarthritis, glaucoma or other ophthalmic diseases, food intolerance, digestive disorders, allergies to all sorts of pollen, materials or chemical substances, side effects from chemotherapy, other chronic illnesses or even quite unusual cases such as allergy to sunlight, to water or to sperm, I have understood that one thing is sure: all these pathologies are based on harmful information and when it is removed, a great many patients are healed and freed of their ills or improve considerably.

Common sports injuries such as torn ligaments and muscles, sprains or wounds due to falling heal more rapidly with this therapy than without. Sometimes surgery can be avoided or the person will recover more quickly from it. This is also true for wounds that remain chronically open, whether they are postoperative or not. The healing energy allows the tissues involved to get a head start on the reconstruction process. This would therefore be beneficial to those who do high level sports and whose margin of recovery is very short, as well as those suffering from chronic wounds. Remember the energized grass in the plant pots in the section "Experiments in energy transmission" and the accelerated time factor.

Information is also present in these domains. If it is harmful, it is therefore possible to remove or neutralize it. It may be pain, inflammation, infection, edema, bruising, coagulation, cicatrization, etc.

Concerning cancerous tumors, there are two aspects to consider. The first is the information that caused the cancer. Whether emotional or physical (absorption of toxic products, permanent contact with carcinogenic substances, etc.), this information can be extracted and, ideally, the body does not reproduce a similar tumor. In this case, the action required is to extract the information; however, the preexisting cancer cells are still there. The second aspect is related to the body's repair mechanisms. In a manner that can be compared to the grass experiment, energization can provide additional support to the patient's self-healing systems and thus help him fight his cancer. Supposing that the information relative to the creation of new cancer cells is removed, the body assisted by the ad hoc medical treatment can then focus solely on the elimination of the dysfunctional cells. If the treatment involves chemotherapy, it is possible to desensitize the patient with respect to the products used so he or she can better tolerate them or at least suffer less from the side effects. Radiation therapy can sometimes cause severe burns. It is public knowledge that Swiss hospitals and clinics keep lists of "faiseurs de Secret", and these people are called upon to relieve burns or stop bleeding, etc. (The "practice of Secrets" is a traditional healing method based on prayer; it is still very common in French and Italian-speaking Switzerland and in some other Swiss cantons, as well as in the Aoste valley in Italy and in some areas of southern France.) You will find examples of the prayers used in the Secrets in the chapter on exercises at the end of the book. They are to be practiced free of charge in order to respect the tradition.

EPI leaves marks that are very strange. At first sight, one may think these marks are normal bruises which are simply caused by friction that is generated by my fingers massaging the spot where the mark appears. This is, however, not the case. First of all for the simple reason that, very often, the mark appears on a spot that I have never even touched during the entire treatment. Secondly, with certain patients I have to work on several areas and on some of these – but not on all – such marks that bear some resemblance to burns appear. It is thus not a matter of skin type. Thirdly, the surface of the marks is often larger than the spot that was massaged. Some marks disappear in a few hours and others remain present up to 30 hours later. This phenomenon may be related to the information that has been removed or to its mass or to the speed of the energetic movement. It is well known that in physical mediumship, the medium can be burned if the ectoplasm returns to his body too quickly. In the case of EPI it would be just the opposite, i.e. the mass would exit at high speed.

I don't try to interpret the nature of this harmful inscribed energy, because we can carry information that is recent or that dates back to our childhood, or is genealogical or even from another life. In general, speculation is therefore useless. As an example regarding rather recently added information: In the case of allergy, the harmful information is usually added through a traumatic event which in some cases may indeed seem ridiculously insignificant to our conscious minds, i.e. the event of being startled by someone while being in contact with the allergen in question.

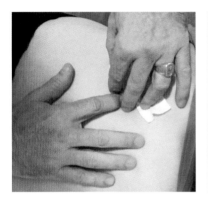 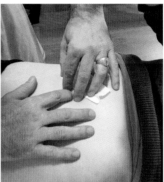

The way my hands and fingers are positioned during the extractions that I perform.

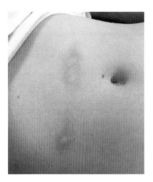 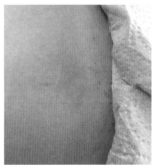

These marks (which are not to be confused with normal bruises that would be caused by friction) on the same patient are shown to explain that in some places you do not see the same type of mark, or sometimes no mark. This is thus not a matter of skin type but rather of the type of information. The marks are most probably different due to the nature of the extracted information.

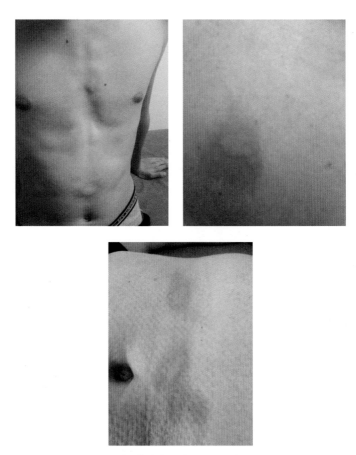

Marks left by the extractions.

During these interventions, I believe the boundaries dissolve: I don't know where my consciousness ends and where the consciousness that works with me begins. It happens as if we were one and the same consciousness. This consciousness must then dissolve the erroneous information in the patient. It would probably be more appropriate or more common to say "extract" given the marks observed on patients I have treated. I am sure of one thing: the information disappears. Since nature loathes emptiness, the memory might return. It is thus absolutely necessary to fill the emptiness left by the extraction with new energy. I am convinced that the medicine of the future is informational medicine.

I can conclude by noting that the EPI healing method allows the practitioner to erase pathological information in the nonphysical part of the patient's body, which in turn finds its material expression in the patient's physical body in the form of disappearing symptoms: we witness a process of *dematerialization*. This healing method can thus be understood as the inverse use of the mechanism which underlies *Pranism* (also known as *Breatharianism* or *Inedia*) where spiritual energy is used to *materialize* matter in the body in order to supply the required nourishment.

Case studies

Jules, 31, is highly allergic to cat dander and horsehair and has hay fever. These allergies may have been triggered by the lung pneumonia he contracted when he was about 11. Since then, Jules can no longer be around cats, horses or hay without getting a runny nose, teary eyes, sneezing repeatedly, and also experiencing severe respiratory difficulty caused by bronchioconstriction. In other words, there was a fixation of the acetylcholine neurotransmitter (notably involved in the vegetative functions) on the appropriate receptors, which produced muscle spasms in the bronchial tubes in the lungs. This led to bronchial obstruction and severe respiratory difficulty which is one of the symptoms of asthma.

Whenever he goes into a home where there are cats, the allergy flares up in less than 15 minutes. Moreover, he and his family live on a farm with hay, horses and cats. He therefore suffers constantly from these symptoms.

To get rid of his allergies, he tried various methods, but without significant improvement.

After the first EPI treatment performed at my clinic, all the symptoms disappeared except for the itchy eyes, but that was the only one left. This while his hands were contaminated by cat hair, horsehair and hay dust and he was constantly rubbing his face.

The mental hurdle is gone as well: he now approaches the stable with joy and serenity, no longer fearing the impact of any allergic symptoms.

The fact that nearly all symptoms have vanished almost instantly with a single treatment – after being part of his life for over 20 years – proves that my treatments directly access the underlying particles which contain the information causing the trouble, in this case the allergies.

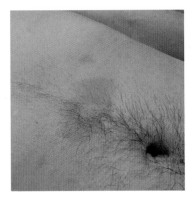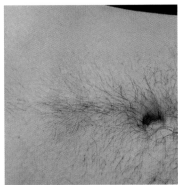

Left: Marks on Jules. First extraction. The exit area is much larger than the zone on which my fingers were placed. Where the density of the ejected energy was the greatest, the skin looks similar to a blister, which, contrary to normal blisters, only remains a day or two. The red halos around the treated area indicate that the movement of the memories when exiting took place beyond the workspace on which my fingers were placed.

Right: Marks on Jules. Second extraction. The obvious difference in size and color of the marks left by my fingers during the second extraction allows me to say that most of the memories were removed the first time.

Allopathic medicine neglects and does not recognize the notion of inscription or memory. Yet everything is based on this. Once again, I want to emphasize that the medicine of the future will be informational medicine!

Our thoughts are inscribed in our cellular memory – our spirit! This inscription can be seen once more in Jules' case, because afterwards, whereas he had not had the least symptom of allergy for three months, his separation from his beloved wife led to almost similar allergic reactions which appeared almost instantly though with less intensity. Thought inscription is also found in cases of food intolerance, for example.

When the particle that forbids eating a certain fruit is removed, the patient must eat some the same day. His system must be informed that everything is now in order and that the intolerance is gone. The few clients that wait several weeks to eat the fruit reprogram the intolerance because in their subconscious mind they hear, "I can't." When they finally try to eat the fruit, the result is much less conclusive.

Florence's case, which is presented hereafter, is also quite eloquent:

In her early forties, Florence is interested in spiritual subjects and meditates regularly. When she came to see me, she had been suffering for 25 years from various allergies and intolerances.

Her digestion is poor and she is constantly constipated. Any product containing lactose causes her to have violent stomachaches that can last from three to five hours. She cannot touch plants or fruit that have fuzz on the surface. As soon as she picks up a fuzzy leaf or fruit, her hands swell and a type of hives breaks out. Thus she cannot pick strawberries or ever walk barefoot in the grass because her feet react in the same manner. It is impossible for her to eat a peach or an apricot because her hands and throat become irritated.

The worst part is probably her allergy to pollen: grasses, hay, birch, and narcissus cause particularly severe reactions. These allergens disfigure her; her eyes can remain glued shut by pus for many hours.

It has been almost three years since I treated Florence. After her first treatment in my clinic, she immediately confronted the allergens that caused the reactions. Her subconscious mind thus did not have time to re-inscribe the erroneous information about the allergy. Right after the first treatment she was able to eat dairy products; after the second she could eat what she liked and she can now touch all fuzzy-skinned fruit and leaves. She can walk barefoot anywhere she wants. While she was getting ready to go jogging through the freshly-cut fields, with grass pollen filling the air, her son begged her, in tears, not to go, saying he would not recognize her when she came home. But to his surprise, she returned without any problem at all!

Three years later, I saw her again and the results of my treatment had not changed: there is no more allergic reaction.

Though the results are spectacular, I am not a super healer and I am not the one that should get the praise! It must be understood that we are information; we trigger our pathologies according to information that is inscribed on a particle in our system. In many cases it "is enough" to remove it. The spirit world and my higher awareness guide me, and the patient's system only has to let go.

When comparing this case to that of Jules, there is a big difference: Florence regularly meditates and practices spirituality while Jules does not. Continuous meditation can indeed play a big role; the inscription of the information in our energy field is done only through thoughts relating to greed or aversion.

EPI can be applied to patients of any age, as Noah's case [https://youtu.be/NRrXwP9tRMI] illustrates:

Noah's beginning of life was hard. At the early age of five months, he was diagnosed with autism, deafness, visual impairment, etc. Moreover, his body showed signs of growth disturbance and rejected countless foods, which reflected in lactose intolerance, gluten intolerance, cereal allergy, egg protein allergy, dust mite allergy, and even various types of vegetables and meat led to complications. These circumstances made achieving a balanced and healthy diet, which is paramount at this age, very difficult.

His various allergies manifested not only in the form of very serious asthma which made the permanent use of an oxygen mask mandatory but also as an enormous generalized skin rash. It started on only one cheek, then grew to cover the entire area around the eyes and finally took over his entire body. His skin had turned so red that it almost looked as if he had suffered burns. It goes without saying that these circumstances had a strong impact on Noah's behavior. His reactions to any ordinary activities were extremely irritated: he cried and screamed as soon as his mother wanted to wash him, but also if she even wanted to simply carry or sit him down. His life amounted to a never-ending ordeal – not only during the days, but during the nights as well.

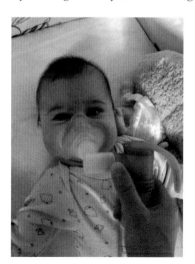 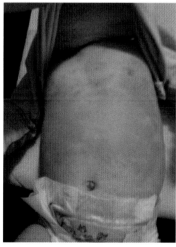

Left: Noah with an oxygen mask.
Right: Noah's skin rash at an advanced stage.

Soon, his mother had to admit that these symptoms had now become chronic and that there was no hope left for any improvement and much less for a healing, since not a single one of the many treatment options that she had desperately tried resulted in the slightest improvement. After two years without any proper sleep and after it had become clear that none of the consulted medical doctors were able to help Noah, his mother fell into a deep hole – she had reached her limit.

It was only upon an unexpected hint from her circle of acquaintances that Noah's mother decided to book an EPI treatment at my practice when he was two years old. Already after three to four weeks, a very strong general improvement had become obvious, which in turn revived his mother as well: the EPI treatments have freed Noah from his oxygen mask which he had been carrying permanently since his third month for two years without interruption, meaning day and night, due to his asthma. Today, Noah is four years old and lives – except for a slight asthma which appears during physical effort – a mostly carefree life.

Left: After the first EPI treatments: Noah's extensive generalized skin rash has strongly improved.
Right: Noah's generalized skin rash completely healed.

Noah's situation is among the rather complex treatment cases, and the achieved success has without any doubt changed his – and his mother's – life in a fundamental way. Given these circumstances it may seem incidental, but the effectiveness of the EPI healing method has become obvious in an additional way: when I had to temporarily interrupt Noah's treatment in order to attend my yearly meditation retreat, Noah suffered a relapse – the symptoms of which immediately improved again as soon as I was able to continue the treatment.

Initial clinical research study

In May and June 2017, I applied the *Extraction of Pathological Information (EPI)* healing method in a clinical research study in Neuchâtel, Switzerland. During this study which was supervised by licensed French doctor and gastroenterology specialist Dr. Jacques Fumex, 81 treatments were applied for allergic rhinitis (also known as "hay fever") and lactose and dairy intolerance (a condition for which science currently offers no treatment).

Ninety-six percent of the patients have shown either complete healing or notable improvement after the treatment, which consisted of two sessions of between ten and 20 minutes each. In most cases, however, there was already complete healing or notable improvement after the first treatment. Dr. Fumex stated:

I have noted quick and surprising results: In my domain of specialization, which is gastroenterology, I met a lot of people during this study who had been suffering long-lasting digestive problems, some of which lasted for decades, and during the study these problems were solved after two rather short treatments, sometimes even after just one treatment. [...]

The goal of medicine is to heal people. If we can achieve this in an easy, non-invasive and gentle way, without suffering any side effects, then that's all the better. I always maintain that the best treatment is the one that works. If it's as simple as herbal tea, then

that's all the better – it's cheap and without danger. Here [during this study], I have seen people who were able to quit taking their medication after one treatment.
(The video of Dr. Fumex's interview is available at: http://www.miraclescome.com/en.)

One medical doctor who was initially very actively and enthusiastically involved in this study chose to step aside later in the process, citing the study's achieved success rate of 96% and noting that this success would seem so impossible in the eyes of his medical and scientific colleagues that their only possible explanation would have to be fraud. He indeed feared to be excluded by his professional peers or to at least suffer some kind of sanctions – a fear that I regretted deeply but nevertheless had not been confronted with for the first time.

Second clinical research study

The astounding healing success rate achieved thanks to the EPI method during the first clinical study in 2017 automatically led me to the next question that needed an urgent answer: If I myself could use EPI to free so many patients from their ills and suffering, could other practitioners do so as well? Could such a soft yet powerful, such a quick yet effective technique eventually be used all over the world? The sheer thought of all the happiness, all the joy and all the bliss that would blossom all over the world thanks to such an evolution – and the thought of all both direct and indirect knock-on effects on people's lives that we usually don't even think of – encouraged me to waste no time.

The two medical doctors Dr. Christian P. Bouillaguet, and Dr. Nicole Cottier, both FMH specialists in internal medicine who practice in Switzerland, had contacted me, seeking to supervise the next study scheduled for the month of May 2018. Again based on a sample size of slightly above 80 patients and keeping all parameters from the first study equal, this second study was to gauge the success rate of the first batch of students that I had trained personally at the *fréquences* school for healing during the months leading up to this study.

Once more, the results proved highly encouraging: My first students have achieved an average success rate of 72% – again defined as "improvement or total disappearance of the symptoms" – for the two categories of hay fever allergy and lactose intolerance. This study thus proves that the EPI healing method can indeed be taught and does not depend on myself. As with the initial study, we are reminded of the fact that the EPI healing method can also be used to cure conditions and diseases for which conventional medicine is unable to offer any solution, as the repeated stellar success in eliminating lactose intolerance shows.

Dr. Nicole Cottier, when asked if the achieved success struck her as an MD, replied:

Yes, absolutely. It shows that in addition to our official and conventional Western medical treatments, other treatment methods are available – different approaches. It makes it clear that we still have a very mechanical view of the human body and that by applying the principles of energetic treatments, we can obtain different results.

The classic medical approach is to wait for the disease to manifest in the body, only to suppress its symptoms afterwards. We have antihistamines, anti-inflammatory and anti-hypertensive drugs, but these never solve the problem, they simply suppress the symptom. What sets these methods [such as EPI] apart is the fact that they act much earlier in the process – they won't try to simply suppress the symptom, but to rather address the cause itself, the root of the problem.

Conventional medicine separates the body and the mind – as the term "psychosomatic" reveals. But in reality, there is no such separation.

Conclusion

We should always keep in mind that we still know very little about the human energetic system and its functions and reactions. So far it's very obvious that we store information in our energetic system through our thoughts. It's also obvious that such information can be read and moved, and even removed if the information is of harmful nature.

The removal of harmful information works very well for a wide array of pathologies – several clinical studies and thousands of treated patients have proven that clearly, as we have shown above. I am very convinced, though, that the EPI healing method cannot change the character of a person.

I still search for medical professors and scientists who are willing to conduct new studies covering the EPI healing method. Areas of particular interest may be the impact of EPI on the aging processes or the HIV virus in humans. These are only two examples out of the many still unknown applications that the EPI healing method may prove to have. We also need to study the human DNA to see if and how it would be impacted by EPI treatments – there is still so much left to do!

But the difficulty lies not solely in finding a doctor or professor who may be interested in working in this field; it most of all lies in finding such professionals who have the courage to publish the results they generate and to speak about them publicly, including their professional colleagues and lobby.

At the very least, the incredible figures resulting from our clinical studies have helped in getting the attention of more medical doctors and some journalists. This technique is so powerful that word of mouth goes around very quickly, leading to long patient waiting lists for all of the EPI practitioners that were trained by myself.

After several thousands of treatments I can come, so far at least, to the following technical conclusions:

The more pathologies or health issues that are treated in one session, the lower the expected success rate becomes. In general, it is thus much wiser to work on one or two problems or "categories" at the same time, but this is even more true for allergies or food intolerances (an example of a "category" would be the family of citrus fruits).

After the treatment of allergies or food intolerances, blood work probing the concentration of the relevant antibodies should ideally be conducted. Such tests offer scientific proof of success and sometimes also indicate that no result or only a weak one was achieved. Blood tests are therefore mandatory especially for patients who may suffer a lethal anaphylactic shock when being confronted with a specific allergen. In these cases, a blood test signals whether the patient may proceed with the final stage of the treatment or not: The confrontation (with the allergen at issue).

Patients who proceed to experience a successful confrontation generally benefit from a stronger result because their subconscious – having itself witnessed the healing – is now much less prone to reprogramming the underlying wrong and harmful information again.

Whenever a treated patient confronting the allergen in my presence still experiences symptoms, I immediately apply an additional treatment which always results in the symptoms either disappearing or getting so weak that they are no longer experienced as a problem.

The results achieved have been accused many times to be only due to the placebo effect. The fact that not only babies and non-believing people but even animals are regularly healed of sometimes highly complex pathologies clearly proves that this accusation has no ground.

I would like to further illustrate this fact by citing the feedback received from a mother who had her baby boy of seven months treated by myself:

As far as my son Adriano is concerned, it should be mentioned that he has had a rough start in life. Due to an emergency, a Caesarean section had to be performed, which led to further complications: due to respiratory arrest, he had to be treated during five days under general anesthesia using antibiotics, morphine and endotracheal intubation, followed by an additional hospital stay of two weeks in Basel (Switzerland).

When Adriano reached the age of three months, the treating neurologist diagnosed cerebral palsy, muscular hypotonia and a general developmental delay. Thereupon, we immediately started physiotherapy; an MRI scan is scheduled for in a few weeks.

Already three days after the first treatment by Mister Jacob which took place a couple of weeks ago, Adriano started catching objects, his concentration had improved significantly. He started laughing as well as crying (which in this case is a truly positive thing!). He stopped sucking on his thumb. His facial expression has become much more relaxed.

After the second treatment, he could catch objects while lying on his back. Two days after the second treatment, we had a child development specialist conduct an assessment, and he reported back that Adriano was now catching up fast: "It is impressive."

There remains a certain delay in his development and our boy still is somewhat apathetic, which is why we continue physiotherapy, but the treating MD was optimistic. I wish to express my deepest gratitude to you and I hope to be able to be admitted to the upcoming OpenDays healing days.

Huge thanks to Mr. Jacob and his team! THANK YOU!

Emilia (Adriano's mother)

Chapter 24

Physical mediumship

Abracadabra
It seems out of nowhere
Abracadabra
Appears before my eyes
Where emptiness reigned
A feather, a bell
A man, a hand
Abracadabra
Traveling particles
Matter were
And become again
Celestial raptures
Delight my senses
What does it take
Faithless one
To shatter your doubt
To enable your reasoning
to share in this magic
If a spirit brings us
before our eyes
solid and real
thousands upon thousands
of heavenly gifts
The bread of Jesus
or just a feather at your feet
What doubt
that the Father
made the earth

Physical mediumship is one of the rarest and also one of the most astonishing forms in the field of mediumship. The fact that an occurrence can be perceived by anyone through the five senses and not just by the medium at work – as is the case with mental mediumship – is amazing.

The photographs below show spoons which Laurence Melet, a healer who lives in neighboring France, has bent during a mediumship session [www.laurencemelet.com]. After a few minutes, the spoon becomes as soft as melted butter. Not only can she then bend it, she is also able to twist it into a ring with no effort at all, nor any need for strength.

Spoons that Laurence twisted without applying any strength at all.

Trying to bend any such spoons by applying physical force would inevitably and immediately break them.

I myself have tried several times to bend a spoon; I focused and applied the energy for more than an hour each time. The result was not as conclusive as it was for Laurence. The spoon did not move; but what did happen was that my hands became swollen to the point where it looked as though I had stuck them in a beehive. On another occasion, in which I was sitting in the lotus position, my hands, which were holding the spoon, were enclosed in a luminous, bright magenta sphere. Without meaning to, I moved slightly and suddenly the hi-fi switched on full blast. I was so startled I nearly jumped through the roof. Now that is what you call levitation! This is a very clear example of a release of kinetic energy triggered only by me; it had nothing whatsoever to do with a poltergeist.

Apports and materializations

Where apports are concerned, the spiritual world explains that the materialized objects do not appear out of nowhere; they are not made out of nothing. The objects are dematerialized in one place by accelerating their particles, then transported and slowed again at the place in which they are to materialize. A very concrete example of this phenomenon occurred about ten years ago at a spiritualist church in England. Chris Denton, the medium and healer presented previously, was in the middle of a public demonstration of mediumship. A deceased person was speaking through him to a woman in the audience. Chris asked this person to come up, and between his hands a white and lilac carnation appeared, complete with stem. The lady was greatly moved, since the day before, she had brought twelve white and twelve lilac carnations to the deceased's tomb. After the demonstration, she went back to the grave and found 23 stalks and eleven flowers in each color. The spirit world had thus taken the matter it needed to thank that person.

Chris has materialized several objects in public. Unfortunately, he always feels physically ill for several days after these demonstrations. He has therefore asked that the apports cease and they have stopped.

For about ten years, in my personal practice, I have had perfumes materialize in my hands. When I am doing certain therapies, I suddenly feel a sort of tickling in one or the other of the palms of my hands. The fragrance is always sweet, often close to the smell of jasmine. The spirit world materializes this wonderful fragrance that is different each time so that the patient can smell it and thus incorporate the information it carries into their system. This is why each time the perfume varies slightly from the others.

This can happen to me twice a week and then not occur for several months. It is really up to the spirit world. I have tried to materialize these fragrances when meditating, with the greatest possible concentration, but nothing ever happens; nothing appears... When I do experience these materializations, I welcome them with humility and gratitude.

As I understand it, fragrance is used mainly in the case of emotional problems, not for physical work. This might be explained by the fact that smell is the only sense in which the mental filter is not involved: information from a smell reaches the brain in a raw state. The clients' reactions to this phenomenon are very different. Some smell the fragrance with no emotional reaction, while others are astonished and much moved. When these materializations first began, I found it difficult to deal with some people's indifference to such a miracle, but being able to distance myself from it was part of learning the detachment of letting go. Not long ago, a young woman came to my clinic for help with a headache that she had had for three months and with her stress which was due to the fact that she was unemployed. During the treatment, vague whiffs of perfume suddenly filled the room. I gave her my hand to smell and asked her if she recognized the scent. She answered that she didn't, not at all. She breathed it in carefully, several times. After that treatment, I held out my hand to the lady doctor with whom I share my clinic. The fragrance was still strong. Even after I had done some shopping at the supermarket, my assistant could still smell it during a meeting. Three days after this treatment, my client called me to tell me she felt calm and that her headache had totally disappeared! What an honor to be able to work with the Holy Spirit who is there to help us and guide us to our peace...

It is very clear that it is easier for the spirit world to materialize something if there is already a matter that they can use and transfer. We know that sometimes the fabric from a tablecloth or a curtain is used in a materialization. The production of a perfume in my hands is easier to do if the patient wears perfume, just as the white noise of clapping hands facilitates EVP in the production of sound on the tape recordings.

The spirit world does not produce new curtains. The fragrances are different from the one the patient is wearing and the white noise opens the way to words. These phenomena are produced in the form of a transfer of matter or rather an "appropriation of matter" – a minor and entirely innocent theft.

My mediumship mentor, Glyn Edwards, also frequented a trance and physical mediumship circle which met every Tuesday. For years, he drove for two hours to attend this circle's session, and two more hours to go home, every week, even if the Tuesday was Christmas Day. After years of sitting with the same group, there was a big noise and then rose petals showered down on everyone there. They were all immensely amazed and many prayers of gratitude were lifted to the spirit world. This shower of rose petals was repeated again and again, to the point where everyone was getting fed up with having to clean up every time. That is when, at the request of the group to the spirit world, the petals ceased to appear.

While on a Vipassana meditation retreat in a monastery, another friend found himself and the entire circle covered by a shower of petals when he sang the mantras between two classes.

These different materializations are part of what is called apport. An apport is when any kind of object appears suddenly. Often it may be jewelry, bells, stones or even a ball of wax like the one that materialized in a physical mediumship circle in Germany, as I will mention later.

For many mediums, the *nec plus ultra* of materialization is to be capable of producing a substance called *ectoplasm*. Ectoplasm first appears as a sort of mist, then becomes denser and turns into a gauzy-looking or bandage-like material. This is said to be the only material that is shared between the earthly realm and the spirit world. This ectoplasm is produced thanks to and with the medium's bodily matter. Ectoplasm can exit through any physical orifice such as the eyes, ears, nose and even the navel. In the entire world, only a few mediums can produce ectoplasm. David Thompson, an Englishman who lives in Australia, can do amazing things with ectoplasm. Another Englishman, Stewart Alexander, has traveled all over the globe to present these extraordinary phenomena. Bill Meadows is a physical medium who stands out from the rest in terms of ability; I will be discussing the phenomena he has generated in greater detail further on.

To date, with 300 available television channels that program what is often debilitating entertainment and promote a way of life in which everything must go faster and faster, there are not enough mediums who take the time to sit down to train in and practice physical mediumship. Moreover, in the physical mediumship groups, the other participants are simply and humbly there to provide the medium with the energy needed for his work. Creating a physical mediumship group implies finding people whose ego is sufficiently silent and who have personalities that are capable of making themselves available. Rooting out such people is not an easy task. In addition, generating materializations takes ten, 15 or even 20 years of work; it requires a great deal of exercise and energy, which can be reassuring for the audience.

In memory of two Swiss mediums who were influential in the field of parapsychology

In this chapter, I would like to pay homage to two people in the human world who have left their mark on the field of parapsychology, not only in Switzerland, but also internationally: Professor Alex Schneider and Lucius Werthmüller.

Professor Alex Schneider

Physicist and professor, Alex Schneider passed away in 2012, and this was a great loss for the parapsychology movement. Born in 1927, he was a man of great dignity. After completing his studies in the field of high-frequency technology and after having worked in industry, he devoted himself enormously to parapsychological phenomena at the international level. He was *the* influential person of the second half of the 20th century in his field. He was among the organizers of the "Psi Days" in Basel and also chaired many parapsychological associations. His work consisted in empirically examining the phenomena he met, notably going deeper into his study by observing Filipino healers. The latter were studied carefully, including the evaluation of all the possibilities for cheating.

Professor Alex Schneider

Professor Schneider has frequently proved he is not dead. His wife Christina often receives hearts or heart shapes when she is outdoors. In 2014, on their wedding anniversary, she kissed the photo of her husband, which is in the kitchen. When she got back to the living room, she picked up a folder and at the same time, another folder which she had not even touched flew off of the shelf and out fell some old photos of their wedding invitation, which Christina had completely forgotten! You can certainly imagine the widow's joy at realizing her dear husband was so near on that happy occasion!

Lucius Werthmüller

Lucius Werthmüller is a fervent advocate for new approaches and discoveries both in medicine and in psychology. He is one of the living and I would like to salute him.

Lucius is the president of the *BPV* – *Basler Psi-Verein* (Basel parapsychology association), where he works with his partner Sabine. He invites lecturers from all over the world and his magazine, *Psi-Info*, is full of articles and announcements about seminars and conferences. True to his activism in combating social inequality, Lucius offers several pages of free treatments in the first pages of his magazine for those seeking help.

Over 30 years ago, when he was a journalist, Lucius was able to film the Psi Days in Basel thanks to his press card. To his great surprise, he was able to see the work of the Filipino healer David Oligane, who incised bodies and even cut medical dressings at a distance with a simple movement of his hands. Lucius was also lucky enough to be able to watch Brazilian gynecologist Edson de Queiroz. Edson operated on patients while in a deep trance, with no sterile instruments, anesthesia or hemostatic powders and without having to ask what the patients were suffering from. His operations were highly successful. It is easy to understand how Lucius became so passionate about this field of research. He has since become a major reference within the parapsychological movement in German-speaking Switzerland. Later, the healer William Nonog showed Lucius, in slow motion, how his clean, exposed hands made incisions in one body after another, with a little bleeding but without leaving the slightest scar after the harmful tissues had been removed from the body. Nonog even accepted to make an incision in a body, place a cotton ball in it, close the wound and reopen it to extract the cotton. I realize this sounds absurd but when we consider that a female student of mine – a very gifted one, of course – can twist a metal spoon into a loop with less than one hour's training, the fact that our mind dominates our body becomes self-evident. Accessing the particles in a metal or in bodily tissues cannot be that different, just as my spirit knew how to teach my cells to refrain from drinking and eating and receive their nourishment solely from Prana, the universal energy.

During his career, Lucius has been present in over 300 physical mediumship circles in ten different groups. He granted me the honor of sharing what happened to him at two of these sittings, in this book.

On the first evening, the session had begun with an opening prayer. The main event of the evening was the apport of a newspaper clipping of an article which had been published in 1955 and had made the front page with a story about a haunted house. Earlier in the same day, one of the participants had discussed the facts related in this article with a member of the *Institut für Grenzgebiete der Psychologie und Psychohygiene (IGPP)*, an institute in Freiburg, Germany, dedicated to research in parapsychology! The spirit world had thus been present during this conversation and brought the proof to this circle.

During the first two hours of another evening in the same circle in which Lucius was present, all the participants had to be very patient because not much happened. Finally, the participants' seating order was changed and immediately the table rose completely off the floor. They all had their hands on the table again when there was a noise, as if something had fallen. Lucius felt a slight touch on the back of his hand and realized that a half-sphere had materialized in his palm. Given the texture and the consistency, he thought it was a chestnut. But to his surprise, it turned out to be a ball of wax. Inside, there was something metallic – a thimble. After a moment's hesitation, Lucius carefully scratched it and removed a note from the paraffin-filled thimble. This note had been "sent" by Albert Hofmann, the Swiss scientist who invented LSD. Albert and Lucius had been good friends until Albert died at over 100 years of age. The message in the rolled piece of paper said:

Lucius schau diese wundervolle Natur, Sie lebt. Ich lebe Albert (Lucius look at this magnificent nature, it's alive. I'm alive Albert)

It was signed "Albert" with the same signature he used when he was 100 years old.

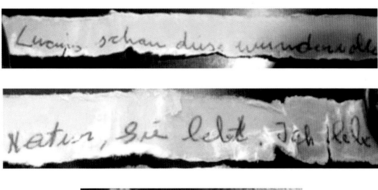

Albert Hofmann

Lucius Werthmüller and the ball of wax

Stanley Krippner, the psychologist, parapsychologist and professor lecturing at the Saybrook University in California, who was one of Albert's friends, confirmed that the writing on the note was the same as in the letters he had received from Albert Hofmann.

There are a great many cases that are just as spectacular dating from the 18th or 19th centuries, but it is very difficult to verify their authenticity. Fortunately the phenomenon relating to Albert Hofmann took place in modern times! I wonder at the lack of political desire to confirm that life does continue after death in the most concrete manner possible. Once again, the question arises: Why is the subject of life after death confined to religion, when it is possible for science to validate the irrefutable proof?

I myself had a lovely meeting with Albert when he was still alive, at a demonstration by Uri Geller, who is well-known for his ability to twist spoons.

When I met Albert, we were both examining a radish sprout that Uri had caused to grow in his hand in about two minutes by transferring energy to it. One of the seeds had sprouted and we all saw it grow in fast forward motion! To our great surprise, a woman who was also watching this happen suddenly took the four-centimeter sprout and ate it right before our eyes. She had been overcome by her greed. She explained that she needed the energy that sprout must have contained too badly to be able to refrain herself...

Helen Duncan

Helen Duncan

When speaking of physical mediumship, it is impossible not to mention Helen Duncan and Winston Churchill.

Helen Duncan was the most famous physical medium of the first half of the 20th century. She was reputed for her ability to produce ectoplasm, but above all she was known for having been the last woman condemned under the "Witchcraft Act". Her condemnation was due to a session in which a sailor materialized. The sailor's mother was in the audience who had come to watch the mediumship demonstration that Helen was giving that evening and was extremely shocked by this apparition as she had believed her son to be alive and serving in the Royal Navy on the submarine HMS Barham. Another spectator who was watching was also in the Navy. He immediately called his superiors to ask why this young man's family had not been informed of his death. This led to Helen Duncan's accusation: the loss of the submarine was still classified "top secret" in November 1941! For Helen Duncan, the horror was only beginning. The British government immediately detained her – officially for fraud – on the grounds of an old law dating back to 1735: the archaic "Witchcraft Act". Helen Duncan was thrown into prison because the government was afraid she would discover other secrets and reveal them to the enemy. Some newspapers were calling it, "the trial of the century"! It was only nine months later that Winston Churchill learned of the details surrounding Helen's arrest and that he immediately ordered her release. This is one of the most documented cases of physical mediumship due to the newspaper coverage and to Winston Churchill's personal intervention! In the case files, there is even a letter from Churchill in which he requests the secretary in charge of the case to release Helen.

Maurice Barbanell, the journalist and author presented in the chapter on "trance", was a spectator at many of Helen's sessions. His accounts are truly fascinating! He witnessed meters of ectoplasm come out of Helen Duncan's mouth and take on various shapes, such as lighted globes that filled the room and disappeared through the floor. One scientist, Harry Price, spread the lie that she swallowed bandage gauzes and then vomited them during the sessions. But Mr. Barbanell had touched the ectoplasm emitted by the medium on several occasions and each time he had found it to be hard and dry, which would certainly not be the case for vomit.

Even today there is still a great deal of controversy about Helen's death. The official version is that she died of a heart attack. The nonofficial version claims she died after the police raided her house: the surprise caused by the arrival of the police made the ectoplasm rush back into her body. The shock of it killed her; in other words, her body could not tolerate this brutal return of the ectoplasm and she died a few weeks later. Even today, you can still find old texts that denigrate Helen Duncan and accuse her of fraud, despite all the official proof that has been provided.

Bill Meadows

A few years ago, Margaret, who is an English healer, and I were invited by physical medium Bill Meadows to his home in England. I was invited because I am the director of *fréquences*. Bill is a small, frail, gray-haired, elderly gentleman who is humble and kind – a very nice person.

Bill Meadows

After a cup of tea as is the custom in the land of Lipton, Margaret and I were invited upstairs to a room and asked to examine it before the session in order to exclude any potential fraud. The room was about six meters by four. In one corner, there was a large wooden armchair. In front of it a curtain which – when closed – was used to contain the energy built up by the medium during his collaboration with the spirit world, like in any cabinet intended for this use. Just next to this was a bookcase in solid wood that was 1 meter wide by 1.2 meters high. Opposite the wooden chair, five straight chairs were placed in a semicircle: one for Bill's wife, one for his assistant, one for another guest, one for Margaret and one for me.

Aside from the previously-mentioned furniture, the room was completely empty and there was no hiding place anywhere. On the top shelf of the bookcase there was a trumpet and a 20 by 30 centimeter piece of cardboard with two phosphorescent strips on it. The trumpet was a light metal or cardboard cone, open at both ends, with a strip of phosphorescent tape on the bottom opening, as shown in the corresponding picture below. The phosphorescent strips on Bill's equipment had just been changed.

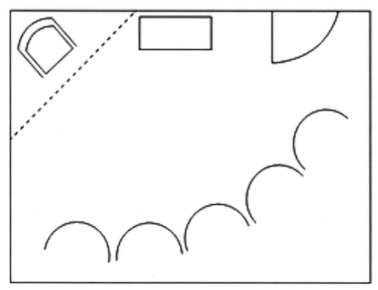

Layout of the room

Example of a cabinet used to contain the energy produced by the medium.

Trumpets

When the room and equipment had been inspected we invited the others to come upstairs and told them the equipment and the room showed no sign of any attempted fraud. Bill sat down in his chair and I personally tied his arms to the armrests and his ankles to the chair legs. The Velcro strips I was using to tie Bill with made a loud and clearly-audible sound. I also tried to take off his wedding band since some mediums do not tolerate contact with metal during a session. Though Bill's hand was thin, I could not take off his ring. He assured me it would not cause any problems.

With the curtains and shutters drawn, it was dark in the room as is customary during physical mediumship sessions. Indeed, it is believed that light hinders the construction of the ectoplasm, which is the only substance that is shared between the spirit world and the earthly one. Ectoplasm looks white and sticky but when touched it is generally dry. The strips on the cardboard and trumpet were new and both objects were so luminous that they lit the room from one end to the other like a dimly-lit lamp. Thus the room was not totally dark. We then sang loudly for a little while though we were certainly off key. The sound produced by our songs, by singing in general or by music generates energy that can be used by the spirit world.

Suddenly we heard a man's voice begin to speak to us very loudly "live". The live voice came from outside the medium, somewhere in the room. This phenomenon is believed possible because the spirit world seems to create a voice box out of ectoplasm. It introduced itself as Father James, Bill's main guide. He was to guide us throughout the evening. As I was a foreign guest who had come expressly to attend the physical mediumship session, he welcomed me specifically. James knew I was the director of the *fréquences* school and congratulated me on my work. He announced that the spirit world would enable the trumpets and cardboard to dance. James asked us especially not to get up or move too much so we would not be hit by the flying objects and get hurt. Everything began, and the physical mediumship session was underway! The trumpet, which we could see all of, began to swoop wildly around the room to the left and right and back again. Its totally erratic movements could not have been due to swinging from a string. These movements continued again and again. No one dared get up; everybody was impressed and stayed obediently seated in their chairs. The curtain in front of the cabinet in which Bill was sitting did not move. As the evening went on, our eyes became better adjusted to the soft light and we had no doubts about what was happening in the room. The trumpet then set itself down and it was the cardboard's turn to dance. "Turn" is a good word because the board was spinning up and down the curtain! Even if there had been someone behind the curtain, it would not have been possible to make it twirl that way, especially through a curtain! It was incredible!

After the cardboard had spun up and down the curtain, James told me that he would be pleased to shake my hand. "Of course!" I replied, without knowing what to expect. Suddenly, the lower part of the curtain began to rise and a stick about two meters long with a fully materialized hand on one end began to reach out toward me!!! It got closer and closer to me. Just as I was going to shake it I saw it was a big man's hand, nothing like Bill's thin one! This hand held mine firmly and the voice – which came from just above my head – thanked me again for all the work I do at my school and all the heart I put into my career as a medium and healer, while assuring me that the spirit world was proud of it. He thanked me for everything that I do in the field of mediumship and healing. Then the stick moved to each participant, and everyone shook hands with it and was spoken to personally. It was such an incredible moment and one that might cause skepticism, but for having experienced it personally I can confirm that it was absolutely exact and true! And that is not all! The stick drew back slowly and we all saw the hand disappear beneath the curtain. Then, it was not – it was no longer – James' voice that we heard, but that of a little girl about six years old whose name was Mary. She was a happy, laughing little girl. She made us laugh, which was certainly to help us produce more energy. She told us that she would like to come see all five of us. "Yes, yes, come, little one!" The curtain went partially up again and we were invited in turn to come closer and touch her head through it. When I touched her, I felt a little girl's head in my hands, and clearly felt her two braids rolled into buns. This materialization, however, was "incomplete": the head was still hard as wood and not soft like James' hand. However, the shape of the head was complete and refined. Even today I can barely find the words to describe the miracles that the spirit world calls "natural phenomena". Since I personally witnessed these events, and many others I no longer have any doubts about Jesus' resurrection, for example.

Little Mary then went away and dissolved behind the curtain where Bill was still seated. We never heard a sound from Bill, nothing that indicated he might be removing the Velcro, nothing. Suddenly there was a tremendous noise in that little room and the bookcase jumped into the middle of the floor, but yet again without the slightest movement of the curtain... or... of... anyone... at... all. Father James then spoke again to say that the session was over. He wished me a *"safe trip back to Switzerland"*. The light was immediately switched on: there was no wooden ball in the room, no two-meter stick – just that bookcase right in the middle. It only took Bill a few minutes to come back to normal. He did not remember anything. He was still wearing his ring and was happy for us. And so were we!

Chapter 25

Jonathan

Jonathan is my guide in philosophical speaking. He often addresses the students during or after meditation and Therapeutic Touch retreats, but also in class at *fréquences*. Usually, the students can ask questions and he will answer, as long as the questions are of general interest. Below I have gathered the most pertinent and most meaningful extracts to show Jonathan's approach when speaking with the students and to share the most touching messages that we have received through him. The reader will understand that these are transcriptions of actual speech and thus do not necessarily respect the standard forms used when writing.

Who are you?

I am with you as Jonathan. The word "I" is not the right word, because I represent a group, so "we" would be more appropriate, wouldn't it? If I were to say, for example, that I was Mahatma Gandhi, your medium would not be able to live with the pressure of that person's fame. If I said I was just a factory worker the students who ask questions wouldn't take our messages seriously. The messages come from a group and not from one person. I, Jonathan, don't have a universal conscience. In each group of guides there are beings that are more or less advanced, more or less knowledgeable; the important thing is to be able to make the energetic connection with our medium.

Doesn't a bee find the pistil? Like bees, we guides find our channel, or in other words, each person. Once and for all, the spirit world is all around you daily; the spirit world surrounds you every second of your life, even if it doesn't intervene in every second of your life. Stop doubting.

How could there be functional collaboration between the two kingdoms – the world of matter and the spirit world – between these two planes if there were no heavenly plan behind it? Not accepting this truth means giving in to suspicion, doubt, and fear. These are feelings that come from lower spheres that can hinder believing and the transparency between the material dimension and the spiritual one.

We speak of two dimensions because that's something that is easy to understand. But in fact there aren't two dimensions. There are different matters, there are different energies and layers, but it's still one world! We understand human worry, human doubt, because we understand their causes. We know how these doubts are born and where these sparks come from, these particles that have been left along the spiritual path that has already been covered. Only the heart that opens up; only the spirit that dares to face the difficulties; only the spirit that dares to go beyond its limits can allow the door to be opened to that spiritual dimension that is more subtle than yours. When the suffering becomes too strong to bear the matter, giving in to the perspective of a spiritual world can ease your pain. Look at your lives – isn't it when you have had problems that you've begged the Great Spirit the most?

What is trance?

Trance is one way the spirit world expresses itself. If the spirit world can control the medium's mind, we can communicate. Trance is the most direct way we have of speaking at the earthly level, especially in the category of mental mediumship. For communication to be possible and thus for us to be able to take control of our medium, it essentially depends on his vibrational frequency.

With regard to the spiritual guides invoked during healing, for example, is our guardian angel one of them?

Yes, he can indeed appear. But you must understand that your guardian angel's role is above all to accompany your spirit. He was there before you were born and he will be there after you die. You have to remember that your guardian angel isn't there to operate on an eye or do any technical things during healing. For these particular operations, there are specialists in your energy fields, according to your occupations. One thing may disappoint some of you: the most important guide in your spiritual team is your higher conscience. It can take on different forms, so as to go beyond your intellect, encourage your confidence and, especially, communicate clear messages that your entire being needs to hear.

This higher conscience can be more enlightened in order to be seen and understood by you and be the most important guide. The incarnated being very quickly forgets that he is conscience and that all knowledge lives within him. Of course, not all knowledge is in you. If we take the medical field, for example, that knowledge is not innate; it's an intellectual knowledge or a manual way of moving certain particles. But at the level of the knowledge of the conscience, that of the true conscience which is your nature, this higher conscience has access to this knowledge and is one of your most important guides. You yourself are the part that you ignore, that part that is so difficult to reach. It's very important to understand that your higher conscience contains knowledge and its true nature is omniscient; it may need a guide to generate the energy for a specific treatment or operation. This guide may perhaps have knowledge that is considerably inferior to your higher conscience, but which can be extremely useful to you. You can have people in your team who are there just to be a wall, to protect you during a public mediumship demonstration or a private sitting. These guides will surround your workspace with their love and their energy. But these particular people, these particular energies, won't necessarily have a high level of knowledge and that knowledge is never called upon. What is organized by the superior hierarchies is, precisely, that energy assistance.

Your higher conscience is almost equal to God. Incredible, isn't it? People on this earth are not aware of their divine spark, because it's hard to believe you are God! Every being is God; every being has that divine spark. Only, it takes a lot of work and a lot of lives or time to get to that understanding or that awakening, to be able to access that spark, and this is what spiritual development is about. The only thing that is real is the movement. From our perspective, everything is in the now. Time is relative.

You also have dear ones who sometimes play the role of guides, helpers, assistants, very often with respect to emotional subjects. When people are going through a hard time, when their energy is low, when their courage fails them or when they need love, it is often their nearest and dearest who are the best energies to help them climb out of their depression.

You have to understand that there are beings at various celestial levels, with various uses in different areas of service. The heavenly hierarchy is organized like the earthly one. This is why some beings that accompany you change and others will stay for years or even much longer, depending on your activities, on your evolution on the path. For example, I, Jonathan, am the being in our group that is able to best connect with our vessel, our medium. I can modestly say that I have a certain amount of knowledge, but I am still a messenger. In our group of beings there are guides that are much more knowledgeable than I. In my last life on this earth, I was listened to for my advice, but that isn't important. It is important for you to understand the mechanisms of how the link between the spiritual world and a medium is woven. Opening up the heart in the context of the guides allows you to establish a real rapport with them. A lot of people talk to their guides but this takes place in their heads; there is no relationship between the souls. It's simply an intellectual debate, so the link you will have with your guides can never reach the level of intensity it could reach if you open up your heart! If there were heart-to-heart communication!

Stay confident. At no time in your existence, on any plane, are you alone; you will never be alone. You will always be accepted by that Love and that Compassion because Love exists on all of the planes!

Is spiritual healing always beneficial?

When you provide spiritual healing, it is always beneficial! Always! There is always energy and information that gets to the patient. What he does with it is not your responsibility.

Is mediumship part of our spiritual development?

It is important to understand the difference between mediumship and spiritual development. Mediumship in itself is not spiritual, no matter what the discipline you choose. It's the accurate use of mediumship that can be spiritual. Each of us develops spiritually at his own pace. It's dangerous to compare ourselves. What we need to look at is the goal you've set. Comparing and judging, for example, trance and inspired writing or healing and mental mediumship is harmful. You are all such different beings and yet you are so much alike. One being cannot be identical to another. We have lived many previous lives, in other places and other times. It's doesn't make any sense to compare oneself to others. Isn't it great to be human? All mistakes are forgiven!

Humans come to this planet to have experiences. It's the struggle and the challenges that forge you, not lazing in a hammock in the sun! The more challenges you encounter, the more mistakes you make. These mistakes are your teachers because they are what make you progress.

Can you give us a key to detachment?

Before being able to define detachment, we have to define love. Love that includes an attachment is not love. Love is a feeling that has no attachment, no personal benefit of any sort. It's more like compassion. Amorous love is purely egotistic. It was created to preserve the species. The benefit of falling in love has nothing to do with divine love. Falling in love is a mental and chemical process. It isn't the same thing as being in the Divine, detached from what we want. Imagine that you are in love: "This is my dream partner!" When you were young, perhaps you met a person that had a special effect on you. So you choose a person who has an identical vibration. It's a matter of inscription, of the information inscribed in your energy particles. You love your spouses as long as they act according to your wishes. Just as a father loves his son until the latter announces he doesn't want to take over the shoe factory! If you are in love you are attached to all the things you love and your lower energies have a lot of trouble getting rid of them. This attraction may come from people you knew in previous lives and who have magnificent vibrations. It's a fact that we have already met many people, in both positive and negative contexts. True love, unconditional and unceasing, is eternal. The souls that find each other without creating ties, who love each other in a disinterested way, will go a long way together. It is always love that saves and heals, because love is detachment and since it is detached, it is eternal. Living in a difficult relationship and loving despite it all allows us to progress.

You consider falling in love to be egotistic, but then what is the reason for the couple, outside of reproduction?

How many hours have you got for me to answer? (Laughter) You already have to make the difference between what is instinct and human nature, which is precisely driven and carried by these instincts, which are very ancient. The survival instinct and the reproductive instinct are the guarantee of the preservation of the species. Every being on earth has them. If we set this aside, we again come to the discussion on interested or disinterested love, with regard to your inscriptions. You live in a rather gregarious culture. Contrary to other animals, humans are generally group-oriented. Inside these groups, there are different behaviors and different consciences, the higher consciences meet for other motivations than interested ones. Everything we call "falling in love" is an interest. Everything that is shared by the heart is disinterested. Love, when tested, is the most difficult, but it is in this difficulty that it is the strongest. It is in these situations that the higher consciences can truly experience love. Where there are interests, or ego, solving issues and settling situations becomes harder. This is of course nothing new; everyone can clearly see it even with their eyes closed. The couple's interests are highly varied. Because the couple that enjoys, outside of any financial or economic logic on which we must not dwell further, true sharing of pain and joy, complicity – this is a magnificent and encouraging thing. This type of sharing can be very rewarding because basically we are not meant to be alone in this state of consciousness of the average human. There are of course a few beings who have no more attachments and who only have one focus: reaching enlightenment and spiritual completeness. But except for this small group of people, everyone else needs to share, to receive love, but also to give it. Those who give to get something back do not do so out of love but out of personal interest. We cannot say what the couple's interest is, because there isn't any definition. But in any case, it's a magnificent way to learn how to love without expectations. This does not mean we can judge couples who separate. It just means that sometimes, we are sorry to see the reasons behind their separation. Many couples who split up do so primarily due to a lack of communication and also a lack of mutual understanding. Human beings are only able to hear what they know and understand. What they don't know is difficult to hear or at least to integrate. There is no celestial judgment with respect to separation. Separation can be beneficial depending on the couple's problems or if there is abuse, or if one of the partners develops respect for himself and gets out of a situation that has a negative effect on his spiritual development and the joy he feels in living. So it is not possible to define the reason for forming a couple, except that of sharing love and tasks.

How do you follow your soul and manage the conflict between the higher and lower conscience?

The struggle between the higher and lower conscience can only be resolved through detachment. The soul has no difficulty distancing itself from this conflict. It never left God because it is equal to God and will therefore always follow its path, and you will have no other choice but to follow it because it is in you. For the spirit the combat is tougher. Sometimes illness is the best solution for the person at that particular time. Even with chronic illness, a being grows. Some illnesses cannot be healed, but the people who suffer from them – for example those who are born with a mental disorder or physical disability – often have a rather advanced level of conscious awareness.

You choose what you want to learn before you incarnate, but you don't know how you will process it. Each path leads to the Light, even if it is difficult to see and even if some people seem to behave very badly.

You understand that pain can be beneficial in some cases and that suffering can allow us to open the door behind which is the Light. For this reason, suffering must be seen from another angle and in a different way. Suffering is the trigger for big steps and significant learning experiences. It is the soil in which humans grow.

When you are feeling euphoric; when everything is going like you want it to; when the world is turning the way you like it you don't make a lot of efforts because everything is running smoothly – you have it all! Understanding the logic and usefulness of difficulty allows you to overcome suffering in a different way.

Don't lose your Faith, grow it!

We would like to talk about attachment. To become attached to something, you have to know it; you have to know the thing. It may be a person, an object, a feeling, a condition, a model, a belief or an illness. When humans know something well, in general they become attached to it. Just as it is interesting to observe that people not only become attached to things they like, which seems logical, but sometimes we do not understand how people become attached to things they dislike. Take, for example, some people who are afflicted with a chronic illness, and who complain all day about their pains and their problems. When they are offered the means of relieving it, they refuse. They need to hang on to what they know. If we come back to attachment and the reason for it, it's because we are afraid of losing something. When we come back to illness, it's the same thing. Some people are afraid of losing it because it is a big part of their identity. That is why some pathology is so hard to treat. Because in the end, it's just a matter of information and particles. The information changes and the particles vibrate, so it's actually child's play to move them. You move particles and energies in each energy treatment. Old models, or even false beliefs, are so firmly anchored that they are part of that identity, that image you have of yourself and which you cannot give up. Human beings have a need to hang on to things. We suggest you look at your being in a slightly different way. We are going to come back to Buddhist philosophies: it's about realizing that the being, even if he appears to be solid, really isn't. You are a large quantity of very small bubbles that vibrate and move. So it is absolutely logical and clear that, since it is only a release, there is no issue with piercing, separating and distancing. But because your thought is your strongest tool, the particles cannot be moved if your beliefs do not allow it. For those who are suffering from lack of confidence, physical problems and especially long-term issues, it's a question of trying to look at them as a vibrating mass, like a ball filled with smaller balls and these smaller balls are filled with even smaller ones, and so on to infinity. These little balls can be separated by just a breath. It even seems to us that there are shamanic techniques allowing the issue to be simply blown away with a breath. One breath is actually enough to heal. But the mind could not accept that a breath can heal. By agreeing to look at yourself from that angle, try to breathe into your hurts and into your lack of confidence. We have already said many times that each of your thoughts is inscribed. In fact each thought separates at its birth. Half of the thought exits and the other half enters; that's all. All of the thoughts make up the collective conscience. Collective conscience is the average of all the thoughts that come from beings. Since the other half of these thoughts enters, you are therefore the average of all your thoughts. That is why positive thinking and prayer are so powerful. The heavenly beings around you have many powers and consciences that will support you. But without your participation, your agreement and your positive thoughts, it is extremely hard for any outside conscience to change anything. We have to have your agreement and your help. It would not be fair, and would even be forbidden at a divine level, to do anything against your will. If all of your thoughts, if your way of thinking is not in agreement with what we are trying to do for you, we have no right to do it, because free will is the main rule on this planet. So we need your energy and your cooperation. To get back to the subject of illness, we cannot take away an illness if you do not agree from your heart that it should go. We are not talking about your mind because in mental reasoning everyone wants to get rid of an illness that is burdening him. Fill yourself with beautiful things, beautiful thoughts, accept compliments. Plant them well inside your being because they will bear fruit, just as a seed does when you plant it. Every seed sprouts. So even if intellectually you don't believe it at the moment, give that positive thought a chance to sprout. Repeat the positive phrases about your life and your being and your being will change. We promise you that.

Obviously we are aware that here we are speaking to people who are already interested in spirituality, so it is easy to approach you and teach you. Please understand that from our point of view, when we are faced with someone who is not interested in improving him or herself, who is not attracted by spirituality or by service at all, that person is difficult to influence in order to be guided on the right path. That is why questions like, "How can he do that? How can God allow that?" are justified, but they are incorrect in their formulation because an ignorant being is presumed ignorant. It is this ignorance that changes with learning and experience. We are all ignorant, but each in his own domain and subjects. Ignorance is the basis for evolution. It is through ignorance that we free ourselves. It's by experiencing the ignorance of our brothers and discovering the abuses that take place that we are able to understand that we ourselves will not carry out the same abuses that we have read about or witnessed. You see how one thing leads to the next.

It must be understood that everyone, absolutely everyone, will free themselves from this ignorance! Each one in his own time and at his own pace and on his own personal path.

We would like to expand a little on the subject of personal paths. We already mentioned the individual a while ago. What part of you is individual? Are you individuals or are you one? The hard thing is to understand that you are individuals, and you are also one and unique. Individuals and all one, at the same time! Imagine the rain falling; imagine the drops. The drops that fall and bounce for an instant before becoming lost on the ground. Are they individuals or are they one?

Nevertheless, there is already a lot of unawareness about yourselves, the aspect that you have, the individual that you are. There is a tremendous amount of unawareness about the All! So this ignorance occurs at two levels. It's intentional; it's normal; it's a matter of evolution. It's enough for now to know and especially to feel that you belong to the same source. This is why the arguments between you humans make us "smile", because you are simply fighting yourselves! The first steps to awareness are working on yourselves and increasing your vibratory rate, in order to perceive more things inside yourselves and only after that outside and in the celestial kingdoms!

Your essence is the same and this individuality is only part of your conscious, and outside of your essence, your individuality is ephemeral. Immediately, some people are going to fear they will not exist anymore. The mistake lies in that fear, because you continue to exist. But your individual aspects will slowly fade, because the only thing that is eternal is the Essence, the Essence filled with Conscience. You will have that Conscience; you will be that Conscience! You already are, but you just can't quite access it. If you could access it, this would be what is called Enlightenment. It's simply that Enlightenment doesn't just happen with a "bang"! Enlightenment is a process, it is work and it requires going through different stages, but it's all part of Enlightenment. Anyone can reach Enlightenment! Everyone! In due time, you cannot fail to reach Enlightenment one day!

Dearest seekers and students, we shall now retire. And if you should forget everything we have said, remember at least this: you are eternal lights and we love you unconditionally.

And if you occasionally lose sight of this Light, know that it will never leave you, because it shines within you.

Are we neglecting any tools needed to reach a high level of spirituality?

In order to reach a high level of spirituality, we invite you to imagine a child at play – no child is incapable of playing! When humans grow up, they stop playing. Many of you stop playing games purely out of love, joy, fantasy and imagination! Why do children talk to their dolls? Why do they engage in role play with bits of wood or rocks? Where does all of that come from? A child has a tremendous natural conscience which is not inhibited or camouflaged by mental aspects; one which is not lost in that fog. Most children perceive the spiritual world. They can see it. We can move; they smile at us and we can feel their smiles. They let themselves be inspired. It is their natural joy that is in all of you! And when you are encouraged to play, you are afraid of looking ridiculous! Yet it is a door, a big door! Play is one of the best doorways to spiritual development! Art is a magnificent way of rising into the vibrations and coming into contact with the sources of the Universe. Play and art. Free time in which you are just yourself, without having to rush. This is a door – a door which works, a door that swings open at the slightest touch on the handle with one finger. Play is light; joy is light – these are energies that carry you and transport you. They are energies that bring you to yourself! It is all well and good to be serious when you work, when you serve, when you give of yourself, but the approach is a game. Try playing! You will gain from it; you can only gain from it!

The reason for all of these efforts is to leave ignorance behind. God, if you like, is a perpetual movement that self-generates; it creates itself. It is a circuit between two polarities – ignorance and awareness – that is constantly in movement and you are a part of that movement. You are all in there; that is why it is worth all the effort; that is why one day, you will all dissolve in the Great Spirit.

You need to understand that there is no regression on the path to the Light. You have different aspects: one aspect of yourself can be very aware, while another wants to experiment, to discover new things and darker energies. The goal is always the same: to rise higher. The same aspect of you does not regress; but aspects of the Whole can be at very different levels!

The ego in all of this – there are many elements to assemble: the soul, the mind. How do you find the way and recognize that which guides us on the right path?

A body has a mind or a soul from birth. Ego is part of what you call mind. Ego is there to define the mind's identity, the need for identity. This is the simplest explanation. Someone who clearly knows what he wants, that the things he wants are happening in the way he wants, has built his own identity in a very strong and even stiff way. The ego can be imagined as a stone tower in the middle of your being. This tower has been built by your reasoning, but also by your fears – the fears of no longer existing, because this existence is defined by the way things happen according to your desires, your greed, and your aversions. As soon as the tower starts losing stones, your ego has to defend itself and immediately re-plaster the stones that have fallen from your walls. You have a mind and you believe it is something that is stable and fixed. "I"; the words "I" and "me", are rock solid. You think that the tower whose shape you forged is something that is stable and unchanging. Therefore, as soon as events remove a stone here and a stone there, you become afraid that the tower will weaken and fall. This is why your ego shows itself, because it does not want to disappear. As if you were in a castle and someone was trying to steal the stones from your wall, you are immediately going to shoot arrows to defend your ramparts. That is how it is; that is simply how it is. Everything is created by the illusion that it must be as you have imagined it, that you are right or you are wrong. You built it that way, always with the illusion that is eternal.

Ego can be defined by the term "identity" or "need for identity." In the mind, there is not only the ego. To follow a certain path, a specific identity is required. It's a question of relation and also of knowing what is ephemeral and changing and accepting that is not going to take your identity away. The first step is to understand that your identity has the right to change. That is the first step to peace. You can always have a tower for your safety, but accept that it will change. This is the first step in the direction of inner peace. But don't forget that intellect is just as important. It is there to discriminate, sort, and make choices. It is just as important, beneficial or harmful as that part of the identity. In the pure sense of explaining a being, higher consciousness would be outside the mind. Outside the mind, as what is mind is ephemeral. What is not ephemeral is part of your essence. We have told you: that which is essence, your essence, can never be destroyed by any act, by any harmful thought, or by any material thing. Nothing that exists on this planet is able to destroy your essence. Your higher conscience in its pure state is part of the essence and not of the mind.

Do we become a medium or a healer of our own choice or is it the guides who tell us to do so?

Choosing to be a medium or a healer... There are reasons for wanting to become a medium and also many reasons to become a healer. We can make these choices based on a desire for power, or a desire to dominate, or to be someone special, out of pure ego for our identity. Or we can make this choice with our conscience, because we understand the need for service around us and have a deep and sincere desire to serve. So there isn't any specific rule. However, there are unfortunately a lot of people who join this profession in order to dominate, even if the decision to join this profession in order to dominate is not a rational one. But the fears that are hiding in the cellar of the tower of Ego lead these people to choose a path in which they have the impression they have increased their power. Thus you will recognize them – not right away, but when you look at the light that is given off by these different beings and observe their actions, you will see who is there to serve and who is there to get rich, or who is there to hide their fears. A guide can encourage a person whose essence seeks to serve to get into it, but he cannot force her, just like he cannot prevent someone who's not cut out for this work from doing it. At the same time, if a guide were to work only with an enlightened being, he would be unemployed.

On a life path, it is not important for everyone to be a medium or a healer. There are incarnations that are not attracted by this, because it is not required as part of the steps in these people's learning processes. These people are not considered as inferior beings simply because they have not developed their clear-senses. It's important to understand and assimilate this. We have given the example of the horse that was not thirsty, so with these people, it's enough to show them the water and when they are thirsty they will go and drink. If their higher conscience knows there is no need to develop their clear-senses, it will not bring these horses to the water. These beings will do what they have come to do. It is important to understand these things and very good for some arrogant people, very good for some mediums who think they are something special because they were born a little more sensitive than the others. As if a musician was vain because he was born with a bit more musical talent than the rest of humanity. So what? It's not important. A person can be extremely Cartesian but also highly developed. He may not have any particular perception but neither will he have ever killed a fly; he will not eat meat because he sees that the animals are mistreated, and so on. You will see many profoundly good actions coming from very Cartesian people.

Those who agree to open their energetic centers, who agree to follow this path to the perceptions, have an advantage provided they do so humbly and for good reasons. Not just believing there is a life after death, but knowing it, enables the person to have deep inner peace. Not just believing there is a life after death, but knowing it is a reality, changes a person. This knowledge has a tremendous effect on one's inner peace. Because your very first fear is fear of dying. Nature made us that way. So develop your clear-senses, but only after having worked on your spirituality!

Some religions condemn people who commit suicide. What about that?

The spirit world does not judge, never judges, people who commit suicide. For a small number of tragic deaths, there may simply be a slower transition period, measured in human time. A spirit that dies in great sadness, in great pain can stay for a while in that state before being able to perceive us. At that moment their spirit is too dense to perceive the Light; they perceive more easily the matter they know than they perceive the heavenly Beings. This is why some mediums, some people on Earth, set up circles in which they help the tiny percentage of spirits who stay in your material spheres, who do not rise up.

But as for any judgment of people who commit suicide – there isn't any. Escaping a challenge through suicide is not the solution in most cases, because the same challenge will be placed on your path at another time. But you are not judged in any case. Your karma takes care of things and our love remains unconditional. We love you exactly the way you are. We chose you because we have a resonance with you. We chose you because we can act through you. We love those who serve. Do not judge harshly those who do wrong, to themselves or to others. They are also spiritual beings; they also have angels and beings that love them and surround them. But in the darkness, it is much more difficult to perceive us than in Love.

And what about assisted suicide?

We have no judgment regarding assisted suicide because once again, it is about the person's free will. It's simply that those who are involved in such actions may ignore the fact that some awareness would be impossible to attain because they left early. If the physical pain is too great, we fully understand. However, one must be aware of the fact that some levels of awareness could not be attained. In terms of light or darkness, there is no judgment with respect to these souls who pass over to our side a little sooner.

We hope with all our souls that you will stay confident, especially in hard times. Don't forget that the Holy Spirit surrounds you every day, every second; that we are never farther away than a breath and that we love you. Never forget that like peace, Love is omnipresent! The only obstacles to Love are your moods. But at no time in your existence does Love ever cease to be.

Many people express their doubts. A very arrogant person who is full of himself will never doubt. It is always those who are seeking who doubt. There is only one harmful side to doubt: holding on to that doubt and carrying it around like a psychological model. Some people need to doubt in order to hide behind or in front of their talent or their gift. Reaching your own light, allowing yourself to let your gifts and abilities flourish, is an issue for some people. But self-doubt is beneficial as it can be overcome – overcome through understanding. It's a way to grow.

Do we have several lives?

Human beings have several lives – that's a fact! But at the same time humans exist on different planes! Because they are All and Nothing! You can thus logically grasp that if you are All you are more than a soul. Is it possible to grasp that if you are more than a soul, or if you are the soul that is the All, that you are dealing with different dimensions? Human beings exist on different planes. It is clear that if you are attached to your individuality, you will only exist on one plane... at least in your head. It is possible in the current incarnation of the human being, to perceive these parallel planes. The only benefit from this awareness is that the horizon opens up or the awareness increases. What keeps the being thus incarnated from grasping this is the veil, that part of illusion that you have. Ignorance and illusion are intended to make human beings progress in their experience. If there were no milestones to reach, no challenges to meet, no suffering to overcome, how would you grow? How could you grasp what is?

Given that you are only part of a whole, you can separate and incarnate in more than one place on Earth. You are aspects of the All. And since the All has different aspects, it is altogether logical that you exist in different places! The conscience will remain individual and just as we have already said, this awareness about opening up will serve no other purpose than to have a broader horizon, because the aspect that you are will make its way anyway. It will follow what the soul has set up for that aspect.

Once you are in the afterlife, all the aspects of yourself will not necessarily be reunited or not right away at least. Take, for example, your dearly departed. These dear ones have not joined with the other aspects; they are still what they are and that's quite right because time only exists in your measurements, not in ours.

Is it the soul that chooses to reincarnate or is it a higher power that commands it to do so?

You are going to be astonished, but the veritable soul is equal to the higher power!

There are a lot of reincarnations for one soul, so there's no need to count them. Have we discouraged you? You see, we are in the techniques, in the discourse on the technical aspects. Very often, in your questioning, it is not about knowing how to better approach Love, how to grow compassion, how to serve better! Sorry to be so frank! After all you have been through, not only in this life, but in all of your lives, the work you have to do here is sometimes tiring, sometimes sad or demoralizing as the new steps you must take are so hard. You are here to perfect yourself in service, no question about it! We are not judging you, but we have to remind you of this.

There is only one essential thing: how can you increase your capacity to love, your capacity to forgive and to be tolerant? In these answers, you will find the deep secrets of life and the brightness of your soul.

How do you rid yourself of anger?

Before you can rid yourself of anger, you have to understand it: the basis of anger is fear! There is only fear. Fear is almost the exact opposite of the higher Conscience, diametrically opposed to Love. It isn't hate that is the opposite of Love, it's really fear. All those feelings like anger or hate are born out of fear. Anger is an emotional reaction. Fear is much deeper, much more deeply anchored than anger. Anger is a passing thing; it changes with the days and the encounters. But fear is a much deeper feeling, not just the simple fear of falling off of a roof or the fear of a shark, but truly existential fear. You have to go back to the root of that fear, to the origin of why there is a need for that fear. In the bases of that existential fear you will find the keys to your life, keys that will increase your conscience and let go of your ignorance.

We are always much moved when we see you find the courage to take steps, forward, and even step off over the precipice for some of you, without knowing where you are going to land. Yet you have the courage to do it and take those steps. Keep on taking your steps, listen to yourselves. It's the

Truth because the answer is always in you, but not in your head.

When you are in a meditation retreat, in silence, it is legitimate to ask yourself about the silence. What is the use of not speaking for part of the day, when you can do it at home? When there is silence all around you, at first there is a roaring noise inside of you. You think that it might be the opposite: you are meditating; you are not speaking all day, so it should be quiet inside you. Alas, since you are not speaking, there is no inner calm! Since you are silent, the inner noise can rise to the surface. If it rises to the surface, it can be cleared. The things you have accumulated inside of you have to be thrown out one way or another. Silence, listening to yourself, is a very strong tool, so give it a chance for your own good.

What about stress?

Like the divine being that inhabits you, peace is omnipresent in you. Stress only lives in your mind. What you must do is to contemplate the stress, not experience it. Meditate and see yourself as a ball of light that has a window. Look through the window at the stress, and it won't affect you. By being in yourself and having access to the higher Conscience, you will avoid a lot of stress. What comes to you comes because there is a resonance.

Karma Yoga

Karma yoga is the household chores that the students perform during retreats. Jonathan would like to talk about this discipline and its benefits.

It's very courageous to accept the humblest tasks such as cleaning the toilets. You know, in India, people touch the feet of those they venerate. Did you know we want to touch the feet of the people who clean the floors and the toilets?

What are the benefits of Karma Yoga?

Karma Yoga has two deep reasons for existing. These are positive reasons that the student often ignores:

You can easily understand the exercise in a protected context, doing an activity in a focused way. In other words, I chop carrots and I only chop carrots, which is very difficult at home when we are cooking for the family, for the husband who is on the way home and the children who are getting home from school, or for ourselves when we know we are going to run to work right afterwards. In a retreat, however, you are in a different state, in a different context. You are much more in the moment. So if you can concentrate with all your heart and take this training moment with your carrot or with the table you are cleaning, you will reap the fruits of your labor when you get back to your daily routine.

The second reason is almost as important: by your actions you allow other people to attend the courses at a reasonable price. If there were no one to clean the toilets, help in the kitchen, or do the washing up, someone would have to be paid to do these tasks and the cost of the course would then be quite different. Many people would be unable to attend classes like these. This principle is applied in many communities that have a spiritual orientation. This activity not only helps others to follow a spiritual path; these actions also influence your karma to a great extent. Any action, even if it is done for personal gain, will, provided it is a positive action, have positive results. A positive action that benefits a group of people has yet another impact. You are planting a seed in your future gardens and the tree that grows will bear many fruits.

Can you teach us a method for opening our hearts to compassion, love and sharing?

You have to look at this from the other end. If your energy system is not purified; if your entire field is not raising its vibration, your heart will not be able to open fully. This is how you should understand how the heart opens up. We have spoken about the balances between the various energetic bodies and between the chakras, which allow us to rise up and enable healthy evolution. In fact, it is unhealthy to work only on some of these centers and ignore the others. This is why your medium, Hannes Jacob, has insisted so much on working on your spirituality and on cleansing your being, and not only on improving your sensitivity and your mediumship. The heart chakra is incapable of opening up by itself, and you would have no chance of acquiring compassion if the lower centers or chakras are not worked upon, that means that the anger, jealousy and fear are not dealt with and that your dense particles cannot dissolve in the light. With that kind of information, a heart cannot open up to compassion, but only to desire. The opening up of your heart is just like any flower that wants to see the other side of the fence; it has to have time to grow so it can look over the fence and into the neighboring garden.

Today the vibrations of time are accelerating but time is movement! Yet time does not exist. The only thing that exists is movement and time is the tool used to describe that movement. The perception of this time, of this movement, is a changing one; vibration is changing; but overall the system will not change.

What is right?

In absolute terms, nothing is right. Or we can also say that in absolute terms everything is right! Take the example of a child who eats in India and another in Europe. In India, his hand will be slapped if he uses a fork and in Europe his hand will be slapped if he eats with his fingers. Some would scold a child for eating a worm, whereas it would be a tasty treat elsewhere. So what is done and not done here or there... Here if you kill someone you will be told you are going to hell. Elsewhere if you kill someone you are made to believe you are awaited in heaven by dozens of virgins that will make much of you and grant all your sexual desires. Do you see how difficult it is to say what is right or wrong? One thing is sure: Divine Law is the same for everyone all over the world.

The next idea that needs to be discussed is why there are these differences. How can there be such deep conviction on one side that is seen as wrong by another side? Of course, the first reason is cultural. The second is evolution. The only tool you have to raise yourself up and out of the density that is in you – the only tool is your free will. This tool is the only thing that can be judged. In other cultures, for example in the ancient Egyptian cultures, you have a god that brought the deceased to his overlord so that the deceased could be judged to determine which heaven he would be sent to. The judgment will thus be made according to the actions of this human who has just left the earthly life. If there were no free will, there would only be chance and no judgment would be possible. All souls would have the same density. Each action would be done unintentionally. Everything that is already chaos would be an unstructured chaos. Because though it is chaos, on your earth, there is organized chaos. What allows everything to be held together is your free will. When you have understood what free will is you will be able to accept cultural differences. Because even in a society where murder is promoted as a beautiful, holy, and beneficial act, some souls would not agree. In your evolutionary stage, you have to accept that you are going to meet some very luminous things and very dense things. Unfortunately it is always easier to understand what is the densest because we have already been there. We've already seen it. You were dense, once. It is much more difficult to understand what is luminous because it is not easy to understand something that doesn't exist in your conscience. Like a child that has missed a few classes and does not understand what the teacher is talking about.

To get the answer to the question "What is right?" a child

will ask his or her parents. But as soon as the child is older and has grasped his own spirit, his conscience will have to act according to his free will. As for you, it's the only thing you can do. Accepting free will is a step not everyone is able to take.

Can you explain what role the conscience plays in conjunction with free will?

What else would make him evolve? What else would make him climb out of his misery? Many people are not aware of the spirit that they are. Many people cannot accept that a flower, a plant or an animal can have an essence and be inhabited by an essence. Moreover, animals are very delicate subjects in a carnivorous society. There was a time when some humans ate other humans. Today no one approves of cannibalism except people who are mentally impaired. The next step is to be aware of the spirit within the animal. The American Indians whose lives depended on animals approached their spirits with respect and no judge would condemn them. On the contrary, the guiding spirits of these Indians led them to their prey because it was the karma of the deer or bison that was being hunted to help ensure the survival of the indigenous people.

Tolerating mass animal suffering is another aspect of evolution or ignorance; a question of free will. How many people consciously agree to cause the animal spirits to suffer by accepting that these living beings endure so much suffering? Who could watch this suffering for one day, in full consciousness, without breaking down? Yet if we are not very hungry, we throw leftovers into the garbage, because there is too much on the plate! We cause animals to suffer and they end up for a large part in the garbage! This is a matter of conscience and evolution! We are not here to tell you to stop eating meat. But we are explaining that all the suffering that exists in some layers, in some densities, will slowly change, through your work among other things. Slowly, you will perceive the same facts in a different manner. The person who eats meat to satisfy his hunger and whose conscience is just and right in his life will not do the same harm as the one who does it with no conscience. By lowering our consumption of meat, we reduce suffering. By ceasing to eat meat, we stop it. We hope we haven't offended anyone. Starting at a certain stage of evolution, you always have free will. It's simply that free will can only be guided by the conscience and that conscience is more or less luminous according to the evolutionary stage. It's a circle. It's a choice or rather a question of free will to focus on one's own misery or to focus on love. Because love exists – and in large amounts! No misery can resist love, just as night is chased away by daylight. This is why there is no absolute truth. And this is why watching some destinies is often extremely painful, destinies or situations which can be terribly painful. What makes everything so beautiful is that one day no being will ever suffer again. That is a promise!

So in that case, what about what is commonly called Karma?

Karma only means cause and effect. One action generates a result, that's all. A person's karma is linked to his actions and his actions will have to do with his conscience and his conscience will be affected by what can or cannot be grasped, with its density or its light, according to its state. The person will act in a certain way and thus meet with results.

Look, you have this Father you see in heaven. That's good, but there is no need to search the sky because He is no more in heaven than he is in you. So pray to yourselves! This essence penetrates everything.

Pray to the Father; but not for the reasons you think. In a way there is no use praying to the Father in heaven because the Father has already organized things. The laws are set and the love is already there. Prayer won't bring you divine love but prayer will help you reach that love which is already there all around you. This universe, and on a smaller scale, this earth, already has its law. The Father who created the earth did so in such a way that it would be organized and experienced through your actions. Prayer is useful only to provide positive thoughts and to invite your teams to support you in your work, because none of the angels and none of the higher beings will interfere in your lives if you do not ask them to do so. Prayer is useful for Faith and letting go.

Up to now, we have tried to explain karma. These are your actions that will generate certain results. So prayer is supposed to help you begin rising in this essence so that this essence will become a living part of you and not just a mental one. So to come back to the question of what karma is, of what your actions and opinions do and when you should intervene because you see humans acting in shocking ways. We have just explained that according to your evolutionary stage, you are going to adopt some types of behavior and act in a certain way. That is why there are the activists on one side, the women's rights advocates, or the animal welfare activists or the political party supporters. We have non-governmental organizations that will intervene in other countries to do good. So in all these circumstances, in all the situations that will come up, some people want to be sent to war zones as their conscience can no longer tolerate seeing suffering inflicted on supposedly innocent people; they can no longer accept that in a place where there is a different conscience some people in power are not afraid to make thousands and thousands of people suffer. Well, the explanation is the same with respect to the level of the densities and of evolution. A lot of people who have killed others in previous lives would rather let themselves be killed rather than committing the same act again. It has to do with your inscriptions, with the evolutionary stage. Every person has different inscriptions and reacts according to resonances. All information has resonance. It's the law of attraction. That's why we have said that the Great

Spirit has already organized everything since the beginning. So lifting prayers to heaven is senseless in that respect because you inscribe yourself and you are going to meet things according to your inscriptions. God has nothing to do with any of that. You are the only ones who are responsible for anything in your misfortune or your happiness. Sooner or later, you will reach that state of conscience where you will no longer tolerate certain things, and then you will get up and say, "This can't go on, I don't agree." If several people and several groups come to the same conclusion that will lead to movements that will change things so that these injustices will no longer happen. That is why in some countries there is national health care, social welfare systems exist, and medical care is available for all while in other countries there is none. This is just an example of to what extent things can happen or not.

You are not the puppets of a supreme power. If you are puppets, it is of your own hidden side, your false belief in your identity, your fight to maintain an identity that you believe to be the only right one. You are the puppets of your ego and your identity.

Reincarnation is a choice. A spirit is never forced by a supreme power to reincarnate into a man or an animal. But despite the suffering that you may experience, don't forget that the most beautiful flowers grow in soil that has been fertilized with manure. Sunflowers never ask toward what direction they should turn; they follow the sun. You must understand that the concept of time is determined by the matter. As soon as you leave the matter you will no longer have this concept of time. When you have understood the movement between the life cycles, when you have reached the other side and grasped the extent of your existence, you will understand how a life on earth is not even a finger snap in comparison. It is only through incarnation that you experience movement as something slow. In reality it is only your brain's ability to comprehend speed or slowness. As soon as you have left your mortal envelope, time will only be a tool to describe movement. Dreams can help compare and grasp the relativity of time. Not only do you have the impression that you have dreamed for hours and yet it has only been seconds, but also as soon as you wake up the dream disappears or its memory fades in the mists of a new day.

Thank you for your attention. May the light be with you, or rather may you become aware of the light that you are!

There is abundant love here and in heaven, but again it's your choice to decide to share it and experience it.

In any case, we have chosen and will never cease to love you no matter what!

Ink that flows
Word by word and sentences
Cannot say or paint
How much I love you

Ink that flows
Like blood in your veins
That touches your soul
As delicate as its feather

Ink that flows
Agile as the river
Rolls its stones
Rocks your grief
Reduces it to sand
And more
Ink that flows
In the dawn and its glow
The dew of the new
Dissolves your fears

Ink that flows
Draws your map
To the day when your joy
Chases your doubt away

Ink that flows
Comes to its end
Leaving behind
The essence of a work
Balm for your hurts

Ink that flows
And will never fade away
Until that day
When you share from above
Love again

Ink that flows
Like the river you are
Ink that dilutes
Ocean you will be

Life

Chapter 26

Conclusion

With this book, I hope I have been able to shed some light on the highly complex and yet so beautiful field of mediumship and healing. Two notions should be retained and comprise my main message. The first is to assimilate that we are information, that absolutely everything is inscribed in us. If you dislike some inscriptions you have the choice of changing them, of transmuting them. You don't have to take my word for it – try it for yourself, verify it yourself and then decide whether you want to believe or not. Your health is your greatest wealth. Take care of that first and then work on your level of "excellence" in mediumship.

The second is to perform spiritual work, because you are Essence before being information. Make this your priority even if it is difficult, more difficult than learning about mediumship. Rest assured that you will learn the latter anyway, as you go. Be patient; be confident. What happened to me can happen to you – and more…

Dear scientists, professors, researchers, clinical practitioners, in the fields of physics, quantum physics, neurology, psychiatry, medicine, mathematics, statistics, etc.: Are you interested in going deeper into the existing studies in the area of sensitivity or in partnering in pilot projects such as the Hannes Jacob Syndrome? A contact address has been reserved specially for you so that we may have the pleasure of discussing research projects: hannes@miraclescome.com.

And why not even solicit donors to this beautiful cause to build a clinic where research on sensitivity can be continued and in which patients would benefit from energy therapy in complement to allopathic treatments.

It is our wish to bring the immense potential that the EPI healing method holds to as many patients as we may reach. If you are interested in bringing EPI to your city by co-hosting an OpenDays event, you may reach out to us at: opendays@ hannesjacob.ch.

For more information about me, please visit my website: www.hannesjacob.ch.

For information about *fréquences* – Swiss School of Healing, please visit: www.frequences.ch.

Thank you for everything.
May faith be with you
to the day of the ocean.

Meditations and exercises

Meditations

Below are two pure meditations that will allow you to work on your spiritual awakening as well as your physical and mental health. Other "meditations" are presented further on. These are tools for improvement work in the various branches of mediumship.

The duration of each meditation is given to provide a time indication if you want to record the meditations or read them to someone. They are an exact translation of the audio version that is provided in French on the *fréquences* website. Before recording them, we recommend that you first read them out loud a few times to find the best way of speaking.

Vipassana
Vipassana is the traditional meditation of Theravada Buddhism. Vipassana means introspection or self-observation. From it we

learn that there are only three forms of thought: equanimous thought, which is neutral, thoughts based on aversion and thoughts based on greed. The two latter ones are harmful and are inscribed in our being. These inscriptions will be the negative resonances of our future, i.e. they are our karmic code. Thus it is all our lives. The good news is that we can dissolve these inscriptions through an in-depth examination of our being. By doing this very attentively, the inscriptions dissolve, provided we do not feed them with reactions of disgust when faced with unpleasant sensations, or with greediness for pleasurable feelings. When we carry out this introspection, we will realize very quickly that these feelings are changing and thus ephemeral. This is the first reason for not paying more attention to them than through simple and equanimous neutral observation.

Every time we bring our attention back to the same place, we notice that the sensations are different. Thus we are also ephemeral. Thoughts wander due to our daily activities, our old inscriptions, and our ego that will do anything to keep from dissolving. Ego must be translated by the term "identity", that which we believe we are, that which we believe to be our identity which we mistakenly want to preserve. Ego will bring up every thought it can to distract us from meditation. Losing focus during meditation is therefore normal. It's not a failure, it's natural. Success, however, is being aware of these thought detours and bringing them back to observing without getting upset. Observing oneself dispassionately dissolves the ego. Our body changes trillions of times in one second, so it is thus anything but solid. Our spirit changes with every thought, so it is anything but stable. The only thing that remains, then, is our essence that is identical to pure conscience, which is pure peace and unconditional love.

Anapana: 10'

Before we practice Vipassana meditation, we first do a form of concentration-meditation which is called "Anapana" or "Anapana meditation". In other words, it is the observation of our breathing, just above the lips, between the upper lip and the nostrils. We observe this space. We just watch the friction of the air that goes into and out of our nostrils.

My breathing, when I inhale and exhale, is done at a natural rhythm. I don't force or otherwise direct my breathing. I simply observe the moment, the truth of the moment which is this friction happening above my upper lip.

The more my mind calms down and the more I observe my breathing, the more I will grasp and feel these sensations that it generates on this little region. The more I observe my breathing, the smaller this region becomes and the sharper my focus gets. And sooner or later, the focal point shrinks. What starts as all the space between my upper lip and my nostrils is going to get smaller and smaller until it finally becomes the size of a pinhead. Just this tiny point, but it will be a tiny focus point. The more my mind calms down, the sharper my focus becomes and I will take the tiniest point and observe the feeling there.

Anapana is useful precisely to calm your mind and sharpen your focus. It is useless to do Vipassana if you haven't taken at least a moment to calm your spirit down and focus your attention. In many courses teaching this form of meditation, it is recommended to take one-fourth to one-third of your available time to observe your breathing, precisely above your upper lip. After that, the three-quarters or two-thirds time remaining will be consecrated to Vipassana meditation, thus to introspection.

A student once complained to his teacher that he could not concentrate and was unable to keep his focus. The teacher said, "Imagine you are alone in a room with a highly venomous cobra; I'm sure you would have no problem focusing on the cobra. So, you see, it's only a matter of priorities."

Vipassana: 40'

Where Vipassana is concerned, it is not about what position you assume, as long as your spine is straight. From there, I would just choose the position you are most comfortable in. You will have to hold this position throughout your work. Once you choose a position, I suggest you not change it. For myself, I sit down comfortably in a position that feels good. I observe my breathing and the feeling it creates between my nostrils and my upper lip. My only intention is to observe this spot. My focus is entirely on this region which gets smaller and smaller as the feeling becomes clearer and clearer. And I can grasp the tiniest fraction of space and manage to feel it. I start first by looking at the palm of my hand. I wonder what I may well feel there. Maybe I will feel warmth, or tingling, perhaps a throbbing sensation – it doesn't matter what comes to me. The main thing is to notice how my hands are at that very moment. Whatever the sensation is, as soon as I feel something, I let it go. I will then observe the soles of my feet: what are they like right now? Again, they could feel hot or cold, tingly or itchy; I don't have a preference for any feeling. The exercise lies in grasping the moment – the truth of the moment. As soon as I feel something I leave that region. I leave the soles of my feet. Next, I concentrate on the top of my head, at the top where the fontanel is. I try very calmly to grasp the sensations that are taking place right now at the top of my head. As soon as I have grasped the feeling in my fontanel, I go around my scalp. What can I feel on my scalp? As soon as I have felt the least little thing, I move on until I have gone all over my scalp. I examine my forehead – what do I feel there? What is happening on my forehead at the moment? Do I feel any tenseness? Tingling? A puff of air? It isn't important whatever I may feel; whatever it may be, that feeling is ephemeral, because everything is ephemeral, and I don't hang on to it. I observe my temples – how do my temples feel? And my eyes? My eyes and all around them. Can I feel the area around my eyes? If in one part of my body, I don't feel anything after a specific time, maybe 30 seconds or a minute, I accept the fact that at that moment I feel nothing. And I continue and move to my nose. I observe my cheeks. How are my cheeks at that moment? I focus on my lips. Are they buzzing? Is there any tickling? Are they vibrating? It isn't important; it isn't important. As soon as I have got it, I go on. I move down to my chin and my jaw line. I examine the back of my neck; what can I feel in the back of my neck? It might be tenseness or it might be throbbing. It isn't important what. That's not important. Everything changes at every moment. I observe my throat; what feelings do I have in my throat? My focus moves on and I observe my trapezoids. Again, is there any tingling, any tenseness, any buzzing? Are there any vibrations of any kind? It's ephemeral; it changes. The word in Pali is "anitcha". "Anitcha" – everything is "anitcha", "ephemeral". Since it is ephemeral, I don't hold onto it and at the same time I observe my shoulders. How are my shoulders? What is the truth of the moment in my shoulders? As soon as I feel something, I go further down. I examine my triceps. I observe my biceps. I move down to my elbow and the hollow of my elbow. I go further down and focus my attention on my forearm.

As a rule, I examine an area about as large as my palm. I go through my entire body. I don't place any importance on what I perceive, not ever. No importance because it changes, nothing is permanent. I go to my wrists. What do I feel in my wrists? I observe the back of my hands. I go over my palms. I examine my two little fingers. As soon as I have felt a sensation, I go to the next finger and so on, all the way to my thumbs. As soon as I have seen, I let go of the spot and go on. And I go back up and observe my wrists. My forearms and elbows – I examine the biceps and triceps. I go over my shoulders and start focusing on my collarbones. Space by palm-sized space, I go down my chest. Both sides at the same time, left and right. Whether I feel buzzing, stretching, pressure, temperature, or the feeling of clothes on my skin. As soon as I have noticed any sensation I let it go and continue. I move gently downwards, stop a moment on my solar plexus and as soon as I have felt something I leave it and go over my entire abdomen.

I go back up my sides above the hips and move up a little at a time until I get to my armpits. No feeling is important. There are pleasant feelings, but I don't get attached to them because they are ephemeral. There will be unpleasant or painful feelings but I don't pay attention to them. They are ephemeral. Everything changes at every moment. I focus on both my back muscles and then just under my neck, all of my upper back. And again at the same time, I slowly go down both sides of my back. I go slowly down my back. If there is a spot where I don't feel anything, I stop for a moment; I can try to approach this spot from one side or the other. Maybe I will gain an access. But if the truth of the moment is that I don't have any feeling I accept that and continue. If my thoughts are wandering, when I become aware of it, I bring them back without judging them or paying any attention to them. Thoughts about my life, any feelings of disgust or greed will inscribe themselves in my body. If I perceive my sensations and do not react, these inscriptions dissolve. That is why I examine myself – to dissolve any negative inscription through observation of my physical body. I free myself from all my future burdens.

I examine my lower back. I examine my entire pelvis, including my buttocks and genitals. I examine my buttocks and the upper part of my thighs. I go around my thighs – how are they at the moment? How are my thighs right now? I go slowly down my thighs, all the way to my knees. I examine my knees, around them and inside them. As soon as I have felt the least sensation, I leave them and check my calves and shins. I remain calm, focused and attentive. I study my ankles; how are my ankles? The condition of the top of my foot and my feet. If I am wearing shoes, do I feel them? And how are my heels? The soles of my feet? Can I feel the touch of the ground? Are my feet cold or hot? I go over my toes, one after the other, just long enough to grasp any sensation. And with my full attention, I examine my body as I move back up. How are my feet? How are my ankles? I move up my shins and calves. What condition are my knees in? And I go back up my thighs, front and back.

As soon as I have felt something, I leave it. I never forget that everything changes. I never hang onto any feeling or to any sensation, and I do not hang on to any thought that distracts my focus. What is happening in my pelvis and in my lower abdomen? I feel my lower back. I go back up from here on both sides of my spine. I focus on my shoulder blades and do them, all around my shoulder blades to the top of my back. Once more I go back and focus on my loins and move back up through my abdomen. If there is any tenseness or cramping, any buzzing or tingling, I don't pay any attention to it. As soon as I have noticed, I go on, and move to my solar plexus. Whether I feel stressed or relaxed, I pay no attention to it. I interpret nothing about these feelings. It's just that; it's just this moment, and every moment changes. I go back up to the top of my chest, step by step, to my collarbones. I feel the ends of my fingers one after the other. How are my forearms? Step by step, I go up my forearms to my elbows. I follow my biceps and triceps to my shoulder. I examine my throat and neck. I go over my face, chin and jaw, all of my mouth, my nose. Everything changes. I examine my cheeks and my eye sockets. I focus on my forehead. I feel the temples. I concentrate on my ears. I go over my scalp again, and all of my head. I take my fontanel. I don't become attached to anything because everything changes. My body changes; my spirit changes. My inscriptions dissolve every time I go over my body from head to toe and toe to head. I am dissolving the inscriptions of the past. With each equanimous examination, I dissolve these inscriptions and get closer to my inner peace, to my essence, to my pure conscience. In this peaceful state, I share the fruits of my labor with everything that is. May all beings be happy. May all life be peaceful. So may it be.

Pranayamas

The two pranayamas that are presented here can be carried out alone as a meditation or in preparation for sensitive work.

Nadi Shodana: 5-10'

I sit down comfortably on a chair or meditation pillow. I keep my back straight, but allow my shoulders and jaws to relax, and I breathe slowly. I simply observe my chest movements. I watch myself inhale and exhale, and watch my chest move in and out. I inhale and exhale and observe my breathing.

I focus on the zone between my upper lip and my nostrils and watch how my breathing goes in and out. I keep focused on this. All of my concentration is on the friction caused by my breathing, just above my upper lip. I visualize and focus on my left nostril and breathe in and out uniquely through it. The next time I exhale through my left nostril, I inhale through my right nostril. Inhale... exhale. The next time I exhale through my right nostril, I inhale on the left and exhale on the right, inhale on the right and exhale on the left – left-right, right-left. With my natural breathing rhythm I alternate: left-right, right-left. I balance my hemispheres and my nervous system; work on my third eye, and practice focusing. One breathing technique and four exercises. I finish by exhaling from the left.

Then I return to my normal breathing.

Kriyas: 10-30'

I focus on my perineum and contract it. (If I am a woman, I focus on my cervix and contract it.) I contract and release; contract, release. I do this several times. And I visualize a light beam extending from my perineum to the middle of my head;

a light beam that surrounds my spine. I visualize a ball of light in my perineum. A luminous ball that completely lights up my loins. And every time I inhale I raise this ball of light through the beam to the middle of my head. Every time I exhale the ball goes down the beam to my loins. While I am doing these pranayamas and this breathing technique, the tip of my tongue is touching my palate (Kechari Mudra). When I breathe in, the energy rises; when I breathe out, the energy goes down. And as I breathe to my own rhythm, I raise and lower this ball of energy through my spine.

Inhale, and the ball rises; exhale, and it goes back down. Never force energy. Be relaxed and the intention will really make the energy move. You can't make energy do anything. But you can guide it and you do that precisely with intention. Every time I inhale, I bring the ball up through my spine. Every time I exhale I evacuate dense particles and dissolve them. Thus with every breath I am lighter: with every breath my vibration field increases and my duality decreases. With every breath I am more balanced and more at peace.

If you want to intensify your breathing you can do "Oms" in a 4-beat rhythm – but silent "Oms". Tell yourself, "I will say four silent Oms when inhaling and four silent Oms when exhaling." Four Oms when inhaling and four Oms when exhaling. I inhale and exhale in a relaxed manner.

People who have high blood pressure or a hiatus hernia cannot hold their breath after inhaling, and people with low blood pressure cannot hold the air out after exhaling. And now, after four inhaled Oms, I will do two apneal Oms, two paused Oms, four exhaled Oms, and two paused Oms. This is a four-timed breathing rhythm: four inhalations, two holds, four exhalations, two holds. In other words I say "Om" four times when breathing in and two when holding my breath, and four Oms when breathing out and two while holding my breath. If my breathing is still slow and balanced, I work on four + four

+ four + four: the Pranayama square. This means that I say four Oms when I inhale, four Oms while holding my breath, four Oms when I exhale and four Oms before breathing in again.

When I have exhaled for the fourth time, I return to my normal breathing and do stretching movements through my spine, from the lower spine to the upper in the middle of my head, and from the middle of my head back down to my perineum.

Grounding: 5'

The word "grounding" is often used. Being well-grounded helps us to live better in the present and to be more present in our thoughts. It also helps balance our energies. Additionally, being well-grounded keeps us in good physical and mental health. But it is nevertheless a good idea to ground yourself every morning before leaving home and also after meditating for long periods in which work was carried out in a state of modified consciousness. You can ground yourself whether you are sitting, standing or lying down. Personally, I really enjoy doing it while standing. I am centered and I connect with my center or with my heart chakra. I breathe into my center and spread throughout my body, but especially I spread to my legs and feet. When I inhale and expand I send beams through my body, through my feet and into the ground. If I want to, I visualize glowing roots growing from the soles of my feet and how I breathe through these roots. With every breath, I pull this earthly energy into my core. I breathe through the roots beneath my feet and fill my being with this vibrant energy. When I exhale, I just think, "I ground myself." I am centered, I am present and in the moment. You can do this exercise in the morning for two or three minutes and repeat it two or three times per hour throughout the day for one or two breathing cycles.

Slow frequency exercises

Slow frequencies are usually used in therapy to transmit healing energy. The medium is in a passive state which varies depending on whether he or she is performing spiritual healing or TT. The lower the medium's brain frequencies, the better this modified consciousness state enables connection with the spirit world, as is notably the case during trance healing.

Spiritual healing

Exercise 1

This exercise is done by two people and takes 15 to 30 minutes depending on how much time you have.

The people are seated, with the healer sitting behind the patient. The latter visualizes either a beam of light falling on him or the Divine Source, according to his beliefs. Through the fontanel, the healer breathes into his energy center, which is usually located in the middle of his chest, and visualizes it growing and expanding. He then relaxes when exhaling. The healer continues in this manner until he sees himself wrapped in a glowing ball of light which has built up around him. In order to have an idea of this construction, you can imagine a balloon which has been placed under a water tap. The water enters through the top and fills the balloon, which expands at the bottom. Every time the healer breathes in, his center builds up accordingly, flows through him and then expands outside his body and wraps him in a bubble. He then invites his spirit guides to join him. This is the best time to observe the energy change that occurs when your guide comes near.

Then from inside the bubble, he inhales and expands into the energy of his guides which builds up around him.

When the connection has been established and the energies between the healer and the spirit world have interwoven, the healer stands up and places his hands lightly on his seated colleague's shoulders. The time needed for this stage of the energy construction and for the establishment of the connection varies according to the healer's experience.

In the soothing rhythm of his breathing, he continues to expand the energy from his center through his arms and into the palms of his hands, so that the patient can benefit from the energy of the spirit world and the Source. I want to insist on the fact that the energy comes from the spirit world or the Source because the healer must not provide his own energy. This can be ensured on condition that the healer does not become personally involved and disregards the patient's identity. The healer's focus is on God and the transfer of this magnificent energy, in absolute confidence because he is led by his higher conscience and his spirit guide. The healer remains thus for ten to 15 minutes.

At the end of the treatment, the healer thanks his guide, who then leaves. Here too you should try to note how the energy changes when your guide leaves you. Finally, the healer grounds himself and the roles can be exchanged.

Therapeutic Touch (TT)

Exercise 2
A short guide to the practice of Therapeutic Touch (according to
Dr. D. Krieger/D. Kunz):

1. **Get in tune with and center yourself:** Use whatever ritual you prefer.
2. **Scan and assess the energy states:** Scan the body's energy fields (front/back).
3. **First contact:** Open up the hand and foot fields.
4. **Solar plexus:** Slowly move your hands above the solar plexus.
5. **Open the secondary chakras:** Touch the joints in the legs and arms on both sides of the body. Let the energy run from one hand to the other until you feel the energy flow. *Legs:* Ankles (interior/exterior), knees, hips (front/back). *Arms:* Wrist (back/underside), elbow (front/back), shoulders (front joint/back joint), collarbones.
6. **Back:** Send energy from the back of the neck to the coccyx. Place your hands on both sides of the spine.
7. **Head:** Place one hand on each temple.
8. **Benediction:** Place three fingers on the third eye chakra and either two or three fingers or the palm of the hand on the heart chakra. Wish for the best healing for the patient.
9. **Closing:** Sprinkle sparks of golden light over the body.
10. **Reassess/compare the energies:** Scan the body and repeat if needed.
11. **Specific application:** Hold your hand above the unbalanced areas.
12. **Finish:** Pull energy from the soles of the feet if necessary.

To help you practice, use the below extended guide to

Therapeutic Touch (according to Dr. D. Krieger/D. Kunz). The two protocols are described for the practice of Therapeutic Touch with the patient either lying down or seated. A session takes between 25 and 40 minutes.

Therapeutic Touch protocol: Patient lying down

1. Centering

After washing his hands, the therapist places himself in the divine ray and breathes it into his energy center (the heart chakra) in order to construct his field. This development allows him to consciously separate himself from his patient's energy field.

2. Scanning and assessing the state of the energies

The therapist moves his hand lengthwise about ten to 20 centimeters above the patient's body in a rapid gesture so that the therapist's thought will not be implicated. The therapist keeps his eyes open to avoid touching the patient.

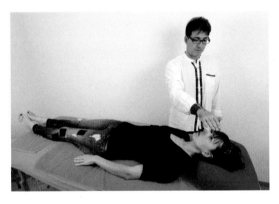

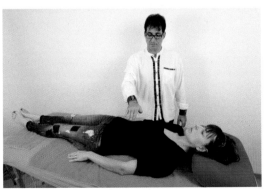

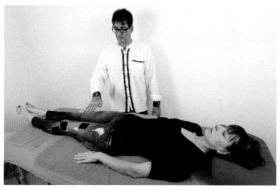

3. Making contact with the patient

The therapist opens the energy fields in the hands and feet. Note: The therapist places his hands on the backs of the patient's hands and feet, *not* on the ankles or wrists.

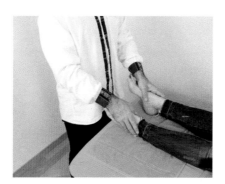

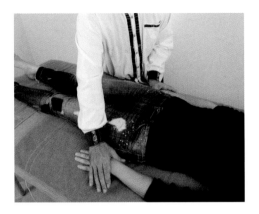

4. Drawing the energies from the solar plexus

This is an important step, because it is used to ease the solar plexus and may already bring relief to the patient. The movement is always towards the feet. The energy that is withdrawn from the solar plexus is placed in a column of white light visualized by the therapist or transferred to the healing guides to be transmuted for the greatest good of the patient.

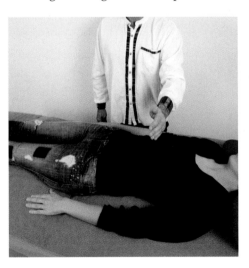

5. Opening the secondary chakras via the main joints in the body

Touch the joints in the legs, arms, and shoulders on both sides of the body. The therapist lets the energy run from one hand to another until he feels this energy flow.

Legs:

The therapist places both hands on one of the patient's ankles, one hand on the outer side and one on the inner side.

Note: As soon as the therapist decides which leg to start with, he will have to do each joint in that leg without changing sides, so that the patient will not feel any imbalance on one side of his body. Moreover, the chakras in both legs must be opened before moving to the arms and the upper body.

The therapist then places his hands on the knee, one hand on either side of the kneecap.

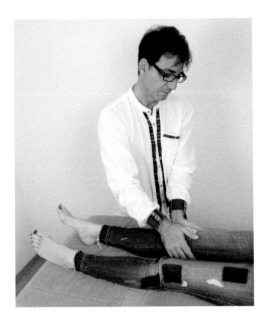

Then the therapist moves his hands to the hip, with the tips of his fingers turned *outwards*. The palm of the hand can be placed on the patient's groin, in line with the hip joint, at the therapist's discretion.

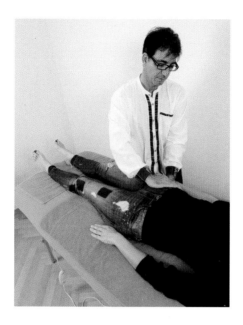

Arms:

The hands are placed on the wrist, one on the inside and the other on the outside.

The hands are then placed on the elbow, one on the inside and one on the outside.

Afterwards, the hands are placed on the shoulder, one on the front of the joint and one on the back of the joint.

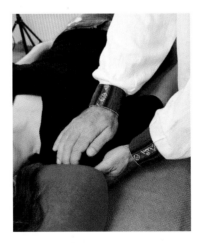

The therapist then places his hands on the collarbones, one hand on each. Here, the therapist must take care *not to breathe on the patient*. To do so, he might, for example, turn his head to the side.

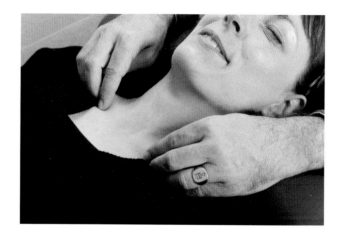

6. Sending energy through the back

In this operation, the therapist sends energy from the neck to the coccyx by placing one hand to the left and one hand to the right of the spine, on the shoulders. During this operation, the therapist must take care *not to breathe on the patient*. To do so, he might, for example, turn his head to the side.

7. Sending energy through the head

The therapist places one hand on each temple. Note: Take care not to cover the ears or the fontanel.

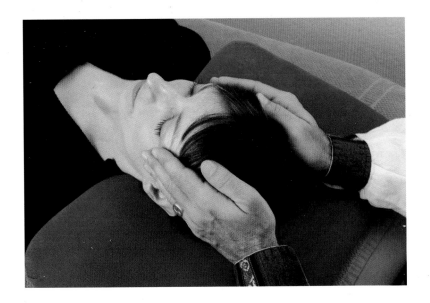

8. Benediction

At the end of the treatment, wish for the best healing for the patient by placing three fingers on the third eye chakra and placing either two or three fingers or the palm of the hand on the heart chakra.

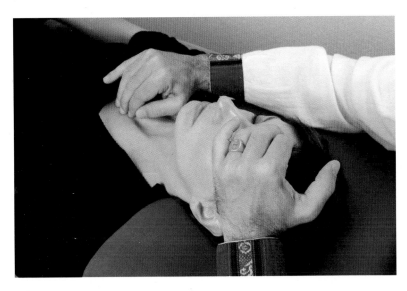

9. Closing
Sprinkle sparks of golden light over the patient's body.

10. Reassess the patient's energies/Compare them with the information collected during the first scan.
Scan the patient's body to detect any residual energy blockage and if necessary treat the unbalanced areas again.

11. Specific applications
For treatments specific to a particular organ, joint or other area, the hand is held above the unbalanced areas.

12. Finish
The therapist visualizes roots under the soles of his patient's feet and extends these roots from the feet by about 10 to 20 centimeters maximum.

Note: The therapist must be careful to only pull towards himself as the goal of this operation is to bring the patient's roots out and not push them back in.

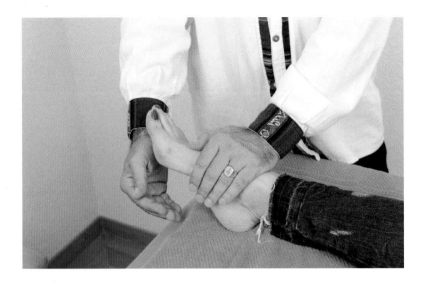

At the end of the treatment the therapist grounds *himself* correctly in order to recover his full material consciousness, and, in the manner that he prefers, thanks the energies that worked with him.

The therapist also looks after his patient, making sure the latter feels well, helping him get down from the table, offering him something to drink, etc.

Therapeutic Touch protocol: Patient seated

Requirements: During the full TT session with a seated patient, the therapist must make sure to keep his back straight. Indeed, as the session will require more or less time, the therapist must always be comfortable and not have a backache after the session is finished. Of course, the therapist must also ensure the patient's comfort and posture as well as his own.

The following photos show the posture in detail and the more general posture with the back straight.

This therapeutic technique is applied to people with limited mobility, in wheelchairs or with back issues that do not allow them to be treated lying down, and also to the elderly.

1. Centering

After washing his hands, the therapist places himself in the divine ray and breathes it into his energy center (the heart chakra) in order to construct his field. This development allows him to consciously separate himself from his patient's energy field.

2. Scanning and assessing the state of the energies

The therapist moves his hand lengthwise about ten to 20 centimeters above the patient's body in a rapid gesture so that the therapist's thought will not be implicated. The therapist keeps his eyes open to avoid touching the patient.

3. Making contact with the patient

The therapist opens the energy fields in the hands and feet. Note: The therapist places his hands on the backs of the patient's hands and feet, *not* on the ankles or wrists.

4. Drawing the energies from the solar plexus

This is an important step, because it is used to ease the solar plexus and may already bring relief to the patient. The movement is always towards the feet. The energy that is withdrawn from the solar plexus is placed in a column of white light visualized by the therapist or transferred to the healing guides to be transmuted for the greatest good of the patient.

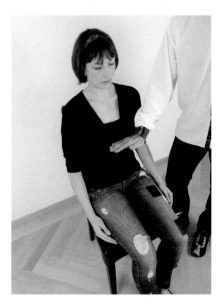

5. Opening the secondary chakras via the main joints in the body

Touch the joints in the legs, arms, and shoulders on both sides of the body. The therapist lets the energy run from one hand to another until he feels this energy flow.

Legs:

The therapist places both hands on one of the patient's ankles, one hand on the outer side and one on the inner side.

Note: As soon as the therapist decides which leg to start with, he will have to do each joint in that leg without changing sides, so that the patient will not feel any imbalance on one side of his body. Moreover, the chakras in both legs must be opened before moving to the arms and the upper body.

The therapist then places his hands on the knee, one hand on either side of the kneecap.

Then the therapist moves his hands to the hip, with the tips of his fingers on the *outside*.

Arms:

The hands are placed on the wrist, one on the inside and the other on the outside.

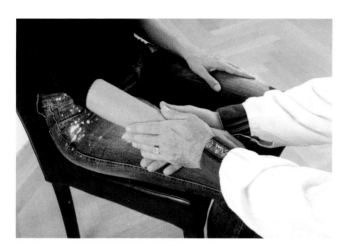

The hands are then placed on the elbow, one on the inside and one on the outside.

Afterwards, the hands are placed on the shoulder, one on the front of the joint and one on the back of the joint.

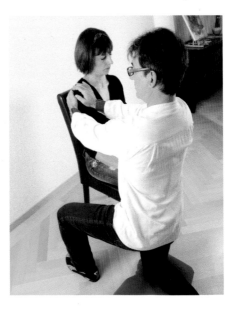

The therapist then places his hands on the collarbones, one hand on each. Here, the therapist must take care *not to breathe on the patient*. To do so, he might, for example, turn his head to the side.

6. Sending energy through the back

In this operation, the therapist sends energy from the neck to the coccyx by placing one hand to the left and one hand to the right of the spine, on the shoulders. During this operation, the therapist must take care *not to breathe on the patient*. To do so, he might, for example, turn his head to the side.

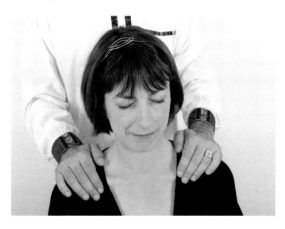

7. Sending energy through the head

The therapist places one hand on each temple. Note: Take care not to cover the ears or the fontanel.

8. Benediction

At the end of the treatment, wish for the best healing for the patient by placing three fingers on the third eye chakra and placing either two or three fingers or the palm of the hand on the heart chakra.

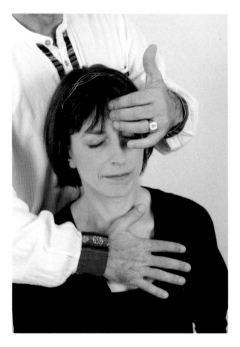

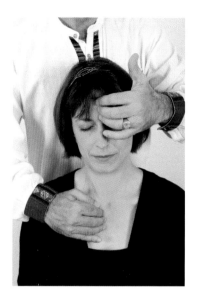

9. Closing
Sprinkle sparks of golden light over the patient's body.

10. Reassess the patient's energies/Compare them with the information collected during the first scan.
Scan the patient's body to detect any residual energy blockage and if necessary treat the unbalanced areas again.

11. Specific applications
For treatments specific to a particular organ, joint or other area, the hand is held above the unbalanced areas.

12. Finish
The therapist visualizes roots under the soles of his patient's feet and extends these roots from the feet by about 10 to 20 centimeters maximum. As the patient is seated, the therapist grasps the patient's calf and lifts his leg to reach the sole of his foot.

Note: The therapist must be careful to only pull towards

himself as the goal of this operation is to bring the patient's roots out and not push them back in.

At the end of the treatment the therapist grounds *himself* correctly in order to recover his full material consciousness, and, in the manner that he prefers, thanks the energies that worked with him.

The therapist also looks after his patient, making sure the latter feels well, helping him get down from the table, offering him something to drink, etc.

Trance

Exercise 3

The following trance meditation is an excellent exercise to do to intensify the link to the guides, whether it is for spiritual healing, TT, trance healing or spoken trance.

Trance: 50′

This trance meditation is in two parts. The first part is relaxation, which can be used alone just to relax and let go of one's thoughts, if you have insomnia or need a moment of peace and quiet. But it is recommended to connect both, i.e. relax in order to prepare to move into a state of trance in the second part.

Relaxation: 10′

I observe my chest movements as I breathe. Any thought that may go through me, I allow to pass without following it. This meditative moment is a moment of peace. Anything that is the future is only projection. This time is now. So there is nothing other than relaxing, nothing more than enjoyment. Any past or future thought will go by without my becoming attached to it. I watch my chest movement as I breathe. I become aware of the soles of my feet, my toes and my feet as a whole. I feel a wave of relaxation flow over them. It's pleasant; my feet relax – their muscles and tendons. I release my feet. This relaxing wave fills my ankles, moves up my shins and calves and I release these muscles which relax. Relaxation in the rhythm of my breathing. The feeling moves to my knees, then to my thighs and hips. My legs are at ease. Relax. Free of tension. Relax. Relax. My legs are totally relaxed, at rest. The wave moves up and fills my lower body. The lower part of my stomach and lower back. I let go. I let go. I let go in the peaceful and regular movement of my breathing. I let go. The feeling of relaxation moves higher and fills all my stomach and my chest. Moves from the lower back to the upper back. All comfortable. All relaxed. Relaxed. Relaxed. Complete relaxation, complete. And the relaxing wave spreads, through my shoulders and my arms, through my hands to the tips of my fingers. Everything is relaxed. Free of any tension. Free. Relaxed. Relaxed. Even more relaxed. I let go of my muscles and all the tension goes away, goes away. While the relaxing wave moves up my neck, my back, I relax my jaw. The wave moves up to my temples, into my face, my forehead and all of my face and head. I am free of tension. Free of strain. Relaxed. Relaxed. I am fully relaxed, from my feet to my head. In a completely relaxed state. I am feeling great peace, that of this so total relaxation. In great peace because this moment of relaxation is peace.

Meditation: 40'

I sit comfortably and loosen anything that might constrain me. My spine is straight, my body is relaxed. I visualize a luminous ray falling on me and surrounding my entire being. This nourishing beam is protective; it comes from the Great Spirit. I work in the light and the light is my guide. I visualize my center, that part of me that is perhaps in my chest. That place to which I retire in my peace, in which I interiorize myself. My center is a source of light. Through my fontanel I breathe into my center. I inhale the light from this ray. With each breath, my center constructs itself from this light. With each breath my center expands. With each breath all my being relaxes. Through my fontanel, I breathe into my center and my center builds itself. With each breath, I am brighter. With each breath, my center expands through my body. Calmly, in the natural rocking motion of my breathing. Calmly. I breathe into my center and from my center I spread through myself. I fill my entire being. From my center I spread through myself. I expand beyond my body and start wrapping myself in a bright, shiny, magnificent bubble. Inhale, build, expand. Exhale, calm. With my conscience, I retreat into my source. I retreat into the home inside me. I retreat into my center. I am bathed in light. Bathed in my shining energy. I am now nothing more than a field of light; my body has disappeared. I am at the center of myself. And inside my center I visualize a spiral staircase, a bright staircase that spirals downward. I am at the top of this staircase, wrapped in my own energy in the middle of the Great Spirit's light beam. Before I go down the first steps, I ask my guides, the light beings, the beings of higher consciousness, to come close to me. And I know that each step I am going further down inside myself; as I go down these steps, at each step, I will connect with my guides, connect more closely, deeper. I will not start any exchange with these beings that are approaching. I am not trying to know who they are. I do not try to communicate with them. If I have a feeling, a vision, I take note of it but I do not dwell on it. All I am doing is going down into myself; going deeper into my source. At each step, I leave my mind behind me. At each step, I leave my emotions behind me. All my conscience and focus is on interiorizing. I breathe into my center, I inhale through my fontanel. And from my center, I expand. And now, each time I inhale, I take one step down. Each time I exhale, I pause on that step and relax. I take the first step. I exhale and relax. I breathe into my center and expand as I take the second step. Slowly, calmly, I go down this spiral staircase.

With each step, I spread through myself and outside of myself, in the energy of my guides that is building up around me. Each time I exhale, I relax. I go down, step by step. Breath by breath. Expansion by expansion. I construct the link with the heavenly energies. My energy builds up; my energy extends in the energy of my guides. Just as they send their beams and make the connection with my field and my energy. I breathe into my center and connect with them. After the next step, I get to the first landing. I imagine stopping for a moment on the landing, consolidating my state, consolidating my energy. Maintaining the link that is being made. No interaction, no curiosity. I am in my center; I am in my peace; I am in my light.

There are more steps in front of me, still going down. I breathe into my center and spread to my guides as I go down the next step. I exhale, and rest, and relax, before inhaling and expanding again and going further down, deeper into my center, further into my deepest conscience and my light. I breathe into my center, and from my center, I spread myself out. One foot after another. Step by step, I deepen this connection with these higher consciousnesses. With my guides. I come to the next landing. I rest for a moment and maintain my state. I strengthen the link that has been made. I maintain my state. I invite my guides to come even closer, to connect more closely with my energy and my being. And I continue down the stairs.

I leave the second landing and go down. I breathe into my center and from my center I spread through myself, outside my body and into my guides. When I exhale, I let go and relax. Step by step in to the rhythm of my breathing. I am more and more detached from everything that is, except for my light, except for my connection with those that guide me; with those who have honored me by choosing me as a tool of light on Earth.

In front of me is the third landing; here there is a comfortable armchair and I sit down. I memorize my state. I memorize my state and my consciousness will know how to find that state. I maintain the connection that has been made. I keep close to my guides. It is a never-ending labor; never ending until we reach unconscious moments when we are no longer anything but tools; when we are no longer anything but light. Like in trance healing or when we sit down to automatic writing, whether it is to pen philosophical thoughts or to provide advice for loved ones. My mind is no longer in that state; I am light. I anchor that state firmly into my consciousness, and my spirit will know how to find that peace. I thank my guides. I thank them for everything that they have done for me without my knowledge and for their great patience. I trust them. I trust them completely because they are the ones that chose me, so I am just. I get up from my seat, with the awareness that with each step I take to go back up, the connection with my guides will gently fade; slowly, with each step I will become a little more myself and a little closer to my normal state of consciousness. So I go up the stairs more nimbly than when I came down. With a light step, I go up, pausing for only a moment at each landing. I take the time I need to come back to myself, in my consciousness. No shortcuts. But my intention is clear: to get back my sense and my awareness. As I go up the stairs, I keep that peace within me. I watch my energy change. Step by step, I go up, by the first landing already I am much more awake, much more present. I go up and keep going up. I climb the last steps. I know when I have reached the top. I open my eyes; I am awake and refreshed. All good, all good, all good. I get to the top and open my eyes. I can feel the soles of my feet; I can feel the soles of my feet and move my toes; and now I can move my feet. If I am seated in the lotus position I can feel my pelvis and my buttocks. I move my fingers and my shoulders. I come back to myself. I am me again.

So be it. May light and peace be with you.

Exercise 4

The aim of this exercise is to recognize the differences in your state and to feel the physical changes that take place as you go deeper into a trance. The exercise has three phases and is done in pairs. First one person will work for the other person, through inspired speaking for five minutes relative to a word that the other has provided. Then the medium will go into a light trance, do the same thing with another word provided by their "client", for another five minutes. Finally, the medium will go deeper into a trance and let themselves be fully guided by the spirit world and the message it has for their "client". The entire exercise lasts 20 minutes and then the roles are exchanged.

Rapid frequency exercises

Rapid frequencies are used in the context of distance therapy (to inquire about a person's physical state), to learn to read a person based on a name, a photo or a place (e.g. a hospital). The following exercises allow these frequencies to be apprehended and materialized, in order to be able to expand and develop them. Here it must not be forgotten that you learn more from your mistakes than from your successes. Indeed, in the case of a mistake, you can find out if it is the mind producing information or if we actually read it in the other person's energy field, or that of the picture or object.

Indeed, information is received in different ways, depending on each person's working method. In addition, what is produced by the mind comes to us in various manners. The differences are easy to detect and it is each medium's responsibility to see these variations in order to establish a sort of map for the mistake: "I see that I have just made a mistake because what I felt was not the same as when I received the right information." Rapid frequencies also enable mediumistic contact with the deceased and therefore with the spirit world.

The following exercises help you learn to better identify

your clear-senses and to have a better physical understanding of what happens when performing sensitive work.

Exercise 5 – Sitting in the power

Introduction

This form of meditation was presented by an English trance medium, Mark Webb, whose guide, James, explained the meditation through Mark. It is a very powerful type of work, one that touches all areas of our being, especially those relating to sensitivity. What is important in this form of meditation is simply having the intention to do things and not doing things on purpose. In other words, when we make contact with various frequencies or energies, all that is necessary is to be ready for this and to remain focused on the objective and intention to reach these energies. Visualizations and feelings must not be forced, made or projected – we just observe. We observe ourselves.

Balancing the cerebral hemispheres: 10′

I sit comfortably on a chair or cushion. I keep my back straight and let my shoulders drop. I relax my jaw and breathe slowly. I observe my chest movements and quiet my thoughts.

I observe the space between my upper lip and my nostril, watching the air flow in and out. I stay focused. I concentrate on my left nostril and inhale only through my left nostril. I inhale and exhale through my left nostril. When I have exhaled again, I do the same with the right nostril. When I have exhaled on the right side, I alternate. I inhale on the left and exhale on the right, and then I inhale on the right and exhale on the left. Left-right, right-left. Left-right, right-left. To the front – to the back. The next time I exhale on the left, I breathe normally again. Additionally, to balance both sides of my brain, I visualize each side. In my left brain I put the letter "A" and in my right brain I put the number "1"; in the left, I put "B" and in the right I put "2"; in the left I put "C" and in the right, "3". I then continue at my own speed and complete the alphabet, placing the letters to the left and the corresponding sequential numbers to the right.

After this, I reverse the process, which means I put the number "1" in my left brain and the letter "A" in the right; "2" in the left, and "B" in the right; "3" in the left and "C" in the right, and so on, going through the numbers and letters at my own speed. In this way I relax... relax...

Meditation: 50'

Whether I believe in God or simply in a higher energy or a Great Spirit – whatever name I give this higher power, I visualize a shining beam that flows down from that source – a magnificent bright light. This beam falls on me and surrounds me, protecting me and rocking me. I make contact with my center, if I know where that is... the place where I feel at home... where I renew my energy... where I go inside myself... the place inside me where I am at peace. If I do not know where this is, I accept that for this meditation it is Anahata, my heart chakra, in the middle of my chest. I visualize a luminous source inside of my center. I breathe in through my fontanel. I inhale the energy from that magnificent source through my center. Every time I inhale, my center builds up. With every breath I take my center lights up and expands. Thus I breathe into my center and from my center I spread through myself, beyond my body. I breathe into my center and from my center I spread through myself, beyond my body and throughout the entire room. I breathe into my center and expand beyond my body throughout the room in which I am sitting. I expand outside this room. I expand into all the levels and layers of nature. I am not going to look for memories in nature; I just have the intention of expanding into all the levels and layers of nature. Every time I inhale, I expand; when I exhale, I relax. When I exhale, I let go; I relax and my field will draw upon the levels and layers and bring me what is important, what is right, everything that my body and my spirit need. The intention is enough for me; my spirit knows what to do.

I breathe into my center and from my center, I spread all over the Earth; I expand into the universe; intention is enough. My spirit knows what to do. My spirit knows that distance is an illusion. My spirit knows it can access everything. So I just breathe in through my fontanel and I just expand into the universe. I breathe into my center and I spread into all the levels and layers of the universe; I expand. When I exhale, I relax and allow my spirit to draw upon the power of the planets, to draw forth everything that is right, everything that is for my greatest good.

I breathe into my center and from my center I expand into all of the levels and layers of thought. All of the levels and layers of thought. The intention is enough. I stay focused and observe myself. I expand into all the levels and layers of thought. I exhale and relax and let my spirit take over.

I breathe into my center and expand into all of the levels and layers of sight, into everything that is visual. I do not try to see yet; I simply have the intention to expand into everything that is visual and all the ways of seeing. My spirit knows what to do. So I relax and remain centered and observe. I expand into all of the layers and levels of vision.

Through my fontanel, I breathe into my center and from my center I expand into all of the levels and layers of hearing and all the ways to hear, and once more I do not force anything; my spirit knows what to do. I am just present, in the rhythm of my breathing, aware that at that moment I am spreading into all of the levels and layers of hearing.

I breathe into my center and from my center I expand into all of the levels and layers of feeling. I am not looking for anything in particular. Again, my spirit knows what to do. Intention is enough for me.

And I am at peace and I observe. I spread through all of the levels and layers of feeling. Again, through my fontanel, the magnificent beam of light is falling upon me and enveloping me.

I breathe into my center and I expand into all the aspects of spiritual healing; I spread into all of the aspects of spiritual healing. I do nothing; I observe; I give my spirit time to draw forth a hand to bring me what I need to serve.

And from my interior light, I expand into all of the levels and layers of trance. I spread into all of the aspects of the trance. I do not fall into a trance; I am not going into a trance. I spread through these different frequencies. I remain centered and I observe myself. I remain centered; I stay focused and I expand into all of the levels and layers, in all of the aspects and frequencies of the trance.

And beyond all perception, beyond all our clear-senses, beyond the Earth, the light and the universe; beyond everything and through everything shines a single light, vibrates a unique Great Spirit. I breathe into my center and from my heart and my center I expand into the Great Spirit. I exhale and let myself go in His peace. I am a sponge in the ocean and the ocean is in me. I am the light; I am the peace because it is in me at all times.

Slowly, gently, at my own speed, I come back to myself. I breathe more intensely; I get back into contact with my body, with the soles of my feet. I can feel my body touching the chair, or the floor or the backrest. Slowly, gently coming back.

And after this type of modified consciousness exercise, it is always recommended to ground yourself properly, to return to the moment, to the present time. I am the light all of the time.

Grounding: 5'

The word "grounding" is often used. Being well-grounded helps us to live better in the present and to be more present in our thoughts. It also helps balance our energies. Additionally, being well-grounded keeps us in good physical and mental health. But it is nevertheless a good idea to ground yourself every morning before leaving home and also after meditating for long periods in which work was carried out in a state of modified consciousness. You can ground yourself whether you are sitting, standing or lying down. Personally, I really enjoy doing it while standing. I am centered and I connect with my center or with my heart chakra. I breathe into my center and spread throughout my body, but especially I spread to my legs and feet. When I inhale and expand I send beams through my body, through my feet and into the ground. If I want to, I visualize glowing roots growing from the soles of my feet and how I breathe through these roots. With every breath, I pull this earthly energy into my core. I breathe through the roots beneath my feet and fill my being with this vibrant energy. When I exhale, I just think, "I ground myself." I am centered, I am present and in the moment. You can do this exercise in the morning for two or three minutes and repeat it two or three times per hour throughout the day for one or two breathing cycles.

Exercise 6

This exercise lets you bring your consciousness into your hands, so as to be able to feel the changes in the energies. It allows you to develop your sensitivity and define how information enters your system. It also lets you practice scanning a patient.

For this exercise, you need half of a vest cut out of a trash bag or other plastic bag, and three people: One person will wear the plastic vest, one person will perform the work, and one person will guide the hand of the person working.

The exercise is done standing, as follows:

The person who will be doing the work (the therapist) stands up and closes his eyes so as not to see which side the vest is being worn on. The person who is to wear the vest puts it on, on the right side or on the left, as he prefers.

The last person (the guide) takes the student therapist's hand and moves it in front of the chest of the person wearing the vest for a few seconds, at a distance of between ten to 15 centimeters, so that the medium can grasp the information and detect which side the vest is being worn on.

When the student has detected a difference between the chest and the plastic vest, he will say so and open his eyes to see if what he felt is correct.

The medium will repeat the exercise five or six times in a row to confirm or negate his feeling. Then the group will exchange roles so each person can work as the medium.

Exercise 7

This exercise is done in a group of at least seven people or more. There must not be a smaller number of participants. One person will direct the exercise and the six others will sit on chairs in a circle on the same side.

The person who is leading the exercise will have prepared six pieces of paper, one for each participant. Five will be blank and one will have a number or a letter written on it.

When the group is seated, the leader will distribute one piece of paper to each participant. The participants must not know what is on each other's papers. The one who has the paper with the symbol will be the "blocker". His role is as follows: while the other participants will have to pass the energy around the circle, the blocker must stop it and not let it pass. He must imagine himself to be surrounded by barbed wire, or ice, or a black veil. The intention to block the energy is enough. He must not reveal his role before the end of the exercise.

Before starting the exercise, the leader decides the direction of the energy flow: clockwise or counterclockwise. When the group is seated and the papers have been handed out, the exercise begins. All the participants close their eyes and start to pass the energy around the circle. The blocker blocks the energy sent by the participants. The participants try to find out which one of them is the blocker through their perception of where the energy is no longer flowing and how that information came to them. It may be perceived in different ways: a vision that the energy is no longer flowing in one place, a noise that means the energy has been blocked, or a cold, warm or tingling sensation.

After one or two minutes the leader stops the exercise by asking all of the participants to stop sending the energy around the circle and open their eyes. When they have opened their eyes, the participants have to say where they saw or felt that the energy was blocked and indicate the blocker, who of course has to participate in the discussion as well and must not reveal his role right away. When all of the participants have given their opinions the blocker reveals himself by showing his paper to the others.

The exercise can be repeated several times. The leader takes up the pieces of paper and shuffles them before handing them out again.

The aim of the exercise is to detect an energy blockage and especially to take note of how this blockage is felt: physically (warm, cold, tingling sensation, etc.), visually (mental image of ice or a wall, etc.); or audibly (whistle, gong, etc.). There are many ways in which it may be perceived and it is up to each participant to determine how he notices the blocked energy.

Being able to detect an energy blockage is pertinent during a treatment because when you are scanning a patient it allows you to detect the zones in which there is no energy flow.

Exercise 8

This exercise requires at least three participants. The aim is to be able to differentiate between different people's energies. Each living being has a different energy field and because of this, it is important to perceive the difference, whether it is for mediumship or for healing purposes.

One person will therefore decide to do this exercise. The other participants will make themselves available. All of the participants are standing.

The person who has chosen to do the exercise will stand a few meters away with his back turned towards the group and with his eyes closed.

One of the people in the group moves slowly towards the participant, one step at a time and without making any noise. Ideally, he will be barefoot or wearing shoes that make the least possible noise.

When the person who is doing the exercise feels the advancing participant's energy field enter his own energy field, he will indicate this by raising his hand or saying something. At that moment the person moving forward stops and remains in place for the rest of the exercise.

When the first person has stopped, the others will do the same thing, i.e. move quietly and slowly forward toward the person doing the exercise. When that person indicates he has felt their energy field, they will stop and go back to their starting points. When each person in the entire group has done this, the person doing the exercise can open his eyes, turn around and speak with the others.

The participants take turns doing the exercise. The one doing the exercise focuses his attention on his own energy field, which will enable him to gain greater awareness of his own energy field and be able to notice when there is a change as another energy field enters into his, whether it is the energy of a living person or that of a being from the spirit world. The person can also evaluate the differences between different people's energy fields. This exercise gives you an understanding of your own energy field and how other energies interact with it.

Exercise 9

There is no ideal number of participants in this exercise; however, it should be an even number so that two groups of equal size can be formed.

The participants remain standing.

One group is lined up on one side of the room with everyone's eyes closed.

The other group spreads out around the room, in silence.

Ideally, this exercise should be done barefoot or wearing shoes that make the least possible noise.

When the participants in the second group have spread out around the room, they indicate this to the group lined up against the wall.

The exercise can now begin. With their eyes closed, the people in the group near the wall start moving. The goal is to cross the room without touching any of the people who are standing around the room. The participants walk carefully and slowly in order to avoid injury if they should bump into anyone.

The people crossing the room with their eyes closed have to pay attention to their energy fields. As soon as they feel a change in their fields, it definitely means that another person's energy field has touched or come into theirs. They must then step aside to avoid bumping into that person. When everyone in that group has crossed the room with their eyes closed, the exercise is over and the group changes roles: the group that was spread around the room will line up on one side of the room and close their eyes, and the group that had to cross the room with their eyes closed first will now spread out around the room, and the exercise will begin again.

The goal for each participant is to cross the room and be aware of his own energy field. This awareness will allow the participant to develop a good level of awareness of his own energy field and learn to notice the changes when another energy field has entered his, and thus be able to avoid bumping into one of the other participants. It also enables you to perceive the different energy fields relating to each person. This understanding of your own energy field allows you to sense the interaction of another being from the living world or the spirit world.

Exercise 10

There is no exact number of participants in this exercise; however, it must be an even number because the members of the first group are going to pair off with the members of the second group.

The groups should arrange themselves as follows: One group is sitting on chairs arranged in a circle. The other group stands in a larger circle around the seated group, at a distance of one to two meters depending on the size of the room.

When all the participants have closed their eyes, the standing group slowly and silently moves in closer to the seated group.

When a member of the seated group feels his partner's energy field, he raises his hand. The approaching person will continue to come closer, until he is close enough to put his arms around his seated partner without touching him.

The standing person stays there for between 30 seconds and one minute. Then he slowly and just as quietly starts backing away.

The seated person, who still has his eyes closed, will raise his hand when he senses that his partner is leaving his energy field.

This is an exercise in self-awareness and awareness of your own energy field. This awareness will enable the participant to develop a good sense of his own energy field. He will be able to notice the changes when another energy field has entered his and when it will leave. This understanding of your own energy field allows you to sense the interaction of another being from the living world or the spirit world.

Exercise 11

This is a collective exercise in which the entire group can work at the same time.

You need to have some cotton, the kind that can be bought at the pharmacy or to remove makeup. You should choose cotton wool and not disks so that it can be more easily divided up. Cotton is an ideal material due to its absorbent properties.

Before starting the exercise, each participant holds the piece of cotton he has been given in order to feel its neutrality. Indeed, no one else has left his energy in it. This is why the cotton used by the participants must be discarded after use.

After this operation, each participant must charge his piece of cotton with his energy. To fill the cotton with energy, you have to build up your energy. Imagine yourself in your beam; breathe in the energy through your fontanel and out through your center or heart chakra, to create your own bubble. When you have done this, the energy will have spread through the cotton. This operation may take several minutes and the participants can do it with their eyes open or closed, as they wish.

When this operation is finished, the participants exchange their cotton in order to feel the energy contained in the cotton. To perceive the cotton's energy, each person must hold the piece of cotton in his hand and take note of how they feel the energy it gives off: a feeling of heat or coldness, a vision, a sound, etc. When this is done the participants exchange their pieces of cotton again. This operation can be done several times.

The aim of this exercise is to sense the energy given off by an object that has been charged with someone else's energy (in this case the cotton) to get practice in the subtleties involved in the perception of an energy field. This awareness enables the participant to notice the subtle differences in the energies given off by different people.

Exercise 12

This exercise is done in pairs. It can only be done once, since the objects used are charged with energy.

For this exercise, you need small objects like little stone animal carvings or small plastic figurines, three objects per working group.

The participants are seated two by two at a table, facing each other. The three small objects are lined up on the table between the participants.

The person who has chosen to work first closes his eyes. The other person then takes one of the three small objects in front of him and charges it with energy after centering himself first. When this has been done, he puts the object back where it was and asks the person who is working to open his eyes.

Using his perception, the person working has to find the object that has been energized by the other person. To do this, he can either bring his awareness to one hand and pass it above the object or bring his awareness to both hands and pick up each object in turn.

The aim of this exercise is to sense the energy given off by an object that has been charged with someone else's energy (in this case the small object) to get practice in the subtleties involved in the perception of an energy field. This awareness enables the participant to notice the subtle differences in the energies given off by different people.

A variant which allows the exercise to be repeated several times is to use gravel picked up outdoors and change it with each turn.

Exercise 13

This is an individual exercise.

Before the exercise, the person can, if they wish, rub his hands together to gain greater perception.

In this exercise, the person places the palms of his hands opposite each other, first close and then slowly and smoothly farther apart, before bringing them slowly closer again. Repeating this movement enables the energy that flows between the hands to be physically felt, such as tingling, heat, cold, etc. The person will be aware that the energy is building up when he feels resistance as he brings his palms close, like two magnets pushing against each other, and a stretching like chewing gum when he moves them farther apart. When the person becomes aware of this energy he makes a ball of it and passes it from one hand to the other, while making it bigger or smaller.

Exercise 14

This is an individual magnetizing exercise to do at home. It takes place over one full month. You need two identical plates or bowls and two food items from the same source (e.g. fruit or vegetables such as tomatoes). For example, if you use tomatoes, put one in each bowl or plate and set it in two different places in the room. One tomato will be the control and will not be touched for the entire month, with no attention given to it at all. On the other hand, the other tomato will be magnetized once or twice a day. To do this, cover the tomato with your hands, without touching it, and send energy, by intention, to magnetize it. Each session should last from ten to 15 minutes, depending on the time available. In order to monitor the process, you can take photos of each tomato in regular intervals.

At the end of one month, the control tomato that was not magnetized should have rotted. On the other hand, the magnetized tomato should only be a bit soft or have started to dry out. There should be no signs of rot (or only very minor ones) on it.

Exercise 15

This individual exercise allows you to practice psychokinesis.

The exercise requires an empty drink can (soda or other) and a teaspoon.

First, the person sits at a steady table and places the can in front of him. He then places his hands on either side of the can, without touching it. To make it move, he simply connects his energy to the energy given off by the can, and then slowly moves his hands at the same time in a synchronized movement. The can will then follow the movement. This has nothing to do with a draft created by the hand movement. When the mechanism is fully integrated, the can will start to move more and more quickly.

In the next step, the person sets the can aside and takes the spoon in hand. He then starts to joyfully rub the spoon on the handle just below the oval part. When the energy vibration has sufficiently increased, the particles in the metal will begin to move faster and faster and will become "malleable". To assist in this process, the person can imagine holding raw spaghetti which softens as he rubs it, as it would during the cooking process, and finally loses all stiffness. With a little luck, the spoon can be effortlessly bent without requiring any strength.

Exercise 16a

This exercise is done in pairs.

The goal of this exercise is to use your senses to find the different-colored card. In this example, you should find the red card.

To do this exercise, you need three cards from an ordinary playing deck; two black cards (spades or clubs) and one red card (hearts or diamonds). Leave out the face cards (king, queen or jack) because they can include both red and black and can mislead the perception of the person who is working.

The two people sit at a table opposite each other with the cards laid out in a line between them and decide which person will go first. Once this is done, the person who is not working will take the three cards and shuffle them. Then he will lay them face down on the table so that the person working will not know which one is the red card. The person who is handling the cards should not look at them so as not to communicate the red card by telepathy.

The person working can use his senses to find the red card in different ways:

- He can transfer his awareness to his dominant hand, which he will then pass over each card in turn and assess whether the feeling in his hand changes above a particular card. He can keep his hand over each card for as long as needed to take note of any feeling.

- He can close his eyes and project the shapes of the cards on his internal screen and ask for a sign indicating which card is red. This operation can be done with his eyes open in order to see any distinguishing sign that directs him to the red card. It could be a color, a symbol, a number, any indication is correct.

When the person working thinks he has found the red card, he turns the card over. This exercise is repeated several times and then the roles are changed.

Exercise 16b

This exercise is done in pairs.

The goal of this exercise is to receive information by telepathy to find the red card. This means that both students will be working. One student transmits the information telepathically and the other has to decrypt it. The student who is sending the information has to find the right frequency and means to indicate where the card is.

For this exercise, you need three cards from an ordinary deck; two black cards (spades or clubs) and one red card (hearts or diamonds). Leave out the face cards (king, queen or jack) because they can include both red and black and can mislead the perception of the person who is working.

The two people sit opposite each other at a table on which the cards have been placed in a line. They decide which person will be the sender and which one will be the receiver. Once this is done, the person who is to be the sender shuffles the cards and before putting them back on the table in front of his partner, he looks to see where the red card is. Then he lines them up on the table, face down, so that the receiver will not know where the red card is. He then transmits where the red card is to the receiver.

There are different ways of transmitting information on the red card:

- Mentally visualizing the position of the card, or
- Mentally visualizing the red card, or
- Mentally saying the position of the card: in the middle, on the left or on the right.

When the receiver thinks he has got the information, he turns the card over.

Exercise 16c

This is an individual exercise. To do it, you need 20 playing cards, ten from the red suits and ten from the black, leaving out the face cards because they can mislead perception.

Shuffle the cards and place them in a pile in front of you. Before drawing each card, send your consciousness into the pile of cards to see if a red or black card is on top. When you have received this information, and to verify it, turn the top card over. Repeat until you have reached the end of the pile. It is important to keep track of your progress by making one pile with the cards you got right and one with the ones that were wrong.

Exercise 16d

This is an individual exercise. First you have to make two sets of cards. To do that, cut out ten pieces approximately 6 x 9 centimeters each out of white cardboard.

To make the first deck, use a black pen to draw six symbols on some white paper, then cut them out and glue them on six of the cardboard cards. The symbols are: a triangle, a circle, a square, a cross, some wavy lines and a star.

To make the second deck, cut sheets of colored paper into 5 x 8 centimeter pieces and glue them on the four cardboard cards. The colors must be "primary" colors, i.e. black, blue, red, and yellow.

Now you can do two exercises. Using the first set of cards with the symbols, shuffle the cards and place them face down in front of you and try to guess which symbol is under each card. Do this exercise a dozen times or so and keep track of your results on a notepad. Do the same with the set of colored cards.

Exercise 16e

This is an individual exercise. First you have to make a set of cards. To do so, cut out nine pieces approximately 6 x 9 centimeters each out of white cardboard paper.

Then, take three pieces of colored paper and cut out three pieces per color measuring about 5 x 8 centimeters each. The colors have to be "primary" colors, e.g. black, red and yellow. Glue these nine colored paper cards onto the nine cardboard cards.

Now, shuffle and lay out the nine cards face down in front of you in three lines of three cards each. The exercise is similar to a memory game, i.e. you have to find two cards of the same color, using your senses, and pair them up.

Do this exercise a dozen or so times and keep track of your results on a notepad.

Exercise 16f

This is an individual exercise. You need five pieces of string of the same length. Tie a knot on the end of one string. Then put all the strings together and hold them in your hand so that only the knotless ends can be seen. By looking only at the ends of the strings, you have to guess which of the strings has the knot.

You can repeat this exercise as often as you like and keep track of your progress on a notepad.

Exercise 17

This is an individual exercise. You need nine small cardboard boxes of similar appearance, such as match boxes, and a small, freshly-picked flower. Place the flower head in one of the boxes and then mix them up. Send your consciousness to your hand and scan the nine boxes to find which one has the flower. You can repeat this exercise several times and keep track of your progress on a notepad.

It is important to use a fresh flower and not a dried one because the respective energy flow is different.

Exercise 18

This is an individual exercise that lets you work with numbers. You need a telephone book, an address book, or a smartphone with a contact list.

To do the exercise, set things up so that the phone numbers are hidden and you only see the names of the people. Choose a name at random and then try to guess the dominant number of the corresponding phone number. The dominant number is the one that is repeated the most often. Check the results as you go and keep track of your progress and your success rate on a notepad. You should not be disappointed if you are not very successful, because numbers are managed by the left side of the brain as has been shown in research by Dr. Julie Beischel in the United States.

Exercise 19

The purpose of this exercise is to develop self-awareness that can also be used for psychic readings relating notably to recent memory, but also in mediumship. The two partners in the exercise each work for 15 minutes, with a three-minute discussion of their experiences in between.

This exercise takes place in two parts, a first part that is done alone and a second part as a pair.

First, the person concentrates on things he likes and lists them by name in his mind, such as going out with friends, knitting, going for walks, cooking with spices, eating sweets, etc., and things he likes less such as queuing at the supermarket, sad films, abstract paintings, reading, etc. and also lists them by name in his mind. Each positive or negative emotion corresponds to a feeling: what I feel when I imagine doing something that I like – butterflies in my stomach, tingling in my chest, feeling like I am on a roller coaster, and so on. What I feel when I imagine doing something I dislike – nausea, a disagreeable tickling in my head, a heaviness of heart, and so on. What feeling goes with the pleasant activity and what feeling with the unpleasant activity? It is important to take note of what is felt. This part of the exercise takes five minutes.

The second part of the exercise is done as a pair and will require working with recent memory.

When the roles have been defined, the medium centers himself, breathes in through his fontanel, builds up his field and extends it to the person in front of him. The medium looks for activities his client has recently done, within the past three to five days, and, using the feelings he took note of in the first part of the exercise, defines whether or not the person in front of him liked what he had done.

After ten minutes' work, the two discuss and assess the reading. Did the medium have an agreeable or a disagreeable feeling about the activities? Did the feeling correspond to the satisfaction the client got from them?

When the two have discussed the reading, they change roles.

Exercise 20

This exercise can be done individually by pet owners. The principle is to call the animal (dog or cat) to you simply by thinking. To do this, center yourself, breathe in through your fontanel, build up your field and extend it to your pet. Communication takes place through imagery and not through words. Therefore, you should mentally imagine your pet coming to you for attention. He or she should come. Aside from this exercise, communication with an animal should always be done through images; for example, if you want to tell it something such as not to urinate in the house or outside of its litter box.

Psychic reading
The following exercises let you practice psychic reading.

Exercise 21

This exercise allows you to read the recent events that have taken place in a person's life. When we say "recent events", we mean noteworthy ones, such as having bought a pair of shoes for oneself, or had a punctured tire, or been unusually late to work, or met someone by chance or by appointment. Things like personal hygiene, meals and so on are part of everyone's daily routine and are ordinary events.

The exercise is done in pairs. The two partners in the exercise sit opposite each other and each work for 15 minutes.

The person working closes his eyes, centers himself, inhaling through his fontanel and exhaling through his center to expand his energy field.

When he has done this for about five minutes, the person working extends his field to that of the other person. The intention is to obtain elements from recent memory, i.e. between one and seven days in the life of the person in front of him.

Then, for about ten minutes, the person working will be receptive to the elements in the other person's memory and mentally take note of them.

After this time the person working will open his eyes and describe the information he received to the other person, who has to reply with "yes" or "no".

If the response is negative, the person working will note the mistake down and see how he received the information, because we learn the most from our mistakes. We learn to detect a mistake also by learning to understand ourselves, i.e. by comparing a situation in which we were wrong to situations in which we were correct.

This exercise in reading another person's energy fields can be done with a different aspect than recent memory. For example, you can read the first ten years of childhood, or the second ten, and so on.

When the 15 minutes are up, the roles are exchanged and the other person works.

A variation on this exercise is to do it alone by extending your energy field through intention to a consenting person who is located at a distance. The information received is then written on a notepad. This is done for about ten minutes. After that you discuss the exercise over the phone, via a video conferencing application or even by text messaging and the other person will confirm the information or not.

Exercise 22

This exercise allows pertinent events in the person's recent past to be read.

It is done in pairs, with the people sitting opposite each other and each work in turn, as in a game of ping-pong. The exercise takes 15 minutes; it may be longer if it is done on a private basis. This is my favorite one.

The partners close their eyes, center themselves (each one breathes in from his light beam from the fontanel and breathes out from his center in order to expand his energy field). When this is done, the two extend their fields into each other's. This is to be able to obtain the elements from recent memory, i.e. between one and seven days in the life of the person opposite.

Each in turn will allow the elements of the other's recent memory to come to him and will say them out loud. The other person answers "yes" or "no" before changing roles and doing the same.

A variation on this exercise is to do this remotely via a video conferencing application, telephone or even text messaging.

Exercise 23

For this exercise, it is best to create two groups of equal size and if possible with an even number of participants. This exercise takes 15 minutes.

One group will work and the other will be the "clients". This should be decided at the beginning of the exercise.

The chairs are to be set up before the exercise: a first row of chairs should be set up and then a row just behind it, though the chairs must not touch.

The group that is going to work will sit in the front row of chairs, close their eyes and begin building their energy, breathing through the fontanel into the center, in order to expand it.

Quietly, the participants in the second group will take their seats behind those of the working group, who will not know who is seated behind whom. Every member of the working group must correspond to one of the clients.

Each person in the working group will have built up their energy field and will extend it to the person behind them, with the intention of getting facts from that person: Is it a man or a woman? Tall, or short? What color hair, and how long? and so on, at first, in order to get a physical description of that person. Then the person who is working will seek more information, still factual, about the client's occupation: In what field do they work? In what place do they work? There are many possibilities. The people working can look for facts about the place in which the "client" lives (house, or flat? If it is a flat, on what floor? How does the front door look? How and in what style is it decorated? Etc.), about their family life: does the person live alone, or with someone; do they have children? Etc. About the main personality traits: is the person emotional, or are they pragmatic? Do they like to be with people or prefer to be alone? Etc. The working participants can also look for information about hobbies or free time activities that the person behind them likes to do. Does the person take long walks in the forest or do they prefer to read in a comfortable armchair? Do they play sports or prefer watching TV? Do they like to do odd jobs, or paint, or do pottery? Etc.

This exercise requires you to stick to the facts, in order to avoid bringing your mind into play: indeed, we tend to try to guess who is behind us, because the participants in the groups have seen each other and may even know each other. If the latter is the case, the working group must put aside what they know and work outside of their familiarity with the others.

When the 15 minutes are up, the participants in the working group open their eyes and turn around to share what they received with the other person, for about three to five minutes.

Exercise 24

This exercise is done alone. It lets you practice your reflexes in opening your field to work and closing it immediately afterwards. The main goal is not to get a correct result but to implement personal discipline when you are perceiving information. What is being practiced here is the following mechanism: opening your field to the desired information, perception or reception, and closing your field then grounding or returning to yourself. If additionally the result is correct, then that is all the better.

A medium can practice this as many times a day as they wish; for example, when receiving a phone call or a text message. When the phone rings, before answering it, the medium opens their field to guess who is calling. When a name comes to mind, they close their field, ground and then answer the phone or check the message.

A fun variation can be done in the same way, when the medium has an appointment. Before actually meeting the person, they take a moment to open their field, guess how the person is dressed (main color, style, unique clothing details, etc.) and whether the person will be on time or not. When the medium has received this information, they close their field, ground and then check whether their perceptions were correct or not when the meeting actually takes place.

Exercise 25 – Setting up a personal color chart

Working with colors is something that is often done whether for care or mediumship. It is important to set up your own personal color chart. To do this, it is recommended to draw up a table with two axes: vertically for the colors you see the most often and horizontally with the four layers: physical, mental, emotional or spiritual.

Then, it is recommended to feel each color: when you approach a new color, you should feel its vibration and ask, where you would put that color: at a physical level, and if so, in which part? Or would you put it on a mental level, and if so, in which type of mental operation? Emotional, and if so, which emotion? Spiritual, and if so, which type of blockage or former regime?

It is important to know where to put which color. The range is never finite.

To define a color in your chart, you need to ask yourself what the color means to you and in which layer of the aura (physical, mental, emotional or spiritual) it can be placed.

As a reminder, I find that dirty yellow makes me think of pus; red makes me think of blood, green brings to mind nausea or stomach pain; gray, the gray matter in the brain, and so on.

On the next page is a color table you can fill in. This is of course just an example because color variation is almost infinite.

Layers of the aura / Colors	Physical	Mental	Emotional	Spiritual
Turquoise				
Sky blue				
Royal blue				
Indigo				
Violet				
Pink				
White				
Silvery-gray				
Black				
Golden brown				
Red				
Orange				
Yellow				
Light green				
Emerald green				
Dark green				

Exercise 26 – The Great Spirit's Gardens

Pranayamas: 20'

I sit down comfortably on a chair or meditation pillow. I keep my back straight, but allow my shoulders and jaws to relax, and I breathe slowly. I simply observe my chest movements. I watch myself inhale and exhale, and just watch my chest move in and out. I inhale and exhale and observe my breathing.

I focus on the zone between my upper lip and my nostrils and watch how my breathing goes in and out. I keep this focus; all of my concentration is on the friction caused by my breathing, just above my upper lip.

I visualize and focus on my left nostril and breathe in and out uniquely through it. The next time I exhale through my left nostril, I inhale only through my right nostril. Uniquely through my right nostril. Inhale... exhale. The next time I exhale through my right nostril, I alternate my breathing, i.e., I inhale on the left and exhale on the right, inhale on the right and exhale on the left – left-right, right-left. With my natural breathing rhythm I alternate: left-right, right-left. I balance my hemispheres and my nervous system; work with my third eye, and practice focusing. One breathing technique and four exercises.

After the next left exhalation, I return to normal breathing. I focus on my perineum and contract it. (If I am a woman, I focus on my cervix and contract it.) I contract and release; contract, release. I do this several times. And I visualize a light beam extending from my perineum to the middle of my head; a light beam that surrounds my spine. I visualize a ball of light in my perineum. A luminous ball that completely lights up my loins. And every time I inhale I raise this ball of light through the beam to the middle of my head. Every time I exhale the ball goes down the beam to my loins. While I am doing these pranayamas and this breathing technique, the tip of my tongue is touching my palate (Kechari Mudra). When I breathe in, the energy rises;

when I breathe out, the energy goes down. And as I breathe to my own rhythm, I raise and lower this ball of energy through my spine.

Inhale, and the ball rises; exhale, and it goes back down. Never force energy. Be relaxed and the intention will make the energy really move. You can't make energy do anything. But you can guide it and you do that precisely with intention. Every time I inhale, I bring the ball up through my spine. Every time I exhale I evacuate dense particles and dissolve them. Thus with every breath I am lighter: with every breath the vibration of my field increases and my duality decreases. With every breath I am more balanced and more at peace.

If you want to intensify your breathing, you can do "Oms" in a 4-beat rhythm – but silent "Oms". Tell yourself when inhaling, "I will say four silent Oms," and when exhaling, "Four silent Oms." Four Oms when inhaling and four Oms when exhaling. I inhale and exhale in a relaxed manner.

People who have high blood pressure or a hiatus hernia cannot hold their breath after inhaling, and people with low blood pressure cannot hold the air out after exhaling. And now, after four inhaled Oms, you do two apneal Oms, two paused Oms, four exhaled Oms, and two paused Oms.

This is a four-timed breathing rhythm: four inhalations, two holds, four exhalations, two holds. Four "Oms" when breathing in and two when holding your breath, and four Oms when breathing out and two while holding your breath. If your breathing is still slow and balanced, work on four + four + four + four: the Pranayama square. This means that you say four Oms when you inhale, four Oms while holding your breath, four Oms when you exhale and four Oms before breathing in again.

When you have exhaled for the fourth time, return to your normal breathing and do stretching movements through your spine, from the lower spine to the upper in the middle of your head and from the middle of your head back down to your perineum. You have balanced your hemispheres and found your balance between heaven and earth. You are now ready to work.

The Great Spirit's Gardens: 40'

I see myself walking somewhere in Asia, in the mountains. There is abundant vegetation with terraced gardens. I am on a little path with hills rising above me. In front of me, I see a staircase cut into the rock, which brings me to the first terrace, the first garden.

At the foot of this staircase, I stop; I am here, surrounded by a beam of light falling on me, enveloping me. Through my fontanel, I breathe in this light, in to my center in the middle of my chest. I breathe in this light, into my own light. Each time I breathe in, I climb up one step. Each time I breathe in, I inhale and build my center. When I exhale, I go up the next step. When I exhale, I relax. I inhale into my center through my fontanel and my center builds up. And I go up the steps of these stairs. Step by step, I illuminate myself, because with every breath I take, I am building my center, I am spreading it through me, outside of me and I am wrapping myself in my own light, still within this magnificent beam. This celestial light. Step by step, I go up. Exhalation by exhalation, I relax. Inhalation and building; exhalation and relaxation.

With every step, I shine more brightly. I get to the top of the stairs. Spread out in front of me is a splendid garden with plants and fruit trees. What is odd is that a strong red light is shining through this garden and across this terrace. Each time I breathe in, I expand into this very vibrant color, this color that revitalizes all the cells in my physical body.

I breathe into my center. From my center, I send my rays into this garden, into this color, into this red vibration. When I exhale, I relax. I charge myself with this electromagnetic energy, re-sourcing and reenergizing my entire system, everything in my physical body. Every time I inhale I expand into the red.

Every time I exhale, I relax and allow my body to recharge, to become more tonic. I am filled with tremendous force.

At the end of the garden, I see the next set of stairs, again hewn out of the rock. Still within my light beam, I go up these next steps. At every step, I inhale and spread through myself. When I exhale, I relax even more. Step by step, in the natural rocking rhythm of my breathing. I can already see a beautiful emerald green light waiting at the next terrace. And indeed I arrive in this garden and this emerald green light and power pierces everything. Again, I walk through this magnificent garden. This green works on my emotional layer. It eases my torments. It balances me and brings me back to harmony. I find peace and distance, peace and distance. Everything is green. With every breath, I expand myself into this brilliant green color. I calm down. Step by step, I go through this emerald green garden.

I come to the end of this beautiful terrace, and in front of me there is another set of stairs to climb. Step by step, calmly and peacefully, I go up, deeper in my center with each step; deeper in my center and in my peace. I can see the blue light. A bright royal blue coming from the next terrace. I go into this garden and see the royal blue light, a bright blue and I go into this garden. This blue eases my mental layer, i.e. the operations of my mind. I breathe into my center and spread out from my center into this magnificent blue that calms my repetitive thoughts. This blue that eases my entire mental system. Even deeper into my peace. Peaceful and reassured. From my fontanel, I breathe into my center and spread into the blue. With each breath, my thoughts calm down; with each breath I focus better. My concentration increases. I am concentrated and calm.

And at the end of the garden, there are more steps to take me even higher. Step by step, I go up. Step by step, I get ready. Step by step, I grow closer to my spiritual layer. A glow, a violet light, violet – almost fluorescent – fills me as soon as I enter this garden. And from my center I spread and welcome this splendid spiritual color. I completely fill my spiritual layer with this violet. It cleanses my doubts, strengthens my faith. It pilots the direction of my spirituality. It irradiates the dogma. With each breath I am getting closer to a free, neutral, and pure spirituality. This magnificent color bears compassion, non-judgment, and clear direction, towards a spirituality without thinking; a free spirituality.

There is a final set of stairs before me which brings me to the last terrace, at the top of this hill. Step by step, I approach, because I know I will be meeting my guides. I am going to meet the Light of the Great Spirit. With each step I am lighter, freer. With each breath I am more at peace. And already the first rays of this white light are upon me and I go into this garden and sit in this magnificent Light of the Great Spirit. I can feel my guides' love draw near to me and surround me. I invite my guides to share, to share in the Light of the Great Spirit. This is not a moment of lively discussion with the beings that guide me; it is a moment of peace and love. It is a moment of peace in the Light of the Great Spirit. I breathe into my center and from my center I extend my rays into the Light of God. Each time I expand my rays, His Light pierces me even more. I am a sponge in the ocean and the ocean is in the sponge. One in the other and even more so with each breath. With each breath I lose myself more and I am nothing more than bright Light. A light within a light. Two lights becoming one. So ham, ham sa, I am this, this I am. I am pure conscience. I am love without intention. I am love and I share my love with all that is. I am the Light of the Great Spirit. At any time it is in me and I remember it is within every being. We are all one. I am in the Great Spirit and the Great Spirit is in me, for eternity. I get up to leave this beautiful garden and memorize this profound state of happiness and peace. I will keep this love throughout my day, my nights, and my entire life.

I go back down the stairs with a joyful step. Happiness

overwhelms me and I cross the violet garden. I go down to the blue garden. I am becoming more and more aware of my body. I go down to the emerald green garden. With each step, so light, I am beginning to feel my body. I go down the stairs toward the fruit trees in that so-invigorating red color that helps me to come back to myself, to my physical body. I can feel the soles of my feet on the ground or on the cushion I am seated on. I come to the bottom, onto that little path that brought me to this hill. I move my hands and fingers. I wiggle my toes, touch my thighs. I come back to myself, back to myself while holding on to that peace.

Psychometry

Psychometry, which is a technique of psychic reading, is reading a person through an object belonging to that person. The objects or photos may belong to someone who is living or deceased. Whether it is energized cotton, as seen in the exercise on self-awareness, or cards, small crystal animals, stones, water, sand, flowers, leaves, balls, numbers, or colored ribbons, the object must be worn or used by the person or have been touched by him or her. The list is not an exhaustive one. The process is as follows: you connect with an object in the same way that you connect with a person. In your light beam, you breathe in through your fontanel and pull energy into your center, to build your energy field. When the field is expanded, you direct it to the object with which you want to work. This type of reading enables the physical, mental, emotional and spiritual layers to be read.

Exercise 27

This exercise is done in pairs. It takes 15 minutes, followed by from three to five minutes of discussion.

For this exercise, small objects belonging to the participants and regularly carried will be required: a piece of jewelry, a watch, glasses, keys, etc. The work is done using two objects per group.

The participants are seated two by two at a table, opposite each other. The person who has chosen to work first closes his or her eyes. The other gives him or her the object.

Through his feeling, the person working will read his colleague through the object held in their hands. He will be inspired by the shapes, repeated shapes, colors, numbers, textures, etc. and talk about their "client's" lifestyle, personality etc., using analogies, symbols, images and metaphors.

When the reading is done, the roles may be exchanged.

Exercise 28

This exercise is done in pairs. The participants are seated opposite each other. The exercise takes 15 minutes, followed by three to five minutes of discussion.

Each person will have brought something belonging to a friend. The person who is working takes the object from the one who brought it. The object must belong to a living person.

After centering themselves, the person working will extend their energy to the object and look for factual information. How did its owner get it? What is the history of this object? Is it new? Was it inherited? Was it a gift? Was it something the owner found? When this information has been received, the person working will look for the owner of the object. Is it a man or a woman? How old? How is the owner related to the person who gave me the object? What sort of personality does the owner have? What is their occupation? Where do they live? Is this object important to its owner? Why is it important or not important?

When the work is finished, the pair will discuss it, and then they will change roles.

Exercise 29

This exercise is done in pairs. The participants are seated opposite each other. The exercise takes 15 minutes, followed by three to five minutes of discussion.

Each person will have brought a photograph of someone they know, either living or deceased, and alone in the photo. The photo is placed in an envelope so that the worker cannot see it.

After centering themselves, the person working will extend their energy into the photo and look for factual information. Is it a man or a woman? How old? How is the owner related to the person who brought the photo? What sort of personality does the owner have? What is their occupation? Where do they live? Is the person married? Does the person have children? How are they at the moment, physically (headache, backache…)?

If the person is deceased the questions are to be considered in the past tense and be about the person's former earthly life.

When the work is finished, the pair will discuss it, and then they will change roles.

Exercise 30

This exercise is done alone. The medium will have previously received, from a consenting person, a photo or first name of someone that person knows. It may be someone who is living or dead.

If it is a photo, it will be placed in an envelope so that the medium cannot see it and given to the medium. The owner of the photo will only tell the medium if the person is alive or dead.

Alone at home, after centering themselves, the medium will extend their energy to the photo and look for factual information. Is it a man or a woman? How old? How is the person in the photo related to the person who brought the photo? What sort of personality do they have? What is their occupation? Where do they live? Is the person married? Does the person have children? How are they at the moment, physically (headache, backache…)?

If the person is deceased the questions are to be considered in the past tense and be about the person's former earthly life.

The medium works for the necessary time and takes notes of the information they receive on a notepad.

After this, the medium discusses the results with the owner of the photo, over the telephone, via a video conferencing application or by text message and checks the accuracy of the information received.

In the case of a first name, the only information the medium receives is whether the person is alive or dead. The work is performed in the same way except that the medium's energy is extended into the first name.

When the exercise is finished, the medium discusses the results with the owner of the photo, over the telephone, via a video conferencing application or by text message and checks the accuracy of the information received.

Exercise 31

This is an individual exercise. To do it, all the medium needs is an Internet connection and to know how to conduct an Internet search online.

The work consists in guessing more or less accurately the birth dates of famous people.

To do this, the medium makes a list of famous people whose birth date he or she does not know.

Alone at home, after centering themselves, the medium extends their energy to the first name and looks for the information relating to the time when the person was born. The work is done starting with the most general and moving to the most detailed: visualize a circle divided into four parts, representing the four seasons. Was the person born in the first quarter (spring), the second (summer), the third (autumn) or the fourth (winter)? With respect to the medium, was the person born before them, or after? How many years' difference is there between them: ten, 20, 30? Etc.

Each season has four months; in which month was the famous person born?

Then visualize a calendar with a full month and the days in it. Is the birth date in the upper or lower part of the month?

Continue in this manner until a full date is obtained, then use a search engine to check accuracy online.

Exercise 32

This exercise enables you to work blind with the least possible influence from your mind. It is carried out in a group of three people; one person who is working and two people to be the "clients". You will need a small ball for this.

The medium sits on a chair with their back to the two others. The "clients" must also be seated behind the medium, near enough to be able to touch their shoulder to signal a right or wrong answer or ask for details. Indeed, the medium must not hear their "client's" voice because they might recognize them and know where the ball is and with whom they are working.

One of the two "clients" has the small ball in their hand. The session can now begin: the medium closes their eyes, centers themselves, exhales from their center, builds their field and extends it to the holder of the small ball. Of course, the medium does not know who is actually holding the ball. They will connect with part of the recent memory of the person holding the little ball and will say what they perceive. If this corresponds to the holder's experience, the holder or their companion will pat the medium's shoulder once, twice if it is incorrect and three times if it was not understood.

After each event described by the medium, the ball can change hands, or it can be kept by the person holding it for several turns.

The medium will have to center themselves again, inhale through their fontanel, and extend their field to the little ball. Their focus must not leave the ball.

After 15 minutes, the medium can turn around and talk about their answers and the information they received with the "clients".

After discussing the exercise for three minutes, the participants in the group change roles.

Exercise 33 – Sand reading

This is a group exercise. The material required is a box and enough sand to be able to make hand prints.

The box is filled with sand. The student who is going to read the sand box leaves the room. In this way, they will not know who they are reading. One of the other participants then makes prints of their hands in the sand. In this way they leave their energy.

Then the person who will do the reading comes back into the room and connects with the sand box as well as with the person who left their hand prints in the sand.

The medium will carry out a psychometric reading and an energy reading. The more often the sand is used, the more energy it will contain. The readings will therefore be more energy-related than psychometric.

Exercise 34 – Ball reading

This is a group exercise. The participants are seated in a circle, and the person doing the reading is seated with their back to the circle. In this way they cannot see the ball being passed around in the group.

To begin the exercise, one person holds the ball and the medium connects with the person holding the ball to obtain an element in that person's recent memory.

When this is done, there are two ways to continue the exercise:

The first variant is that the medium gives a correct element and the ball is passed to another person in the group.

The second variant is that as soon as the medium has given a correct element, they exchange places with the holder of the ball and the latter becomes the medium.

Exercise 35

This exercise is done individually. The medium needs a recently-worn article of clothing loaned by one of their friends (pullover, scarf...) or belonging to the latter's partner (but certainly not the panties belonging to the lady at the next dryer in the Laundromat!).

This exercise is to practice doing a reading of places that have been recently visited by the friend or partner in question.

First the medium connects with the person through the garment that was given to them. They then look for recently-visited places and describe them as best they can (was it in the country, in the city, to the north/south/east/west of the country; is there a lot of concrete or is there a lot of vegetation? Etc.). The medium takes notes of all this on a notepad in order to share it later with the actual person by telephone, a video conferencing application or text message. The owner of the garment will tell the medium whether the information received was correct.

Exercise 36 – Water reading (for experienced mediums)

This exercise is done as a group and requires a glass of water.

The glass is filled and energized by a person while the medium is not in the room, so that they will not know who energized the glass.

The medium will connect with the glass of water to do an energy reading of this water.

Exercise 37 – Working with stones

This exercise is done alone. It allows you to connect with an object and this will facilitate the connection when doing psychic readings with objects. It is not required to be knowledgeable about the physical properties of the stones. This exercise takes five minutes, after which there is a three-minute discussion period with the rest of the group.

When you are alone, choose a stone at random, pick it up and close your eyes. Center yourself, breathe in through your fontanel, build your field and extend yourself to the stone.

On which part of your body would you put the stone? How does it make you feel? Onto which meditative path does it seem to want to lead you? Does it have a pleasant or unpleasant feel? Why do you have these feelings? What period(s) in your life does it remind you of?

In most cases, without knowing it, the physical place on which we want to put the stone corresponds to its physical properties; the same is true for the emotions on which it might work. The meditative path is very personal and can only be verified through personal experience.

Exercise 38 – Working with stones

This exercise enables you to sharpen your observational skills and thus enter into a psychic or mediumistic contact. It is done in pairs and takes ten minutes, after which there is a three-minute discussion period.

When the pair have decided who will be the medium, the latter picks up a stone while thinking of their client and looking for information in the latter's recent memory.

Then the medium centers themselves, breathes in through their fontanel, builds their field and extends it to the stone. When this is done, they can open their eyes and observe the stone: does the color say anything about an event that took place recently? Does the stone's vibration tell them anything about recent memory? The medium has to look into the stone for information about recent memory. They will then say what they have perceived. After ten minutes, the pair can discuss what took place, before changing roles.

Exercise 39 – Remote viewing

This exercise is done alone. The medium can ask their partner, or a friend, to make a list of ten places they have never visited before, or make his or her own list. These places must be able to be found on the Internet, in the search engine's pictures section, etc.

Then the medium works alone, focusing on one place at a time. They make detailed notes about all the elements that come to them.

After that, the medium does an Internet search for pictures relating to each place. Services such as "Google Street View" can be very useful here. In this way the medium can verify the accuracy of the information they received during the remote viewing.

Mediumship

The purpose of the following exercises in mediumship is to work on the connection with the deceased in the spirit world, but also to help structure the contact with the deceased, in order to improve the quality of the information.

These exercises are done with the help of a person from the spirit world. You need to know how to create a connection with a person from the spirit world. In these exercises, the connection is made with a deceased person, not with a guide or the people with whom you work. Therefore, except for the meditation with the guides, these exercises must be done with your client; they cannot be done alone.

Let's first review the steps required for establishing the connection with a person in the spirit world: The medium is going to center themselves: inhale the energy from your light beam through the fontanel, exhale from the center, in order to build your energy field, your glowing work bubble. When this is done, you invite someone from the spirit world to join you in the bubble, and the mediumistic work can begin.

A contact must be rigidly structured at first, so that mediums, whether beginners or not, start off with the same things. But this is especially necessary to provide the client with the most factual information. Indeed, it must be remembered that the more factual the information, the better the client will recognize the visitor from the spirit world. Consequently, the message delivered by the medium will be all the more pertinent and adapted to the person who has come to consult.

Let's review some of the main elements of the structure the medium is to use.

After creating a contact with a person from the spirit world, the medium will use their clear senses to look for the following factual information in order to structure the session:

- Is it a man or a woman?
- How old are they?
- How did they die? Did it happen at the hospital, at home, or elsewhere?
- How is the messenger related to the person for whom they have come? Is it a member of the family, a friend, a lover or just someone the client knew?
- What was the messenger's family situation? Were they married, or living with a partner; were there children? How many children? Was there someone in their relations with whom they had a special relationship?
- What was the messenger's occupation?
- What were their hobbies? Did the messenger like to do manual things rather than intellectual ones, or the opposite? What evidence is there of this?
- Did the messenger have a pet?
- What sort of personality did they have? More extroverted or introverted?
- Was the messenger a highly social person or a more solitary one?

This is not an exhaustive list, but it provides a framework for building a mental classification system: where to look for information. It is also important for the medium to structure their mind in this way, so as not to receive information they did not ask for.

Exercise 40 – Meditation with the guides

Pranayamas: 20'

Repeat the pranayamas that you already know in order to ensure optimal preparation for this very precious work:

I sit down comfortably on a chair or meditation pillow. I keep my back straight, but allow my shoulders and jaws to relax, and I breathe slowly. I simply observe my chest movements. I watch myself inhale and exhale, and just watch my chest move in and out. I inhale and exhale and observe my breathing.

I focus on the zone between my upper lip and my nostrils and watch how my breathing goes in and out. I keep focused on this. I keep this focus; all of my concentration is on the friction caused by my breathing, just above my upper lip. I visualize and focus on my left nostril and breathe in and out uniquely through it. The next time I exhale through my left nostril, I inhale only through my right nostril. Uniquely through my right nostril. Inhale... exhale. The next time I exhale through my right nostril, I alternate my breathing, i.e., I inhale on the left and exhale on the right, inhale on the right and exhale on the left – left-right, right-left. With my natural breathing rhythm I alternate: left-right, right-left. I balance my hemispheres and my nervous system; work with my third eye, and practice focusing. One breathing technique and four exercises.

After the next left exhalation, I return to normal breathing. I focus on my perineum and contract it. (If I am a woman, I focus on my cervix and contract it.) I contract and release; contract, release. I do this several times. And I visualize a light beam extending from my perineum to the middle of my head; a light beam that surrounds my spine. I visualize a ball of light in my perineum. A luminous ball that completely lights up my loins. And every time I inhale I raise this ball of light through the beam to the middle of my head. Every time I exhale the ball goes down the beam to my loins. While I am doing these pranayamas and this breathing technique, the tip of my tongue is touching my palate. When I breathe in, the energy rises; when I breathe out, the energy goes down. And as I breathe to my own rhythm, I raise and lower this ball of energy through my spine.

Inhale, and the ball rises; exhale, and it goes back down. Never force energy. Be relaxed and the intention will make the energy really move. You can't make energy do anything. But you can guide it and you do that precisely with intention. Every time I inhale, I bring the ball up through my spine. Every time I exhale I evacuate dense particles and dissolve them. Thus with every breath I am lighter: with every breath the vibration of my field increases and my duality decreases. With every breath I am more balanced and more at peace.

If you want to intensify your breathing you can, do "Oms" in a 4-beat rhythm – but silent "Oms". Tell yourself when inhaling, "I will say four silent Oms," and when exhaling, "Four silent Oms." Four Oms when inhaling and four Oms when exhaling. I inhale and exhale in a relaxed manner.

People who have high blood pressure or a hiatus hernia cannot hold their breath after inhaling, and people with low blood pressure cannot hold the air out after exhaling. And now, after four inhaled Oms, you do two apneal Oms, two paused Oms, four exhaled Oms, and two paused Oms.

This is a four-timed breathing rhythm: four inhalations, two holds, four exhalations, two holds. Four "Oms" when breathing in and two when holding your breath, and four Oms when breathing out and two while holding your breath. If your breathing is still slow and balanced, work on four + four + four + four: the Pranayama square. This means that you say four Oms when you inhale, four Oms while holding your breath, four Oms when you exhale and four Oms before breathing in again.

When you have exhaled for the fourth time, return to your normal breathing and do stretching movements through your spine, from the lower spine to the upper in the middle of your head and from the middle of your head back down to your perineum. You have balanced your hemispheres and found your balance between heaven and earth. You are now ready to work.

Working with the guides: 50'

I am sitting comfortably. I visualize a beam of light falling on me. A magnificent bright light that surrounds me. I visualize an opening at the top of my head, in my fontanel. Through my fontanel, I am going to inhale this energy, down to my center. If I do not know where my center is, I will work with Anahata, my heart chakra, in the middle of my chest. I breathe in through my fontanel, down to my center. Every time I inhale, my center glows, when I exhale, I relax. I inhale and expand, exhale and relax. I expand through all of my upper body. I inhale to my center and expand through my pelvis; I spread through my legs to my feet. I inhale and release. I inhale into my center and expand through my shoulders and arms to my hands. I fill my neck and throat and head. I inhale and expand outside of my body. I breathe into my center and build my field; I surround myself with my bright cocoon, still enveloped with that magnificent beam that falls on me and nourishes me. I breathe into my center and build my field.

Thus protected by my ray of light, surrounded by my own luminous bubble, I visualize myself at the top of a very high mountain. I am in this space that is sacred in me, this space that is far from the torments and storms of my daily life. In the energy of my guides, the storms are far from me and are no more than a distant rumble.

Sitting on this mountaintop while the clouds below me dance, I let go in the light of the higher beings. Some mountaintops are higher than the black storm clouds. Above them, in my peace, I contemplate this magnificent landscape. I am sitting on top of this mountain, in the middle of my shining bubble, protected by my light beam. I know I am here to meet one of my guides, or several; I will begin humbly working to give my time to the spirit world so that it can also find its way to my spirit or my soul. I know that in a moment, one of these light beings will approach me.

On the top of this mountain, I inhale through my fontanel, into my center, and I extend myself. I know that this light being is coming closer to me and I can already feel a slight change in my field. Slowly, slowly I can feel that this energy is increasing, that the beams in my field are starting to touch the beams of my guide. Though I am deeply relaxed and fully at peace, I do not fall into a passive state. I remain in an interactive state, an awakened state that allows perception. I am therefore calm and alert at the same time. I ask my guides to come nearer. I observe the changes in my field. "Come, come," I ask them, "come closer so I can perceive you." I inhale into my center and from my center I expand into my guides' energy; when I exhale I observe myself and relax. I am calm but alert. Attentive and relaxed. Closer and closer, and even closer yet; more and more One. I inhale and expand. I expand and ask them to come even closer, closer than ever. I extend into my guides and observe myself. I move as little as possible so as not to disturb the increasing energy.

To practice my awareness, I ask my guides to step back just a moment so that I can see the changes in my field. Now. Again I ask them to come very close and I observe myself; I watch how the energy builds back up. And systematically, I am now going to practice my different clear-senses. First of all I ask my guides to manifest themselves through my clairsentience. I ask them to manipulate my energy or to touch me in a way that I can feel. When this has been asked, I remain in observation and sharing.

I inhale into my center and expand into my guides and ask them to work with my clairaudience. When this has been asked, I return to observing. Often, I hear them near my ear, behind my head. Sometimes, I hear an inner voice in my head. I do not expect anything specific. I let things happen and I watch and remain attentive.

I inhale through my fontanel, into my center and I expand into my guides and ask them to work with my claircognizance, my clear-knowing, to bring me ideas and thoughts through my fontanel.

I inhale into my center and expand and ask my guides to bring a fragrance. To try to bring me a celestial fragrance.

I inhale into my center and expand into my guides. I ask them to bring me visual impressions. I ask them to work with my clairvoyance. If I have difficulty remaining focused, I silently note each image I see and every impression I receive.

I breathe through my fontanel, into my center and from my center I extend to my guides. And once more I ask them to come even closer, closer than ever. I ask them to just spend some time with me. And each time my thoughts stray, which is normal, each time I center myself again by inhaling and expanding. I never get upset if my thoughts stray. "Come closer, help me become a better tool, a better tool for the work of the Light." I pay attention; I stay aware. I try to be aware of my state and I memorize that state; I memorize that state with respect to my normal state. What is different? How do I feel when I am surrounded? What is the sign that tells me, that proves to me that I am not fooling myself and that I am really in the company of a light being?

Slowly the time comes when I have to leave my guides. I am very aware of myself; I am observing myself. And now I ask my guides to leave. I watch myself more closely. What is happening in my field? How can I become aware of their presence or their departure? I breathe faster and at my own pace I come back to myself, back to the present, in this room, on this seat or cushion. I thank them for their visit and work, and I come back to myself. I come back to myself.

The question

Very often when we are communicating with our guides, we get an answer about which we have doubts as to whether it is really information from a higher consciousness or if our mind has created this answer. To clarify this, we proceed in several steps.

The first step is to formulate the question properly.

The second step is to stay calm for a moment to hear the answer.

When I think I have understood the answer, I repeat it, and then, to see if I really have understood, I ask for a sign confirming that what I have repeated is indeed correct.

We are now going to take the time to go through this experience, step by step.

I center myself well, taking a place in my center in my own light, and I clearly ask my guides what I need to know. Thus I have asked my question.

Now I step back for a moment, to interiorize and wait for the answer.

Now I repeat what I think I have understood: "I think I have understood that…"

I now ask them to confirm that I have understood correctly. This confirmation may be a symbol, an image, or a situation that I will come across in the next few days, in my daily life, without my looking specifically for it. It can be a palm tree in an unexpected place, or a feather that falls at my feet. Anything that may happen to me in my daily life at a time when I do not expect it. Then I step back again and wait for a thought, a feeling, a word, or an image.

Then I write my question down on paper, with the answer and the sign or symbol confirming it.

Exercise 41

This exercise allows use of all the clear-senses. As we have seen, most mediums are visual people, but we also have other clear-senses. To do this exercise, you must not let yourself be distracted by your strongest clear-sense and bring your attention back to the clear-sense you want to work with.

This exercise is done in pairs for 15 minutes and then the pair discusses it for three to five minutes.

When you are establishing the contact to the spirit world and still before the contact becomes interactive (through the use of the remaining clear-senses), you will only solicit your clairvoyance in order to obtain information about the deceased person through observation: is the person I see a man or a woman? In appearance, how old does he or she look? Can I see any physical problems? Can I see how this person died?

If another clear-sense interrupts, bring the focus back to sight.

The medium must tell the client what they see.

Then, to get more details, the medium will focus solely on their clairaudience: What can the person tell me about their appearance? According to the voice, is it a man or a woman? What do I hear about the cause of death? What are they saying about their family?

Again, if another clear-sense interrupts, bring your attention back to what you hear.

The medium must tell the client what they hear.

To get more information, the medium will now use clairsentience: what can I feel about the cause of death. Can I feel the deceased's emotions?

Can the medium feel joy, sadness, resentment or compassion?

Again, if another clear-sense interrupts, bring your attention back to what you feel.

The medium must tell the client what they feel.

At the end of the exercise, the pair exchanges roles.

Exercise 42

This exercise is done in a group of three people.

The purpose of this exercise is to practice feeling energy and to be able to connect with a person in the spirit world who is already present. The exercise takes 15 minutes. The conversation takes place during the exercise, with three to five minutes of discussion at the end of the exercise.

Before beginning, the role of each participant is defined:

One person will construct the contact, with the intention that someone from the spirit world is coming to see the client. When the contact has been set up, the person will give a physical description of the visitor and their relation to the person for whom they have come, a cause of death, and an occupation.

The second person will then enter into the contact and find out more about the deceased's family and personality and where they lived.

The third person will be the client.

When each person's role has been defined, the first medium will take a moment to connect with the spirit world and invite someone to come forward for the client. The medium will then give a physical description of the visitor and their relation to the person for whom they have come, a cause of death, and an occupation. After having given the physical description and stated the family or friendship relation, the medium will pause and ask the client if the information provided makes sense to them. If the client does not understand all of the information, the medium will have to go back to the visitor from the spirit world and ask for more details about their appearance, occupation, cause of death or family.

When the contact is recognized, the second medium will take over and get more information about the contact, asking about the family situation, the deceased's personality, and where they lived. This second medium will pause several times between messages in order to ensure the person to whom the contact is attributed continues to properly understand the information provided.

The mediums do not speak at the same time and respect the order decided on at the start. However, each medium may provide additional information to what the other has said.

Exercise 43

For this exercise, ideally there should be two groups with equal numbers of people, if possible an even number. The exercise takes 15 minutes and there is an additional discussion time of three to five minutes.

One group will be the mediums and the other the clients. This should be decided at the beginning of the exercise.

The chairs should be set up in advance. There should be two rows of chairs, and the chairs must not touch.

The group who will be working sits in the front row of chairs. They close their eyes and begin to build their energy field, inhaling from the fontanel to the center in order to grow their field and then to make the connection with a person from the spirit world.

The second group quietly takes seats in the second row behind the mediums. It is important that the participants in the working group do not know who is sitting behind whom. Each participant in the group of mediums must have a corresponding client partner.

The exercise consists of three parts: the goal of the first part is to establish the deceased person's identity; the second part consists of describing the client sitting behind the medium with the help of the deceased person; and during the last part a description of the nature of the relationship between the client and the person in the spirit world is given.

The mediums will have built up their energy field and invited a person from the spirit world to visit for the person who is the "client". When this connection is established, the medium will first give factual information about the person from the spirit world: Is it a man or a woman? Tall or short? What color's the hair, and how long? How did the person die? What was their relation to the client?

When this description has been made, the medium must

interact with the person from the spirit world and ask for information about the client who is sitting behind the medium: is it a man or a woman? What do they look like? What is their occupation? Where do they live?

Then the medium will ask about mutual memories: what things did the client and the person from the spirit world experience together? Did they go somewhere in particular together? Did they do a particular activity together?

To finish, the medium will ask the deceased if they have a message for the client.

In this exercise, you need to stay as close to the facts as possible in order to prevent your mind from intervening. In fact, we tend to try and guess who is behind us because the participants in the groups have met and may even know each other.

After 15 minutes, the working group will open their eyes and turn around to share what they received with the others. This should take three to five minutes.

Exercise 44

This exercise is done in pairs: a medium and a client seated opposite each other. It takes 15 minutes, after which the partners talk about the exercise for three to five minutes.

The medium who is going to work must make two connections with two messengers from the spirit world, for the same client, i.e. the person seated across from the medium.

The purpose of this exercise, for the medium, is to feel and differentiate between the two different energies from the spirit world, to be capable of holding their concentration on one messenger without mixing up the sources of information, and to transcribe the information received while stating from which messenger it was received. The medium must discipline their mind in order to identify from which messenger they are getting the information and thus avoid the impression that both messengers are speaking at the same time.

The medium will begin by stating the intention to invite a person from the spirit world to come on behalf of the medium's client. Then they will make contact with this person from the spirit world.

The medium will start the session by describing the deceased: man/woman, age, height, cause of death, relation to the client. The medium will then pause to make sure the client can understand and recognize the messenger as part of the client's entourage.

When the client has recognized the messenger the medium will then ask the messenger to step to his right or left and wait a few moments.

Then the medium will state the intention to invite a second messenger from the spirit world to visit on behalf of their client who is opposite the medium. The medium will make a second connection, and when this is done, will describe the visitor: man/woman, age, height, cause of death, relation to the client and to the other messenger. The medium will pause and ensure that their client can understand and recognize the messenger as part of the client's entourage.

When the two messengers have been recognized by the client, the medium asks the second messenger to step to his right or left, depending on where the first messenger has placed themselves.

Then the medium will alternate between the two messengers. He will get facts from one messenger, tell them to the client, then get facts which may be different from the other messenger and tell them to the client, and so on until the end of the exercise.

The medium will close the session either with a message from each visitor or a mutual message from both visitors (the medium will take care to let each messenger speak so that they do not talk at the same time).

When the exercise is finished, the pair discusses it and then switches roles.

Exercise 45

This exercise is done in pairs: a medium and a client. It takes 15 minutes, followed by three to five minutes of discussion between the participants. To do this exercise, the medium must grasp the difference in energy between a messenger from the spirit world and his client's energy field. Indeed, the spirit world is considered to be of a high-frequency vibration in comparison with that of the human energy field, which is considered to be lower, and this is normal since humans are also made of matter.

The medium's goal is to grasp and understand how the information was given to him. In psychic readings, this information is important because a communicator from the spirit world may want to say something and provide information about the client. In mediumistic readings, the medium is going to know when his focus will move from his communicator to his client's energy field in order to gather information about the person from the spirit world.

The medium who is working creates his glowing work bubble and with intention asks a person from the spirit world who can be recognized by the client to appear. He then begins to describe the communicator to his client: man/woman, age, height, cause of death, relationship to the client.

When the person opposite him has acknowledged the facts provided by the medium as relating to a person he is familiar with, the medium politely asks this communicator to stay nearby and wait for a few minutes. The medium then connects with his client, as we have already seen in the exercises relating to psychic readings: he expands his energy field, his glowing bubble, into his client's energy field. When the connection has been made, he goes to look for additional factual information in his client's energy field, relating to the spirit who has appeared.

While maintaining his connections with the person facing him and with the deceased, the medium alternates between the messenger and his client's energy field. He focuses on the way he receives the information: does it have a different vibration? Did he have an easier time with either of the two energies? How did the differences in the energy or vibration appear when he was working with the deceased's energy and when he was working with the energy from his client's energy field?

When the exercise has been completed and the discussion has taken place, the roles are reversed.

Exercise 46 – Double blind (see chapter on the Ouija board)

After having informed the audience of any possible sources of error, whether it springs from the participants' minds or is the work of a playful spirit, here is the procedure for this exercise which is called "double blind". In a group of at least three people, one person writes down the letters given by the spirit world and the two others are, ideally, blindfolded or at least keep their eyes closed.

If anyone really wants to use the Ouija board as a means of communication, it being clear that this is only to be done for learning or helping others, the following procedure must be used:

A spirit working in the light is called upon for the exercise. When the disc is touched lightly with the tips of the fingers, it should move from one letter to another and spell legible words. Once this movement is regular the participants must cover their eyes with the exception of the person who silently notes down each letter indicated by the board. The best thing to do, which absolutely ensures that there is no implication from a participant, is that the person who is taking notes turns the board several times so that the blindfolded participants cannot see how the letters are placed. This is the only way to be 100% sure that the message or lesson comes from the spirit world.

Secrets

What do we mean by "secret" and who are the *"faiseurs de secrets"* ["secret makers"]?

Faiseurs de secret are traditional healers who can be found in French- and Italian-speaking Switzerland and southern France and who use prayer to heal and/or relieve pain from those who ask. This is not a profession and there are no academic studies for it; it is handed down from one generation to the next.

Faiseurs de secret have a special gift and are usually middle-aged or older. Some are highly renowned and sought after although as a rule they do not advertise publicly and you would have to find them by word of mouth. Traditional *faiseurs de secret* generally consider that their gifts are to be given freely and not in exchange for money.

The "secrets" themselves are prayers or formulas that are recited for the afflicted person, often along with the Lord's Prayer and the Hail Mary. They are requested to help relieve burns, earache, anxiety, hemorrhoids, skin problems such as warts, shingles and psoriasis, and other afflictions. As their name implies, the secrets are carefully kept in order to be able to pass them on to the younger generation.

With the increasing interest in the use of alternative medicine, some hospitals in Switzerland and France have begun looking into and implementing collaboration with traditional healers and *faiseurs de secret*. The practice has been the object of official studies and the overall results have been shown to be very positive for the patients.

The secrets shared here are extracts from the work of Abbot Julio, *Prières Merveilleuses – Pour la guérison de toutes les maladies physiques et morales* [*Marvelous Prayers for the Healing of all Physical and Moral Ills*] (Éditions Bussière, 1995; reproduction of the book published in 1896).

Secret for healing burns of all kinds: Prayer to Saint Laurence

Blow on the burn three times in the form of a cross († from top to bottom and left to right) and say:

> † Oh great Saint Lawrence,
> Over the coals burning
> Turning and re-turning,
> You did not suffer.
> † Grant me your blessing
> That this trial shall be passing:
> † Fire of God, lose thy heat,
> just as Judas paled,
> When he betrayed, through his greed,
> Jesus in the Garden of Gethsemane.

> *Original text (in French):*
> *† Ô grand Saint Laurent,*
> *Sur un brasier ardent*
> *Tournant et retournant,*
> *Vous n'étiez pas souffrant.*
> *† Faites-moi la grâce*
> *Que cette ardeur se passe:*
> *† Feu de Dieu, perds ta chaleur,*
> *Comme Judas perdit sa couleur,*
> *Quand il trahit, par passion juive,*
> *Jésus au Jardin des Olives.*

Then say the Lord's Prayer and the Hail Mary, five times each.

The Lord's Prayer
Our Father, who art in Heaven,
Hallowed be Thy name,
Thy kingdom come,

Thy will be done on Earth as it is in Heaven.
Give us this day our daily bread,
And forgive us our trespasses
As we forgive those who trespass against us.
Lead us not into temptation.
But deliver us from evil.
For Thine is the Kingdom and the Power and the Glory,
Amen.

The Hail Mary
Hail Mary, full of grace.
Our Lord is with thee.
Blessed art thou among women,
and blessed is the fruit of thy womb, Jesus.
Holy Mary, Mother of God,
pray for us sinners,
now and at the hour of our death.
Amen.

Secret for healing wounds or other ills

While saying the following prayer, make the sign of the Cross (†
from top to bottom and left to right) several times on the wound
or wounds or over the places where the pain is located:

**† In Jesus' Name,
† and in the name of his servant Jean Sempé,
Evil, stop hurting me.
† In Jesus' Name, I want it and I command it:
Go away, go back where you came from and stay
there forever.
Amen!
† Evil, whoever you are, wherever you come from, whatever
your nature or purpose is, I order you in the Name of Jesus,
who is obeyed by all in Heaven,**

on Earth and to the depths of Hell,
to leave (person's name),
God's own here before me.
I order you to do it in the Name † of the Father, † and
the Son,
† and the Holy Ghost.
Amen!

Original text (in French):
† Au nom de Jésus,
† et au nom de son serviteur Jean Sempé,
Mal, cesse de me faire souffrir.
† Au nom de Jésus, je le veux et je te le commande:
Va-t'en, retourne d'où tu viens et restes-y toujours.
Ainsi soit-il!
† Mal, qui que tu sois, d'où que tu viennes, quel que soit
ta nature ou ton principe, je t'ordonne au Nom de Jésus,
à qui tout obéit au ciel,
sur la terre et jusque dans les enfers,
de quitter (nom de la personne)
cette créature de Dieu ici présente.
Je te l'ordonne, au Nom † du Père, † et du Fils,
† et du Saint-Esprit.
Ainsi soit-il!

Secret for healing toothaches

Blow three times on the affected cheek in the form of a cross (†
from top to bottom and left to right) and say:

Saint Apolline
Beautiful and divine
Was sitting at the foot of a tree,
On a white marble stone.
Jesus, our Savior,

Fortunately happened by,
Asked: "Apolline
Why do you look chagrined?"
"I am here, Divine Master
Out of pain, not chagrin:
I am here for my head, for my blood
And for the pain in my teeth."
Jesus told her, "Apolline have faith:
† On my word, O pain, go away!
† If it is a drop of blood, it will dry
† If it is a worm it will die."

Original text (in French):
Sainte Apolline,
Belle et divine,
Était assise au pied d'un arbre,
Sur la blanche pierre de marbre.
Jésus, notre Sauveur,
Là passant par bonheur,
Lui dit: Apolline
Qui donc te chagrine?
Je suis ici, Maître Divin,
Pour douleur, et non pour chagrin:
J'y suis pour mon chef, pour mon sang
Et pour mon mal de dents.
Jésus lui dit: Apolline a la foi:
† Sur ma parole, ô mal, détourne-toi!
† Si c'est goutte de sang, elle séchera;
† Si c'est un ver, aussitôt il mourra.

Then repeat the Lord's Prayer and the Hail Mary five times each, in honor of the five wounds of our Savior.

About the author

Hannes Jacob has been a spiritual healer at his clinic in Neuchâtel, Switzerland since 1990. As director of *fréquences* – Swiss School of Healing, which he founded in 2005, and graduate professor of mediumship with a SNU degree from the Arthur Findlay College in London, he teaches various healing methods (such as EPI – Extraction of Pathological Information, spiritual healing, Therapeutic Touch, Kahuna, Reiki), mediumship and meditation techniques. He is also a SNU Approved Healer and lectured for six years at the Swiss Parapsychology Association in Bern. Since 2002, he has taught at the Centre for Preventive Health in Colombier, Switzerland. He studied Kriya Yoga with Swamiji Dharmananda Saraswati Maharaj who gave him his spiritual name, Mahān, and goes on regular retreats to Buddhist monasteries to practice silent meditation. For many years he has been keenly interested in modified consciousness states and carried out numerous studies in the field. He has been the subject of a number of articles in various countries, and has also participated in television shows, radio interviews, and conferences in Switzerland.

BOOKS

O-BOOKS

SPIRITUALITY

O is a symbol of the world, of oneness and unity; this eye
represents knowledge and insight. We publish titles on general
spirituality and living a spiritual life. We aim to inform and help
you on your own journey in this life.
If you have enjoyed this book, why not tell other readers by
posting a review on your preferred book site?

Recent bestsellers from O-Books are:

Heart of Tantric Sex
Diana Richardson
Revealing Eastern secrets of deep love and intimacy to Western
couples.
Paperback: 978-1-90381-637-0 ebook: 978-1-84694-637-0

Crystal Prescriptions
The A-Z guide to over 1,200 symptoms and their
healing crystals
Judy Hall
The first in the popular series of eight books, this handy little
guide is packed as tight as a pill-bottle with crystal remedies for
ailments.
Paperback: 978-1-90504-740-6 ebook: 978-1-84694-629-5

Take Me To Truth
Undoing the Ego
Nouk Sanchez, Tomas Vieira
The best-selling step-by-step book on shedding the Ego, using the
teachings of *A Course In Miracles*.
Paperback: 978-1-84694-050-7 ebook: 978-1-84694-654-7

The 7 Myths about Love...Actually!
The Journey from your HEAD to the HEART of your SOUL
Mike George
Smashes all the myths about LOVE.
Paperback: 978-1-84694-288-4 ebook: 978-1-84694-682-0

The Holy Spirit's Interpretation of the New Testament
A Course in Understanding and Acceptance
Regina Dawn Akers
Following on from the strength of *A Course In Miracles*, NTI
teaches us how to experience the love and oneness of God.
Paperback: 978-1-84694-085-9 ebook: 978-1-78099-083-5

The Message of A Course In Miracles
A translation of the Text in plain language
Elizabeth A. Cronkhite
A translation of *A Course in Miracles* into plain, everyday
language for anyone seeking inner peace. The companion
volume, *Practicing A Course In Miracles*, offers practical lessons
and mentoring.
Paperback: 978-1-84694-319-5 ebook: 978-1-84694-642-4

Rising in Love
My Wild and Crazy Ride to Here and Now, with Amma, the
Hugging Saint
Ram Das Batchelder
Rising in Love conveys an author's extraordinary journey of
spiritual awakening with the Guru, Amma.
Paperback: 978-1-78279-687-9 ebook: 978-1-78279-686-2

Your Simple Path
Find Happiness in every step
Ian Tucker
A guide to helping us reconnect with what is really important in
our lives.
Paperback: 978-1-78279-349-6 ebook: 978-1-78279-348-9

365 Days of Wisdom
Daily Messages To Inspire You Through The Year
Dadi Janki
Daily messages which cool the mind, warm the heart and guide
you along your journey.
Paperback: 978-1-84694-863-3 ebook: 978-1-84694-864-0

Body of Wisdom
Women's Spiritual Power and How it Serves
Hilary Hart
Bringing together the dreams and experiences of women across
the world with today's most visionary spiritual teachers.
Paperback: 978-1-78099-696-7 ebook: 978-1-78099-695-0

Dying to Be Free
From Enforced Secrecy to Near Death to True Transformation
Hannah Robinson
After an unexpected accident and near-death experience, Hannah
Robinson found herself radically transforming her life, while a
remarkable new insight altered her relationship with her father, a
practising Catholic priest.
Paperback: 978-1-78535-254-6 ebook: 978-1-78535-255-3

The Ecology of the Soul
A Manual of Peace, Power and Personal Growth for Real People
in the Real World
Aidan Walker
Balance your own inner Ecology of the Soul to regain your
natural state of peace, power and wellbeing.
Paperback: 978-1-78279-850-7 ebook: 978-1-78279-849-1

Not I, Not other than I
The Life and Teachings of Russel Williams
Steve Taylor, Russel Williams
The miraculous life and inspiring teachings of one of the World's
greatest living Sages.
Paperback: 978-1-78279-729-6 ebook: 978-1-78279-728-9

On the Other Side of Love
A woman's unconventional journey towards wisdom
Muriel Maufroy
When life has lost all meaning, what do you do?
Paperback: 978-1-78535-281-2 ebook: 978-1-78535-282-9

Practicing A Course In Miracles
A translation of the Workbook in plain language, with
mentor's notes
Elizabeth A. Cronkhite
The practical second and third volumes of The Plain-Language
A Course In Miracles.
Paperback: 978-1-84694-403-1 ebook: 978-1-78099-072-9

Quantum Bliss
The Quantum Mechanics of Happiness, Abundance, and Health
George S. Mentz
Quantum Bliss is the breakthrough summary of success and
spirituality secrets that customers have been waiting for.
Paperback: 978-1-78535-203-4 ebook: 978-1-78535-204-1

The Upside Down Mountain
Mags MacKean
A must-read for anyone weary of chasing success and happiness
– one woman's inspirational journey swapping the uphill slog for
the downhill slope.
Paperback: 978-1-78535-171-6 ebook: 978-1-78535-172-3

Your Personal Tuning Fork
The Endocrine System
Deborah Bates
Discover your body's health secret, the endocrine system, and
'twang' your way to sustainable health!
Paperback: 978-1-84694-503-8 ebook: 978-1-78099-697-4

Readers of ebooks can buy or view any of these bestsellers by
clicking on the live link in the title. Most titles are published
in paperback and as an ebook. Paperbacks are available in
traditional bookshops. Both print and ebook formats are
available online.

Find more titles and sign up to our readers' newsletter at
http://www.johnhuntpublishing.com/mind-body-spirit

Follow us on Facebook at https://www.facebook.com/OBooks/
and Twitter at https://twitter.com/obooks